Global Issues in Contract Law

By

John A. Spanogle, Jr.
Professor of Law
William Wallace Kirkpatrick Research Professor of Law
The George Washington University Law School

Michael P. Malloy
Distinguished Professor and Scholar
University of the Pacific McGeorge School of Law

Louis F. Del Duca
Edward N. Polisher Distinguished Faculty Scholar
Penn State University Dickinson School of Law

Keith A. Rowley
Professor of Law
University of Nevada, Las Vegas, William S. Boyd School of Law

Andrea K. Bjorklund
Acting Professor of Law
University of California, Davis, School of Law

AMERICAN CASEBOOK SERIES®

THOMSON
™
WEST

Mat #40449803

American Casebook Series and West Group are trademarks
registered in the U.S. Patent and Trademark Office.

© 2007 Thomson/West
      610 Opperman Drive
      P.O. Box 64526
      St. Paul, MN 55164–0526
      1–800–328–9352

Printed in the United States of America

ISBN: 978–0–314–16755–2

 TEXT IS PRINTED ON 10% POST
CONSUMER RECYCLED PAPER

To Brynne Learman, granddaughter.

— JAS

To my daughter Sophia Grace Malloy.

— MPM

To Frances, with appreciation for her support,
understanding, and patience.

— LFDD

In loving memory of my parents, John and Earlene Rowley.

— KAR

To my parents, who have always supported me
in my endeavors, with gratitude and love.

— AKB

*

Preface

Our work on this book began—or at least our thinking about it began—during a Workshop on Globalizing the Law School Curriculum held by Pacific McGeorge's Center for Global Business and Development at Lake Tahoe, California, in August 2005. There the authors, along with our colleagues Professor Ronald A. Brand of the University of Pittsburgh School of Law and Professor Victor P. Goldberg of the Columbia Law School, came to realize that the basic law school Contracts course was particularly well-suited for incorporating global perspectives. Unlike, say, Civil Procedure, Property or Torts, the body of U.S. contract law *already* includes basic, globalizing federal law, *i.e.*, the Convention on Contracts for the International Sale of Goods (CISG). Hence, for many of us the basic question was not *whether* globalized issues should be included in a core Contracts course, but *to what extent* should they be explored. This book represents our collective answer to that latter question.

There is also a very important comparative law element in the materials that follow. The Civil Law presents a quite different attitude towards what a contractual promise is. Although the contract law rules of individual jurisdictions other than the U.S. states are useful sources of comparative study and analysis, a more accessible source is the PRINCIPLES OF INTERNATIONAL COMMERCIAL CONTRACTS, an integrated set of international contract law rules developed by the Institute for the Unification of Private Law (commonly known by its French acronym "UNIDROIT"). The UNIDROIT PRINCIPLES is in some respects a "Restatement" of international contract law, and it is invoked throughout this book as a convenient point of entry into the comparative study of Contracts.

Convenience is a legitimate concern in any attempt at globalizing the core law school curriculum. In most U.S. law schools, the first year Contracts course is now limited to four credits or so, and so coverage of international contract law issues must be limited as well. We consider it important to include coverage of basic CISG and comparative concepts in the Contracts course (scope, contract formation, performance and remedies) and to leave more extensive discussion of complex topics to upper division courses like Sales, Payments Systems, and the like. Hence, the modest objective of this book is to ensure that law students will graduate at a minimum with a solid understanding of the basic principles that govern contracts undertaken in a globalized environment.

This book is the result of a happy collaboration among colleagues who have long been concerned with the issues raised in these pages. We thank the Pacific McGeorge Center for Global Business and Development for initiating the Workshop process that led to this collaboration, and the *Global Issues Series* Editor Franklin A. Gevurtz for encouraging it. We also thank Thomson West, and especially Louis Higgins, for creating the conditions that made the collaboration a practical possibility.

Michael P. Malloy thanks his co-authors for their collegiality, creativity, guidance, and patience. He also thanks his wife, Susie A. Malloy, Esq., who provided—as always—unerring editorial insights and assistance. Finally, he thanks the administrative staff of the Center, Connie Neumann and RK Van Every, for their invaluable service.

Louis F. Del Duca thanks Dean Elizabeth Rindskopf Parker, Franklin Gevurtz, and Michael P. Malloy for their energetic and imaginative leadership in contributing to the globalization of legal education.

Keith A. Rowley thanks Michael Malloy, Elizabeth Rindskopf Parker, and Frank Gevurtz for bringing this merry band together in the first place, and Michael, Andy Spanogle, and Louis Higgins and the other folks at West for their understanding and accommodation when a series of family medical crises and deaths arose half a continent away. He also thanks his wife, Katherine, for her love, support, and excellent proofreading skills, and their son, James, for bringing joy into an otherwise difficult year.

Andrea K. Bjorklund is especially grateful to Seán Duggan, Stefan Kröll, Michael Malloy, Rob Mikos, David Snyder, Andy Spangole, and Sir Guenter Treitel for assistance in preparing her portions of this joint endeavor.

JOHN A. SPANOGLE, JR.
MICHAEL P. MALLOY
LOUIS F. DEL DUCA
KEITH A. ROWLEY
ANDREA K. BJORKLUND

December 2006

Acknowledgements

We gratefully acknowledge permission to reprint excerpts from the following materials:

Franco Ferrari, *Fundamental Breach of Contract under the UN Sales Convention—25 Years of Article 25 CISG*, 25 J. L. & COM. 489 (2006).

John Y. Gotanda, *Awarding Damages Under the United Nations Convention on the International Sale of Goods: A Matter of Interpretation*, 37 GEO. J. INT'L L. 95 (2005).

Amy Kastely, *The Right to Require Performance in International Sales: Toward an International Interpretation of the Vienna Convention*, 63 WASH. L. REV. 607 (1988).

K. ZWEIGERT & H. KÖTZ, AN INTRODUCTION TO COMPARATIVE LAW (Oxford University Press 1998). By permission of Oxford University Press.

*

Global Issues Series

Series Editor, Franklin A. Gevurtz

Available for Spring 2007 Classes

Global Issues in Civil Procedure by Thomas Main, University of the Pacific, McGeorge School of Law
ISBN 978–0–314–15978–6

Global Issues in Contract Law by John A. Spanogle, Jr., George Washington University, Michael P. Malloy, University of the Pacific, McGeorge School of Law, Louis F. Del Duca, Pennsylvania State University, Keith A. Rowley, University of Nevada, Las Vegas, and Andrea K. Bjorklund, University of California, Davis
ISBN 978–0–314–16755–2

Global Issues in Corporate Law by Franklin A. Gevurtz, University of the Pacific, McGeorge School of Law
ISBN 978–0–314–15977–9

Global Issues in Criminal Law by Linda Carter, University of the Pacific, McGeorge School of Law, Christopher L. Blakesley, University of Nevada, Las Vegas and Peter Henning, Wayne State University
ISBN 978–0–314–15997–7

Global Issues in Property Law by John G. Sprankling, University of the Pacific, McGeorge School of Law, Raymond R. Coletta, University of the Pacific, McGeorge School of Law, and M.C. Mirow, Florida International University College of Law
ISBN 978–0–314–16729–3

For Fall 2007 adoption, we also expect to have titles available in Constitutional Law, Employment Discrimination, Family Law, Labor Law, and Professional Responsibility.

*

ix

Summary of Contents

*

Table of Contents

*

Table of Cases

Global Issues in Contract Law

*

Chapter 1

INTRODUCTION

A. CONTRACTS IN A GLOBALIZED ECONOMY

A few generations ago, many U.S. lawyers took as their basic frame of reference the law of the state in which their firm (and, perhaps, most of their clients) were located. Such a perspective is no longer practical. Given the constant movement of persons, goods and services across state boundaries, lawyers must take into account laws of states other than their own, as well as the body of federal law which has grown since the New Deal. One obvious result of the transition of the U.S. economy into a truly interstate, national market was the emergence and adoption of the Uniform Commercial Code (UCC)—state-based commercial legislation that has encouraged uniform or harmonized approaches to legal issues involving contracts for the sale of goods.

The national economy has continued to be dynamic, however, and the growing movement of persons, goods and services across *national* boundaries in an increasingly *global* economy requires lawyers to be aware of the laws of other nations and of emerging international sources of law. This development has immense practical consequences. Think about the products and services that you purchased in, say, the six months prior to your arrival at law school. How many of these came from outside the United States? (And how many of the goods and services made in the United States are also sold outside the United States?)

If there is a contract dispute between the purchaser and seller of any of these goods or services, could the lawyers representing them provide competent advice without being familiar with the *Convention on Contracts for the International Sale of Goods*

1

(CISG)?[1] Could the lawyers for a small U.S. company selling goods in Europe provide competent representation if they are unfamiliar with applicable contracts and commercial law in the European Union? If there is a dispute involving these goods or services, can the lawyers represent their clients adequately if they are unfamiliar with the available remedies in the non-U.S. jurisdictions in which the goods or services have been marketed?

Similar questions arise in other basic areas of the law that comprise the typical first-year law school curriculum. In a world in which the economy is increasingly global, future lawyers must think globally—and they should begin by being taught to understand a global frame of reference.

Globalizing the Contracts course involves a different situation from most other subject matter areas in a law school core curriculum. The corpus of U.S. contract law *already* includes basic, globalizing federal law, *i.e.*, the CISG, negotiated by the United Nations Commission for International Trade Law (UNCITRAL). It was ratified by the United States in 1986 and entered into force as to the United States in 1988. As one writer has described the situation, "The United States has two laws of contracts: a state law of contracts, represented by the UCC, and a 'federal' law of contracts, the CISG."[2] As we shall see in *Asante Technologies*, the CISG is automatically applicable to contracts for the sale of goods between parties located in two CISG states unless the parties agree otherwise. Because the CISG might well intrude in a contract through inadvertence or ignorance of counsel, minimum knowledge of the convention's potential applicability becomes an issue of basic professional competence.[3] Hence, the basic question is not *whether* globalized issues should be included in a Contracts course, but *to what extent* should they be explored.

Beyond the CISG, which is binding U.S. law for the transnational contracts to which it applies, contract law rules of individual jurisdictions other than the U.S. states may be useful sources of comparative study and analysis. In this regard, potential sources of pertinent contract law principles in the comparative context include the PRINCIPLES OF INTERNATIONAL COMMERCIAL CONTRACTS, a product of the Institute for the Unification of Private Law (commonly known

---

1. United Nations Convention on Contracts for the International Sale of Goods, Apr. 11, 1980, U.N. Doc. A/CONF.97/18 (codified at 15 U.S.C. App.), *reprinted in* 19 INT'L LEG.MATERIALS 668 (1980).

2. Larry A. DiMatteo, *The CISG and the Presumption of Enforceability*, 22 YALE J. INT'L L. 111, 156 (1997).

3. *See, e.g.*, Ronald A. Brand, *Professional Responsibility in a Transnational Transactions Practice*, 17 J.L. & COM. 301, 336 (1998) ("If . . . the lawyer determines that the [CISG] applies to the transaction, he or she then has a duty to understand fully the rules of the Convention and the application of those rules to the transaction in question").

by its French acronym UNIDROIT), and the PRINCIPLES OF EUROPEAN CONTRACT LAW prepared by the Commission on European Contract Law. These sources will be examined in subsequent chapters of this book.

Notes

1–1. *Identifying the "Law of Contracts."* We are used to finding the law of contracts in reported case decisions and in statutes like the Uniform Commercial Code. Another source, not directly binding on courts,[4] is of course the RESTATEMENT OF THE LAW OF CONTRACTS (2d), approved in 1981 by the American Law Institute, a scholarly organization of practitioners, judges, and professors. In its attempt to summarize or "restate" the U.S. common law of contracts, for the most part the Restatement follows the specific rules endorsed by the common law of the majority of states within the United States, and occasionally in a minority jurisdiction if a particular minority rule seems better on the merits, or more logical or consistent with other rules. It tends to be very influential as a short-hand expression of current trends in common law, and courts and commentators regularly refer to it for insights as to the state of the law.[5] In international commercial practice, another important source of law is the CISG.

1–2. *Contrasting the Restatement and the CISG.* As of 1 January 1988, the CISG applies in many situations to the sale of goods between a U.S. national and a national of any other nation state that is a signatory of the CISG. Unlike the Restatement, however, the CISG is *binding federal law* applicable to international transactions that fall within its scope.[6] As one commentator has emphasized, "the [CISG] is not merely a form of restatement of (international) contract law, nor is it simply a 'model law' which would be subject to modification by contracting states to address local concerns; rather ... CISG applies of its own force to all proposed contractual relationships that satisfy its 'internationality' requirements."[7] The CISG does not simply "reflect" or "restate" contract law; it is *part of the contract law* of every state in the United States.

1–3. *Comparing the Restatement and the UNIDROIT PRINCIPLES.* An international equivalent of the Restatement is actually the UNI-

4. *See, e.g., Brewer v. Erwin*, 287 Or. 435, 600 P.2d 398, 410 n.12 (1979) (comparing statutes and restatement provisions as authority).

5. For discussion and analysis of the RESTATEMENT (2d), see *Symposium*, 81 COLUM. L. REV. 1 (1981); 67 CORNELL L. REV. 631 (1982).

6. CISG, art. 1, para. (1). For a useful discussion of the alternative bases for applicability of the CISG, see Louis F. Del Duca and Patrick Del Duca, *Selected Topics Under the Convention on International Sale of Goods*, 106 DICK. L. REV. 205, 207–218 (2001).

7. Michael P. Van Alstine, *Consensus, Dissensus, and Contractual Obligation Through the Prism of Uniform International Sales Law*, 37 VA. J. INT'L L. 1, 9 (1996) (footnotes omitted).

DROIT PRINCIPLES,[8] first issued in 1994 and republished with slight revisions in 2004.[9] Like the Restatement, the UNIDROIT PRINCIPLES are not legally binding; rather, they reflect commonly accepted rules of contract law. Unlike the Restatement, however, the PRINCIPLES do *not* draw on a single body of contract law—like, for example, the generally accepted rules of U.S. common law of contracts—but are derived from a wide range of sources, sometimes antithetical, and attempt to construct a single, unified body of principles.[10] Hence, there is a certain abstracted or generalized quality to the PRINCIPLES that is not characteristic of either the Restatement or the CISG.[11]

B. STATUS AND SCOPE OF THE CISG

Under Article I of the CISG, two basic jurisdictional questions arise: (*i*) an "internationality" requirement that the parties to the contract are located in different nation states that are parties to the convention; and, (*ii*) the substantive requirement that the contract involve a sale of "goods." The following case focuses on the internationality requirement. The substantive requirement will be examined in some of the notes following this case.

ASANTE TECHNOLOGIES, INC.
v. PMC–SIERRA, INC.

164 F.Supp.2d 1142 (N.D.Cal. 2001).

WARE, DISTRICT JUDGE.

[Asante, a manufacturer of computer-network switchers, sued PMS–Sierra, a supplier of application-specific integrated circuits ("ASICs"), in state court, alleging breach of contract and express

---

8. INTERNATIONAL INSTITUTE FOR THE UNIFICATION OF PRIVATE LAW, UNIDROIT PRINCIPLES OF INTERNATIONAL COMMERCIAL CONTRACTS (2004).

9. For discussion of the 1994 version of the UNIDROIT PRINCIPLES, see M. BONELL, AN INTERNATIONAL RESTATEMENT OF CONTRACT LAW (2d ed. 1997); Joseph M. Perillo, *UNIDROIT Principles of International Commercial Contracts: The Black Letter Text and a Review*, 63 FORDHAM L. REV. 281 (1994); *Symposium*, 69 TULANE L. REV. 1121 (1995). For discussion of the current version of the UNIDROIT PRINCIPLES, see M. BONELL, AN INTERNATIONAL RESTATEMENT OF CONTRACT LAW (3d ed. 2004) (hereinafter "BONELL 2004").

10. UNIDROIT PRINCIPLES 2004, *supra* at xv ("For the most part the UNI-

DROIT PRINCIPLES reflect concepts to be found in many, if not all, legal systems. . . . [T]hey also embody what are perceived to be the best solutions, even if still not yet generally adopted.").

11. *Cf.* COMMISSION ON EUROPEAN CONTRACT LAW, THE PRINCIPLES OF EUROPEAN CONTRACT LAW (2003) (setting forth general contract rules to be applied within European Union). For comparative analysis of the UNIDROIT PRINCIPLES and the European PRINCIPLES, see BONELL 2004 at 335–359. For an insightful comparison of the UCC and the European PRINCIPLES, see Ole Lando, *Salient Features of The Principles of European Contract Law: A Comparison with the UCC*, 13 PACE INT'L L. REV. 339 (2001).

warranties. PMS–Sierra removed the action to federal court.[a] On Asante's motion to remand to state court, the District Court had to consider whether the CISG applied to the contract, thus raising a federal question that would keep the case in federal court.]

Plaintiff is a Delaware corporation having its primary place of business in Santa Clara County, California. . . . Plaintiff purchases [ASICs], which are considered the control center of its network switchers, from Defendant.

Defendant is also a Delaware corporation. Defendant asserts that, at all relevant times, its corporate headquarters, inside sales and marketing office, public relations department, principal warehouse, and most design and engineering functions were located in Burnaby, British Columbia, Canada. Defendant also maintains an office in Portland, Oregon, where many of its engineers are based. Defendant's products are sold in California through Unique Technologies, which is an authorized distributor of Defendant's products in North America. It is undisputed that Defendant directed Plaintiff to purchase Defendant's products through Unique, and that Defendant honored purchase orders solicited by Unique. Unique is located in California. Determining Defendant's "place of business" with respect to its contract with Plaintiff is critical to the question of whether the Court has jurisdiction in this case.

Plaintiff's Complaint focuses on five purchase orders. Four of the five purchase orders were submitted to Defendant through Unique as directed by Defendant. However, Plaintiff does not dispute that one of the purchase orders, dated January 28, 2000, was sent by fax directly to Defendant in British Columbia, and that Defendant processed the order in British Columbia. Defendant shipped all orders to Plaintiff's headquarters in California. Upon delivery of the goods, Unique sent invoices to Plaintiff, at which time Plaintiff tendered payment to Unique either in California or in Nevada.

. . . Defendant asserts that . . . documents upon which Plaintiff relies emanated from Defendant's office in British Columbia. . . . It is furthermore undisputed that the Prototype Product Limited Warranty Agreements relating to some or all of Plaintiff's purchases were executed with Defendant's British Columbia facility. . . .

Defendant does not deny that Plaintiff maintained extensive contacts with Defendant's facilities in Portland Oregon during the

a. A defendant is permitted to remove to federal court any civil action brought in a state court that originally could have been filed in federal court. 28 U.S.C. § 1441(a). When a case originally filed in state court contains separate and independent federal and state law claims, as PMC–Sierra claimed in this case, the entire case may be removed to federal court. *Id.* § 1441(c).—Eds.

"development and engineering" of the ASICs.... These contacts included daily email and telephone correspondence and frequent in-person collaborations between Plaintiff's engineers and Defendant's engineers in Portland....

The [CISG] is an international treaty which has been signed and ratified by the United States and Canada, among other countries. The CISG was adopted for the purpose of establishing "substantive provisions of law to govern the formation of international sales contracts and the rights and obligations of the buyer and the seller." U.S. Ratification of 1980 United Nations Convention on Contracts for the International Sale of Goods: Official English Text, 15 U.S.C.App. at 52 (1997). The CISG applies "to contracts of sale of goods between parties whose places of business are in different States ... when the States are Contracting States." 15 U.S.C.App., Art. 1(1)(a). Article 10 of the CISG provides that "if a party has more than one place of business, the place of business is that which has the closest relationship to the contract and its performance." 15 U.S.C.App. Art. 10....

Defendant asserts that this Court has jurisdiction to hear this case pursuant to 28 U.S.C. section 1331, which dictates that the "district courts shall have original jurisdiction of all civil actions arising under the Constitution, laws, or treaties of the United States." Specifically, Defendant contends that the contract claims at issue necessarily implicate the CISG, because the contract is between parties having their places of business in two nations which have adopted the CISG treaty. The Court concludes that Defendant's place of business for the purposes of the contract at issue and its performance is Burnaby, British Columbia, Canada. Accordingly, the CISG applies. Moreover, the parties did not effectuate an "opt out" of application of the CISG. Finally, ... the Court concludes that the CISG preempts state laws that address the formation of a contract of sale and the rights and obligations of the seller and buyer arising from such a contract....

A. FEDERAL JURISDICTION ATTACHES TO CLAIMS GOVERNED BY THE CISG

Although the general federal question statute, 28 U.S.C. § 1331(a), gives district courts original jurisdiction over every civil action that "arises under the ... treaties of the United States," an individual may only enforce a treaty's provisions when the treaty is self-executing, that is, when it expressly or impliedly creates a private right of action. The parties do not dispute that the CISG properly creates a private right of action. *See Delchi Carrier v. Rotorex Corp.,* 71 F.3d 1024, 1027–28 (2d Cir.1995); *Filanto, S.p.A. v. Chilewich Int'l Corp.,* 789 F.Supp. 1229, 1237 (S.D.N.Y.1992)....

Therefore, if the CISG properly applies to this action, federal jurisdiction exists.[12]

B. The Contract in Question Is Between Parties From Two Different Contracting States

The CISG only applies when a contract is "between parties whose places of business are in different States."[13] 15 U.S.C.App., Art. 1(1)(a). If this requirement is not satisfied, Defendant cannot claim jurisdiction under the CISG. It is undisputed that Plaintiff's place of business is Santa Clara County, California, U.S.A. It is further undisputed that during the relevant time period, Defendant's corporate headquarters, inside sales and marketing office, public relations department, principal warehouse, and most of its design and engineering functions were located in Burnaby, British Columbia, Canada. However, Plaintiff contends that, pursuant to Article 10 of the CISG, Defendant's "place of business" having the closest relationship to the contract at issue is the United States.[14]

The Complaint asserts *inter alia* two claims for breach of contract and a claim for breach of express warranty based on the failure of the delivered ASICs to conform to the agreed upon technical specifications. In support of these claims, Plaintiff relies on multiple representations allegedly made by Defendant regarding the technical specifications of the ASICS products at issue.... It appears undisputed that each of these alleged representations regarding the technical specifications of the product was issued from Defendant's headquarters in British Columbia, Canada....

Rather than challenge the Canadian source of these documents, Plaintiff shifts its emphasis to the purchase orders submitted by Plaintiff to Unique Technologies, a nonexclusive distributor of Defendant's products. Plaintiff asserts that Unique acted in the United States as an agent of Defendant, and that Plaintiff's contacts with Unique establish Defendant's place of business in the U.S. for the purposes of this contract.

Plaintiff has failed to persuade the Court that Unique acted as the agent of Defendant. Plaintiff provides no legal support for this

---

12. Diversity cannot serve as a basis for jurisdiction in this case, because both parties are incorporated in the state of Delaware. *See Bank of California Nat'l Ass'n v. Twin Harbors Lumber Co.,* 465 F.2d 489, 491–92 (9th Cir. 1972).

13. In the context of the CISG, "different States" refers to different countries. U.S. Ratification of 1980 United Nations Convention on Contracts for the International Sale of Goods: Official English Text, 15 U.S.C.App. at 52 (1997).

14. Article 10 of the CISG states *inter alia:*

For the purposes of this Convention:

(a) If a party has more than one place of business, the place of business is that which has the closest relationship to the contract and its performance, having regard to the circumstances known to or contemplated by the parties at any time before or at the conclusion of the contract.

proposition. To the contrary, a distributor of goods for resale is normally not treated as an agent of the manufacturer. Restatement of the Law of Agency, 2d § 14J (1957) ("One who receives goods from another for resale to a third person is not thereby the other's agent in the transaction."). . . . Plaintiff's dealings with Unique do not establish Defendant's place of business in the United States.

Plaintiff's claims concern breaches of representations made by Defendant from Canada. Moreover, the products in question are manufactured in Canada, and Plaintiff knew that Defendant was Canadian, having sent one purchase order directly to Defendant in Canada by fax. . . . Moreover, Plaintiff directly corresponded with Defendant at Defendant's Canadian address. . . . In contrast, Plaintiff has not identified any specific representation or correspondence emanating from Defendant's Oregon branch. For these reasons, the Court finds that Defendant's place of business that has the closest relationship to the contract and its performance is British Columbia, Canada. Consequently, the contract at issue in this litigation is between parties from two different Contracting States, Canada and the United States. This contract therefore implicates the CISG.

C. The Effect of the Choice of Law Clauses

Plaintiff next argues that, even if the Parties are from two nations that have adopted the CISG, the choice of law provisions in the "Terms and Conditions" set forth by both Parties reflect the Parties' intent to "opt out" of application of the treaty.[15] Article 6 of the CISG provides that "[t]he parties may exclude the application of the Convention or, subject to Article 12, derogate from or vary the effect of any of its provisions." 15 U.S.C.App., Art. 6. Defendant asserts that merely choosing the law of a jurisdiction is insufficient to opt out of the CISG, absent express exclusion of the CISG. The Court finds that the particular choice of law provisions in the "Terms and Conditions" of both parties are inadequate to effectuate an opt out of the CISG.

Although selection of a particular choice of law, such as "the California Commercial Code" or the "Uniform Commercial Code" *could* amount to implied exclusion of the CISG, the choice of law clauses at issue here do not evince a clear intent to opt out of the CISG. For example, Defendant's choice of applicable law adopts the

---

15. Plaintiff's Terms and Conditions provides "APPLICABLE LAW. The validity [and] performance of this [purchase] order shall be governed by the laws of the state shown on Buyer's address on this order." . . . The buyer's address as shown on each of the Purchase Orders is San Jose, California. . . .

Defendant's Terms and Conditions provides "APPLICABLE LAW: The con-
tract between the parties is made, governed by, and shall be construed in accordance with the laws of the Province of British Columbia and the laws of Canada applicable therein, which shall be deemed to be the proper law hereof. . . . " . . . It is undisputed that British Columbia has adopted the CISG.

law of British Columbia, and it is undisputed that the CISG *is* the law of British Columbia. (International Sale of Goods Act ch. 236, 1996 S.B.C. 1 *et seq.* (B.C.).) Furthermore, even Plaintiff's choice of applicable law generally adopts the "laws of" the State of California, and California is bound by the Supremacy Clause to the treaties of the United States. U.S. Const. art. VI, cl. 2 ("This Constitution, and the laws of the United States which shall be made in pursuance thereof; and all treaties made, or which shall be made, under the authority of the United States, shall be the supreme law of the land.") Thus, under general California law, the CISG is applicable to contracts where the contracting parties are from different countries that have adopted the CISG. In the absence of clear language indicating that both contracting parties intended to opt out of the CISG, and in view of Defendant's Terms and Conditions which would apply the CISG, the Court rejects Plaintiff's contention that the choice of law provisions preclude the applicability of the CISG.

D.   FEDERAL JURISDICTION BASED UPON THE CISG DOES NOT VIOLATE THE WELL-PLEADED COMPLAINT RULE

[The court also rejected Asante's argument that removal was improper because of the "well-pleaded complaint" rule. This rule states that a cause of action arises under federal law only if a plaintiff's well-pleaded complaint raised issues of federal law. While the complaint did not refer to the CISG, PMC–Sierra argued that the preemptive force of the CISG converted the state breach of contract claim into a federal claim. The court concluded that "the expressly stated goal of developing uniform international contract law to promote international trade indicates the intent of the parties to the treaty to have the treaty preempt state law causes of action."]

Notes

1–4.   If both Asante and PMC–Sierra are Delaware corporations, how could the "internationality" requirement of CISG Article I have been satisfied?

1–5.   Compare CISG Article 10 (quoted in *Asante*) with the following provision from the UCC:

§ 1–105. Territorial Application of the Act; Parties' Power to Choose Applicable Law.

(1) Except as provided hereafter in this section, when a transaction bears a reasonable relation to this state and also to another state or nation the parties may agree that the law either of this state or of such other state or nation shall govern their rights and

duties. Failing such agreement this Act applies to transactions bearing an appropriate relation to this state. . . .

Would it have made any difference to the outcome in *Asante* if the court had applied UCC § 1–105 instead of CISG Article 10?

1–6. It seems that both the UCC and the CISG would allow parties to agree as to the law to be applied to their contract. If Asante chose the law of California, and PMC–Sierra chose the law of British Columbia, why does *neither* choice remove the contract from the application of the CISG? *See BP Oil International, Ltd. v. Empresa Estatal Petroleos de Ecuador*, 332 F.3d 333 (5th Cir. 2003) (holding that CISG applied to contract with clause choosing Ecuadorian law, because parties were located in signatory countries, contract did not explicitly opt out of CISG coverage, and CISG was Ecuadorian law). What would the contract have to say to remove it from the CISG?

1–7. By its own terms, UCC § 1–105 seems to apply to the contract and the resulting dispute. How is it possible that the court replaces otherwise applicable UCC provisions with the corresponding provisions of the CISG? As you may discuss at greater length in your Constitutional Law course, this is possible—indeed, legally required—by a principle known as federal preemption of state law. This is based on the U.S. Constitution, art. VI, cl. 2, which states that "[t]his Constitution, and the Laws of the United States which shall be made in Pursuance thereof; and *all Treaties made, or which shall be made, under the Authority of the United States*, shall be the supreme Law of the Land; and the Judges in every State shall be bound thereby, any Thing in the Constitution or Laws of any State to the Contrary notwithstanding." (Emphasis added.) Thus, because an applicable treaty is part of the "supreme law of the land," state law has no legal effect contrary or inconsistent with the provisions of the treaty.[16] In another portion of its opinion, *Asante* applies preemption as follows:

> In the case of federal statutes, "[t]he question of whether a certain action is preempted by federal law is one of congressional intent. The purpose of Congress is the ultimate touchstone." *Pilot Life Ins. Co. v. Dedeaux,* 481 U.S. 41, 45 (1987) (internal quotations and citations omitted). Transferring this analysis to the question of preemption by a treaty, the Court focuses on the intent of the treaty's contracting parties. *See Husmann v. Trans World Airlines, Inc.,* 169 F.3d 1151, 1153 (8th Cir.1999) (finding Warsaw Convention preempts state law personal injury claim); *Jack v. Trans World Airlines, Inc.,* 820 F.Supp. 1218, 1220 (N.D.Cal.1993) (finding removal proper because Warsaw Convention preempts state law causes of action).
>
> In the case of the CISG treaty, this intent can be discerned from the introductory text, which states that "the adoption of

---

16. For a thorough historical analysis of the preemption principle in the courts, see Mary J. Davis, *Unmasking* *the Presumption in Favor of Preemption,* 53 S.C. L. Rev. 967 (2002).

uniform rules which govern contracts for the international sale of goods and take into account the different social, economic and legal systems would contribute to the removal of legal barriers in international trade and promote the development of international trade." 15 U.S.C.App. at 53. The CISG further recognizes the importance of "the development of international trade on the basis of equality and mutual benefit." *Id.* These objectives are reiterated in the President's Letter of Transmittal of the CISG to the Senate as well as the Secretary of State's Letter of Submittal of the CISG to the President. *Id.* at 70–72. The Secretary of State, George P. Shultz, noted:

> Sales transactions that cross international boundaries are subject to legal uncertainty—doubt as to which legal system will apply and the difficulty of coping with unfamiliar foreign law. The sales contract may specify which law will apply, but our sellers and buyers cannot expect that foreign trading partners will always agree on the applicability of United States law.... The Convention's approach provides an effective solution for this difficult problem. When a contract for an international sale of goods does not make clear what rule of law applies, the Convention provides uniform rules to govern the questions that arise in making and performance of the contract.

Id. at 71. The Court concludes that the expressly stated goal of developing uniform international contract law to promote international trade indicates the intent of the parties to the treaty to have the treaty preempt state law causes of action.

The availability of independent state contract law causes of action would frustrate the goals of uniformity and certainty embraced by the CISG. Allowing such avenues for potential liability would subject contracting parties to different states' laws and the very same ambiguities regarding international contracts that the CISG was designed to avoid. As a consequence, parties to international contracts would be unable to predict the applicable law, and the fundamental purpose of the CISG would be undermined. Based on very similar rationale, courts have concluded that the Warsaw Convention preempts state law causes of action.... The conclusion that the CISG preempts state law also comports with the view of academic commentators on the subject. *See* William S. Dodge, *Teaching the CISG in Contracts,* 50 J. Legal Educ. 72, 72 (March 2000) ("As a treaty the CISG is federal law, which preempts state common law and the UCC."); David Frisch, *Commercial Common Law, The United Nations Convention on the International Sale of Goods, and the Inertia of Habit,* 74 Tul. L.Rev. 495, 503–04 (1999) ("Since the CISG has the preemptive force of federal law, it will preempt article 2 when applicable.").

Asante Technologies, Inc., 164 F.Supp.2d at 1150–1153.

1–8. The CISG applies to contracts for the sale of goods. Would it apply to a contract calling for delivery of goods and performance of services? Consider the following situation. Genpharm Inc., a Canadian pharmaceutical manufacturer, entered into a contract with Pliva–Lachema A.S., a Croatian supplier of warfarin sodium, under which Pliva–Lachema was to supply warfarin sodium to be used by Genpharm in an anticoagulant drug to be sold in United States. Genpharm was beginning the preliminary development work necessary to prepare and submit an Abbreviated New Drug Application (ANDA) to the Federal Drug Administration (FDA) for generic warfarin sodium tablets. As part of this effort, Genpharm needed a supplier to provide the drug and to assist it in obtaining ANDA approval from the FDA. (Among other things, Pliva–Lachema would provide information to the FDA about its equipment, manufacturing steps, raw materials, laboratory controls, and facilities and agreed to allow Genpharm to act as sole distributor of Pliva–Lachema warfarin in the United States, Canada, and other designated countries.) Is this a contract for the sale of goods for purposes of the CISG, or a goods-and-services agreement not covered by the convention? In *Genpharm Inc. v. Pliva–Lachema A.S.*, 361 F.Supp.2d 49 (E.D.N.Y. 2005), the district court held that it had subject matter jurisdiction under the CISG with respect to a contract dispute between the parties. In reaching this conclusion, the court relied on CISG Article 3, which states:

> (1) Contracts for the supply of goods to be manufactured or produced are to be considered sales unless the party who orders the goods undertakes to supply a substantial part of the materials necessary for such manufacture or production.

> (2) This Convention does not apply to contracts in which the preponderant part of the obligations of the party who furnishes the goods consists in the supply of labour or other services.

1–9. Would Genpharm have entered into a contract for the purchase of warfarin sodium from Pliva–Lachema if the seller had *not* also agreed to send a "Letter of Access" to the FDA, authorize the FDA to refer to its explanation of its operations and facilities in support of Genpharm's FDA filing, and provide advance notice to both Genpharm and the FDA of any change in its manufacturing site? If not, does this mean that the Genpharm/Pliva–Lachema contract is *not* a contract for the sale of goods, but something else?

1–10. Being a contract for the sale of goods is essential for a contract to be covered by the CISG—as it is for coverage by the UCC. Consider how the *Genpharm* court uses the UCC in deciding whether the contract is covered by the CISG:

> This result [holding that the contract was for goods under the CISG] would also be appropriate if analyzed under the UCC. The Second Circuit has recognized that "[c]aselaw interpreting analogous provisions of Article 2 of the Uniform Commercial Code ('UCC'), may also inform a court where the language of the

relevant CISG provisions tracks that of the UCC. However, UCC caselaw 'is not per se applicable.' " *Delchi Carrier,* 71 F.3d at 1028 (quoting *Orbisphere Corp. v. United States,* 726 F.Supp. 1344, 1355 (Ct. Int'l Trade 1989)).

Here, the Court finds that caselaw interpreting contract formation under Article 2 of the UCC is helpful. Courts look to the "essence" or main objective of the agreement when deciding whether an agreement is a contract for the sale of goods covered by the UCC. *Medinol Ltd. v. Boston Scientific Corp.,* 346 F.Supp.2d 575, 593 (S.D.N.Y.2004). "If the provision of services or rendition of other performance predominates and is not merely incidental or collateral to the sale of goods, then the contract will not be subject to" the UCC. *Dynamics Corp. of America v. International Harvester Co.,* 429 F.Supp. 341, 346 (S.D.N.Y.1977); *see also Triangle Underwriters, Inc. v. Honeywell, Inc.,* 604 F.2d 737 (2d Cir.1979); *Cary Oil Co. v. MG Ref. & Mktg., Inc.,* 90 F.Supp.2d 401 (S.D.N.Y. 2000).

There can be no question that the instant dispute involves an agreement to supply goods. Indeed, it is clear that the only reason Genpharm and the Defendants had any relationship at all was for the international sale of warfarin, which is undeniably a "good." In addition, it makes no difference whether the agreements may or may not contain price or quantity. The CISG expressly provides that it "governs only the formation of the contract of sale and the rights and obligations of the seller and buyer arising from such contract." CISG, art 4. The applicability of the CISG is not restricted to contracts after formation or contracts containing definite prices or quantities. Therefore, this dispute falls within this Court's treaty jurisdiction, and this Court's subject matter jurisdiction. . . .

Genpharm Inc., 361 F.Supp.2d at 55.

1–11. In the course of its analysis, the *Genpharm* court referred to CISG art. 7(1)-(2), which states:

> (1) In the interpretation of this Convention, regard is to be had to its international character and to the need to promote uniformity in its application and the observance of good faith in international trade.

> (2) Questions concerning matters governed by this Convention which are not expressly settled in it are to be settled in conformity with the general principles on which it is based or, in the absence of such principles, in conformity with the law applicable by virtue of the rules of private international law.

How does this provision compare with the following provision of the UCC?

> § 1–102. Purposes; Rules of Construction; Variation by Agreement.

(1) This Act shall be liberally construed and applied to promote its underlying purposes and policies.

(2) Underlying purposes and policies of this Act are

(a) to simplify, clarify and modernize the law governing commercial transactions;

(b) to permit the continued expansion of commercial practices through custom, usage and agreement of the parties;

(c) to make uniform the law among the various jurisdictions.

Could the court have decided that the Genpharm/Pliva–Lachema agreement was governed by the UCC? Would it make any difference to your answer if the agreement had contained a provision stating that "[t]he parties agree that this contract shall be subject to the UCC"? If Genpharm and Pliva–Lachema had been *U.S.* companies and entered into the agreement described in note 1–8, *supra*, would the UCC have applied to the agreement? What if these two U.S. companies had agreed "that this agreement shall be subject to the laws of Canada"?

1–12.   Articles 1–3 of the CISG provide:

Article 1

(1) This Convention applies to contracts of sale of goods between parties whose places of business are in different States:

(a) when the States are Contracting States; or

(b) when the rules of private international law lead to the application of the law of a Contracting State.

(2) The fact that the parties have their places of business in different States is to be disregarded whenever this fact does not appear either from the contract or from any dealings between, or from information disclosed by, the parties at any time before or at the conclusion of the contract.

(3) Neither the nationality of the parties or the civil or commercial character of the parties or of the contract is to be taken into consideration in determining the application of this Convention.

Article 2

This Convention does not apply to sales:

(a) of goods bought for personal, family or household use, unless the seller, at any time before or at the conclusion of the contract, neither knew nor ought to have known that the goods were bought for any such use;

(b) by auction;

(c) on execution or otherwise by authority of law;

(d) of stocks, shares, investment securities, negotiable instruments or money;

(e) of ships, vessels, hovercraft or aircraft;

(f) of electricity.

Article 3

(1) Contracts for the supply of goods to be manufactured or produced are to be considered sales unless the party who orders the goods undertakes to supply a substantial part of the materials necessary for such manufacture or production.

(2) This Convention does not apply to contracts in which the preponderant part of the obligations of the party who furnishes the goods consists in the supply of labour or other services.

What if Genpharm were a U.S. company and Pliva–Lachema were a French company? (Both France and the United States are signatories to the CISG.) Could the court have decided that the Genpharm/Pliva–Lachema agreement was governed by the UCC? Would it make any difference to your answer if the agreement had contained a provision stating that "[t]he parties agree that this contract shall be subject to the UCC"?

1–13. For a case with similar facts reaching the same conclusion as the *Genpharm* case, see *Geneva Pharms. Tech. Corp. v. Barr Labs., Inc.*, 201 F.Supp.2d 236, 281 (S.D.N.Y.2002), *rev'd on other grounds*, 386 F.3d 485, 489 (2d Cir.2004) (involving contract for sale of clathrate, raw material used in production of warfarin). In *Geneva Pharms.*, the plaintiff alleged that a contact existed because it purchased research and development quantities of clathrate, invested a substantial amount of money in developing warfarin based on the defendants' raw material, and relied on a reference letter provided by the defendant-supplier in connection with the ANDA that it submitted to the FDA. The court not only applied the CISG but also determined that an implied contract existed between the parties. *Geneva Pharms.*, 201 F.Supp. 2d at 284.

1–14. Is the CISG a jurisdictional device, or a source of substantive law of the contract? The excerpts from *Asante*—and the *Genpharm* case as well–focus on the jurisdictional implications, but as the materials in the following chapters will demonstrate, the CISG also has application as the substantive law of the contract. In confronting CISG issues, however, U.S. courts sometimes seem to waffle on the issue of subject matter jurisdiction under the CISG. One such case is *Mitchell Aircraft Spares, Inc. v. European Aircraft Service AB*, 23 F.Supp.2d 915 (N.D.Ill. 1998). In that case, Mitchell Aircraft brought suit against European Aircraft (EAS), a foreign seller of aircraft parts, for breach of contract and breach of warranty. As a preliminary matter, the court considered whether it had jurisdiction, based either on the diversity of the parties (a U.S. national and a Swedish national), or on federal question jurisdiction based on the applicability of the CISG. The court seemed to become confused over the interplay of the parties' choice of applicable law and subject matter jurisdiction. The court determined that it had diversity jurisdiction under 28 U.S.C. § 1332(a)(2). If it was a diversity case, then was the substantive law governing the contract the law of Sweden, Illinois, or the CISG? However, as *Asante* suggests, if the CISG applies, does that mean that the court has *federal question* jurisdiction over the case under 28 U.S.C. § 1331? The court in effect ducked the issue in the following terms:

> . . . [I]t is clear that this court has subject matter jurisdiction over this case pursuant to 28 U.S.C. § 1332. Thus, this court has jurisdiction over the case regardless of whether the CISG provides an independent basis for subject matter jurisdiction. The court's opinion would not change in any way if it found that its jurisdiction were based on the CISG. Thus, the court need not reach the issue of whether the CISG provides an independent basis for subject matter jurisdiction.
>
> . . . [T]he CISG governs most of the issues in this case because the United States, where Mitchell has its place of business, and Sweden, where EAS has its place of business, are both States Party to the CISG. CISG art. I. . . .

Mitchell Aircraft Spares, Inc., 23 F.Supp.2d at 918. If the court is right in concluding that it has diversity jurisdiction over the case, why does it say that "the CISG governs most of the issues" in the case? In negotiating the contract, if Mitchell Aircraft had wanted its agreement to be subject to the Illinois version of the UCC, could it have done so?

Chapter 2

CONTRACT FORMATION

A. INTRODUCTION

At common law, the basic legal framework for the formation of a contract requires an offer and an acceptance matching the terms of the offer.[1] To what extent is that framework altered if the parties to a purported contract are nationals of two respective states that are signatories of Convention on Contracts for the International Sale of Goods (CISG)? The following cases illustrate the effect of application of the CISG to contract formation.

FILANTO, S.p.A. v. CHILEWICH INT'L CORP.
789 F.Supp. 1229 (S.D.N.Y.1992).

BRIEANT, CHIEF JUDGE.

[Filanto, an Italian footwear manufacturer, brought an action against Chilewich, a New York import-export firm, alleging breach of a contract for the purchase of footwear from Filanto to fulfill Chilewich's contract with its Russian buyer. Chilewich moved to stay the action pending arbitration, and Filanto moved to enjoin arbitration or alternatively that arbitration be held in Southern District of New York, rather than in Russia. The District Court held that the question of whether the parties had agreed to arbitrate their dispute was governed by the Federal Arbitration Act, rather than by New York law, and that the record established that the parties had agreed to arbitrate disputes by incorporating a provision from Chilewich's contract with the Russian buyer requiring arbitration. The court ordered arbitration in Russia, despite unsettled conditions there. In the course of its decision, the court

---

1. This framework is adjusted by the provisions of Article 2 of the Uniform Commercial Code (UCC), which applies to sales of *goods* within the United States. The implications of these adjustments are discussed in § D, *infra.*

17

considered whether the "general principles of contract law" relevant to the action included the Uniform Commercial Code (UCC) or the federal law of contracts to be found in the CISG.]

Plaintiff Filanto is an Italian corporation engaged in the manufacture and sale of footwear. Defendant Chilewich is an export-import firm incorporated in the state of New York with its principal place of business in White Plains. On February 28, 1989, Chilewich's agent in the United Kingdom, Byerly Johnson, Ltd., signed a contract ["Contract No. 32–03/93085"] with Raznoexport, the Soviet Foreign Economic Association [in what is now Russia], which obligated Byerly Johnson to supply footwear to Raznoexport. . . .

However, the focus of this dispute, apparent from the parties' submissions, is not on the *scope* of the arbitration provision included in the Russian contract; rather, the threshold question is whether these parties actually agreed to arbitrate their disputes at all. . . .

. . . The central disputed issue, therefore, is whether the correspondence between the parties, viewed in light of their business relationship, constitutes an "agreement in writing".

Courts interpreting this "agreement in writing" requirement have generally started their analysis with the plain language of the Convention [on the Recognition and Enforcement of Foreign Arbitral Awards and its implementing legislation, codified at 9 U.S.C. § 201 *et seq.*, to which the United States, Italy and the USSR are all signatories], which requires "an arbitral clause in a contract or an arbitration agreement, signed by the parties or contained in an exchange of letters or telegrams", Article I(1), and have then applied that language in light of federal law, which consists of generally accepted principles of contract law, including the Uniform Commercial Code. *See, e.g., Genesco*[, *Inc. v. T. Kakiuchi & Co., Ltd.*, 815 F.2d 840, 845–846 (2d Cir.1987)] (holding under "general contract principles" that buyer agreed to arbitrate disputes arising under unsigned sales confirmation forms due to parties' course of dealing and buyer's signatures on related sales confirmation forms); *Sen Mar, Inc. v. Tiger Petroleum Corp.*, 774 F.Supp. 879, 883–84 (S.D.N.Y.1991) (denying seller's motion to compel arbitration since arbitration clause not in signed writing or in exchange of letters); *Midland Bright Drawn Steel, supra*, 1989 WL 125788, at 4, 1989 U.S.Dist.Lexis 12368, at 3–4 (holding seller entitled to stay of arbitration since arbitration clause represented material alteration of contract not accepted by seller); *Beromun Aktiengesellschaft v. Societa Industriale Agricola, Inc.*, 471 F.Supp. 1163, 1171–72 (S.D.N.Y.1979) (denying seller's motion to compel arbitration since no contract ever formed between parties). *But see Astor Chocolate* [*Corp. v. Mikroverk, Ltd.*, 704 F.Supp. 30, 33–34 (E.D.N.Y.1989)], (applying state contract law in case governed by Convention). *See also Zambia Steel & Building Supplies Ltd. v. James Clark & Eaton Ltd.*, 2 Lloyd's Rep. 225 (1986) (United Kingdom) (seller's oral assent to sales note containing arbitration clause sufficient under Convention to compel arbitration).

However, as plaintiff correctly notes, the "general principles of contract law" relevant to this action, do *not* include the Uniform Commercial Code; rather, the "federal law of contracts" to be applied in this case is found in the United Nations Convention on Contracts for the International Sale of Goods (the "Sale of Goods Convention"), *codified at* 15 U.S.C. Appendix (West Supp.1991). This Convention, ratified by the Senate in 1986, is a self-executing agreement which entered into force between the United States and other signatories, including Italy, on January 1, 1988. *See* Preface to Convention, *reprinted at* 15 U.S.C. Appendix (West Supp. 1991).... [A]bsent a choice-of-law provision, and with certain exclusions not here relevant, the Convention governs *all* contracts between parties with places of business in different nations, so long as both nations are signatories to the Convention. Sale of Goods Convention Article 1(1)(a). Since the contract alleged in this case most certainly was formed, if at all, after January 1, 1988, and since both the United States and Italy are signatories to the Convention, the Court will interpret the "agreement in writing" requirement of the Arbitration Convention in light of, and with reference to, the substantive international law of contracts embodied in the Sale of Goods Convention.

Not surprisingly, the parties offer varying interpretations of the numerous letters and documents exchanged between them. The Court will briefly summarize their respective contentions.

Defendant Chilewich contends that the Memorandum Agreement dated March 13 which it signed and sent to Filanto was an offer. It then argues that Filanto's retention of the letter, along with its subsequent acceptance of Chilewich's performance under the Agreement—the furnishing of the May 11 letter of credit—estops it from denying its acceptance of the contract. Although phrased as an estoppel argument, this contention is better viewed as an acceptance by conduct argument, *e.g.*, that in light of the parties' course of dealing, Filanto had a duty timely to inform Chilewich that it objected to the incorporation by reference of all the terms of the Russian contract. Under this view, the return of the Memorandum Agreement, signed by Filanto, on August 7, 1990, along with the covering letter purporting to exclude parts of the Russian Contract, was ineffective as a matter of law as a rejection of the March 13 offer, because this occurred some five months after Filanto received the Memorandum Agreement and two months after Chilewich furnished the Letter of Credit. Instead, in Chilewich's view, this action was a proposal for modification of the March 13 Agreement. Chilewich rejected this proposal, by its letter of August 7 to Byerly Johnson, and the August 29 fax by Johnson to Italian Trading SRL, which communication Filanto acknowledges receiving. Accordingly, Filanto under this interpretation is bound by the written terms of the March 13 Memorandum Agreement; since that agreement incorporates by reference the Russian Contract containing the arbitration provision, Filanto is bound to arbitrate.

Plaintiff Filanto's interpretation of the evidence is rather different. While Filanto apparently agrees that the March 13 Memorandum Agreement was indeed an offer, it characterizes its August 7 return of the signed Memorandum Agreement with the covering letter as a counteroffer. While defendant contends that under Uniform Commercial Code § 2–207 [discussed in § D, *infra*] this action would be viewed as an acceptance with a proposal for a material modification, the Uniform Commercial Code, as previously noted does not apply to this case, because the State Department undertook to fix something that was not broken by helping to create the Sale of Goods Convention which varies from the Uniform Commercial Code in many significant ways. Instead, under this analysis, Article 19(1) of the Sale of Goods Convention would apply. That section, as the Commentary to the Sale of Goods Convention notes, reverses the rule of Uniform Commercial Code § 2–207, and reverts to the common law rule that "A reply to an offer which purports to be an acceptance but contains additions, limitations or other modifications is a rejection of the offer and constitutes a counter-offer". Sale of Goods Convention Article 19(1). Although the Convention, like the Uniform Commercial Code, does state that non-material terms do become part of the contract unless objected to, Sale of Goods Convention Article 19(2), the Convention treats inclusion (or deletion) of an arbitration provision as "material", Sale of Goods Convention Article 19(3). The August 7 letter, therefore, was a counteroffer which, according to Filanto, Chilewich accepted by its letter dated September 27, 1990. Though that letter refers to and acknowledges the "contractual obligations" between the parties, it is doubtful whether it can be characterized as an acceptance.

More generally, both parties seem to have lost sight of the narrow scope of the inquiry required by the Arbitration Convention. . . . All that this Court need do is to determine if a sufficient "agreement in writing" to arbitrate disputes exists between these parties. *Cf. United Steelworkers of America v. Warrior & Gulf Co.*, 363 U.S. 574, 582, 80 S.Ct. 1347, 1352–53, 40 L.Ed.2d 1409 (1960) (party cannot be required to submit to arbitration absent agreement). Although that inquiry is informed by the provisions of the

Sale of Goods Convention, the Court lacks the authority on this motion to resolve all outstanding issues between the parties. Indeed, contracts and the arbitration clauses included therein are considered to be "severable", a rule that the Sale of Goods Convention itself adopts with respect to avoidance of contracts generally. Sale of Goods Convention Article 81(1). There is therefore authority for the proposition that issues relating to existence of the contract, as opposed to the existence of the arbitration clause, are issues for the arbitrators. . . .

The Court is satisfied on this record that there *was* indeed an agreement to arbitrate between these parties.

There is simply no satisfactory explanation as to why Filanto failed to object to the incorporation by reference of the Russian Contract in a timely fashion. As noted above, Chilewich had in the meantime commenced its performance under the Agreement, and the Letter of Credit it furnished Filanto on May 11 *itself* mentioned the Russian Contract. An offeree who, knowing that the offeror has commenced performance, fails to notify the offeror of its objection to the terms of the contract within a reasonable time will, under certain circumstances, be deemed to have assented to those terms. Restatement (Second) of Contracts § 69 (1981); *Graniteville v. Star Knits of California, Inc.*, 680 F.Supp. 587, 589–90 (S.D.N.Y.1988) (compelling arbitration since party who failed timely to object to sales note containing arbitration clause deemed to have accepted its terms); *Imptex International Corp. v. Lorprint, Inc.*, 625 F.Supp. 1572, 1572 (S.D.N.Y.1986) (Weinfeld, J.) (party who failed to object to inclusion of arbitration clause in sales confirmation agreement bound to arbitrate). The Sale of Goods Convention itself recognizes this rule: Article 18(1), provides that "A statement made by or other conduct of the offeree indicating assent to an offer is an acceptance". Although mere "silence or inactivity" does not constitute acceptance, Sale of Goods Convention Article 18(1), the Court may consider previous relations between the parties in assessing whether a party's conduct constituted acceptance, Sale of Goods Convention Article 8(3). In this case, in light of the extensive course of prior dealing between these parties, Filanto was certainly under a duty to alert Chilewich in timely fashion to its objections to the terms of the March 13 Memorandum Agreement—particularly since Chilewich had repeatedly referred it to the Russian Contract and Filanto had had a copy of that document for some time.

Notes

2–1. If the relevant federal transactional law under the Arbitration Convention "consists of generally accepted principles of contract law, including the Uniform Commercial Code," how does the *Filanto* court come to apply the CISG to the issue of formation of a contract to arbitrate?

2–2. Seller *A* offers to sell goods to Buyer *B*. By letter *B* responds by agreeing to purchase the goods at the stated price, with arbitration of any disputes to be held in the city where *B*'s own purchaser is located. At common law, do *A* and *B* have a contract? If *A* and *B* are nationals of two states that are signatories of the CISG, do they have a contract? What leads the *Filanto* court to the answer that it would give to these questions?

2–3. Are the parties in *Filanto* arguing about the applicable law, or the factual interpretation of their actions? With the factual dispute in mind, would one really reach a different conclusion if the common law or the UCC applied to the case?

2–4. Assume that *A* and *B*, after a lengthy series of negotiations, reach agreement over the amount of goods to be purchased and the unit price of the goods, but have left other terms of their agreement— such as the date(s) and place(s) of delivery of the goods—to be worked out. Would they have a binding contract at common law? What if *A* and *B* were nationals of two states that were signatories of the CISG? In answering these questions, consider the following case.

GENEVA PHARMACEUTICALS TECHNOLOGY CORP. v. BARR LABORATORIES, INC.

201 F. Supp. 2d 236 (S.D.N.Y. 2002), *aff'd in part, rev'd in part and remanded on other grounds*, 386 F.3d 485 (2d Cir. 2004).

[GPTC, a pharmaceutical drug manufacturer, brought antitrust and related state law claims against Barr, a competitor and raw material supplier, and related defendants. On Barr's motion for summary judgment, the District Court granted the motion as to the antitrust claims. As to GPTC's state law claims, the District Court considered, among other things, whether GPTC and Barr had an implied contract and whether the CISG preempted GPTC's state law contract claims against Barr.]

The CISG, intended to ensure the observance of good faith in international trade, CISG Art. 7(1), embodies a liberal approach to contract formation and interpretation, and a strong preference for enforcing obligations and representations customarily relied upon by others in the industry. *E.g., MCC–Marble Ceramic Center, Inc. v. Ceramica Nuova d'Agostino, S.p.A.*, 144 F.3d 1384, 1387 (11th Cir.1998) (CISG abandons parol evidence rule); *Delchi Carrier SpA v. Rotorex Corp.*, 71 F.3d 1024, 1028 (2d Cir.1995) (UCC case law is not *per se* applicable to cases governed by the CISG). A contract may be proven by a document, oral representations, conduct, or some combination of the three. CISG Art. 11. The usages and practices of the parties or the industry are automatically incorporated into any agreement governed by the Convention, unless expressly excluded by the parties. CISG Art. 9.

While embodying a liberal approach, the CISG does not vitiate the need to prove concepts familiar to the common law, including offer, acceptance, validity and performance. ACIC/Brantford challenges all of these elements.

1. OFFER

Article 14 of the CISG states two requirements for the creation of an offer: it must (1) be "sufficiently definite," meaning that it indicates the goods and expressly or implicitly fixes or makes provision for determining the quantity and price; and (2) indicate the intention of the offeror to be bound in case of acceptance. CISG Art. 14(1).

Invamed [GPTC's name before its purchase by Geneva Pharmaceuiticals, part of an Austrian conglomerate] claims that a well-established custom in the industry was to rely on implied, unwritten supply commitments. Defendant Sherman [Chairman of one of the defendants, a Canadian company named Apotex Inc.] affirmed under oath that "the predominant practice is for these commitments not to be embodied in formal legal documents." Further, he stated, "When a supplier provides access to a manufacturer to its Drug Master File and the manufacturer relies upon such access as the basis of its New Drug Submission [to its regulator], it is the custom and the understanding of both the manufacturer and the supplier that, upon the issuance of the Notice of Compliance, the supplier will supply the product."

The alleged contract clearly identifies the goods at issue, clathrate. Invamed alleges that the parties had already agreed to a price and to the production of "commercial quantities" of clathrate and admits no discussion took place regarding a delivery schedule. However, accepting as true Invamed's allegations of an industry custom, the contract was sufficiently definite. Further, the alleged contract indicated Invamed's intention to be bound; it would only send in a purchase order if it in fact needed a commercial quantity of clathrate.

2. ACCEPTANCE

Relying on the provision of the CISG addressing oral offers, defendants argue that the offer had to be accepted immediately. However Invamed is relying on a contract established by the conduct of the parties. In such a situation CISG Art. 18(3) applies. It states that "the offeree may indicate assent by performing an act, such as one relating to the dispatch of goods or payment of the price," [and] "the acceptance is effective at the moment the act is performed, provided the act is performed" either within the time fixed by the offeror, if no such time is fixed, within a reasonable time. CISG 18(3). Invamed alleges that it was industry custom that the provision of a reference letter indicates acceptance. That defendants dispute this material fact only argues against summary judgment being granted.

MAGELLAN INT'L CORP. v. SALZGITTER HANDEL GmbH

76 F. Supp. 2d 919 (N.D. Ill. 1999).

SHADUR, SENIOR DISTRICT JUDGE.

Salzgitter Handel GmbH ("Salzgitter") has filed a motion pursuant to Fed.R.Civ.P. 12(b)(6), seeking to dismiss this action brought against it by Magellan International Corporation ("Magellan")....

FACTS

In considering a Rule 12(b)(6) motion to dismiss for failure to state a claim, this Court accepts all of Magellan's well-pleaded factual allegations as true, as well as drawing all reasonable inferences from those facts in Magellan's favor (*Travel All Over the World, Inc. v. Kingdom of Saudi Arabia*, 73 F.3d 1423, 1429 (7th Cir.1996)). What follows is the version of events set out in the Complaint, when read in that light.

OFFERS, COUNTEROFFERS AND ACCEPTANCE

Magellan is an Illinois-based distributor of steel products. Salzgitter is a steel trader that is headquartered in Dusseldorf, Germany and maintains an Illinois sales office. In January 1999 Magellan's Robert Arthur ("Arthur") and Salzgitter's Thomas Riess ("Riess") commenced negotiations on a potential deal under which Salzgitter would begin to act as middleman in Magellan's purchase of steel bars—manufactured according to Magellan's specifications—from a Ukrainian steel mill, Dneprospetsstal of Ukraine ("DSS").

By letter dated January 28, Magellan provided Salzgitter with written specifications for 5,585 metric tons of steel bars, with proposed pricing, and with an agreement to issue a letter of credit ("LC") to Salzgitter as Magellan's method of payment. Salzgitter responded two weeks later (on February 12 and 13) by proposing prices $5 to $20 per ton higher than those Magellan had specified.

On February 15 Magellan accepted Salzgitter's price increases, agreed on 4,000 tons as the quantity being purchased, and added $5 per ton over Salzgitter's numbers to effect shipping from Magellan's preferred port (Ventspills, Latvia). Magellan memorialized those terms, as well as the other material terms previously discussed by the parties [price, quantity, delivery date, delivery method and payment method had all been negotiated and agreed to by the parties], in two February 15 purchase orders. Salzgitter then responded on February 17, apparently accepting Magellan's memorialized terms except for two "amendments" as to prices. Riess asked for Magellan's "acceptance" of those two price increases by return fax and promised to send its already-drawn-up order confirmations as soon as they were countersigned by DSS. Arthur consented, signing and returning the approved price amendments to Riess the same day.

On February 19, Salzgitter sent its pro forma order confirmations to Magellan. But the general terms and conditions that were attached to those confirmations differed in some respects from those that had been attached to Magellan's purchase orders, mainly with respect to vessel loading conditions, dispute resolution and choice of law.

Contemplating an ongoing business relationship, Magellan and Salzgitter continued to negotiate in an effort to resolve the remaining conflicts between their respective forms. While those fine-tuning negotiations were under way, Salzgitter began to press Magellan to open its LC for the transaction in Salzgitter's favor. On March 4 Magellan sent Salzgitter a draft LC for review. Salzgitter wrote back on March 8 proposing minor amendments to the LC and stating that "all other terms are acceptable." Although Magellan preferred to wait until all of the minor details (the remaining conflicting terms) were ironed out before issuing the LC, Salzgitter continued to press for its immediate issuance.

On March 22 Salzgitter sent amended order confirmations to Magellan. Riess visited Arthur four days later on March 26 and threatened to cancel the steel orders if Magellan did not open the LC in Salzgitter's favor that day. They then came to agreement as to the remaining contractual issues. Accordingly, relying on Riess's assurances that all remaining details of the deal were settled, Arthur had the $1.2 million LC issued later that same day.

Post-Acceptance Events

Three days later (on March 29) Arthur and Riess engaged in an extended game of "fax tag" initiated by the latter. [Essentially Salzgitter was demanding an amendment to the LC, and Magellan refused, demanding instead an amendment to Salzgitter's order confirmations.] At the same time, Magellan requested minor modifications in some of the steel specifications. Salzgitter replied that it was too late to modify the specifications: DSS had already manufactured 60% of the order, and the rest was under production.

Perhaps unsurprisingly in light of what has been recited up to now, on the very next day (March 30) Magellan's and Salzgitter's friendly fine-tuning went flat. Salzgitter screeched an ultimatum to Magellan: Amend the LC by noon the following day or Salzgitter would "no longer feel obligated" to perform and would "sell the material elsewhere." On April 1 Magellan requested that the LC be canceled because of what it considered to be Saltzgitter's breach. Salzgitter returned the LC and has since been attempting to sell the manufactured steel to Magellan's customers in the United States.

MAGELLAN'S CLAIMS

Complaint Count I posits that—pursuant to the [CISG]—a valid contract existed between Magellan and Salzgitter before Salzgitter's March 30 ultimatum. Hence that attempted ukase is said to have amounted to an anticipatory repudiation of that contract, entitling Magellan to relief for its breach....

Formation of a contract under either UCC or the Convention requires an offer followed by an acceptance (*see* Convention Pt. II). Although analysis of offer and acceptance typically involves complicated factual issues of intent—issues not appropriately addressed on a motion to dismiss—this Court need not engage in such mental gymnastics here. It is enough that Magellan has alleged facts that a factfinder could call an offer on the one hand and an acceptance on the other.

Under Convention Art. 14(1) a "proposal for concluding a contract addressed to one or more specific persons constitutes an offer if it is sufficiently definite and indicates the intention of the offeror to be bound in case of acceptance." So, if the indications of the proposer are sufficiently definite and justify the addressee in understanding that its acceptance will form a contract, the proposal constitutes an offer (*id.* Art. 8(2)). For that purpose "[a] proposal is sufficiently definite if it indicates the goods and expressly or implicitly makes provision for determining the quantity and the price" (*id.* Art. 14(1)).

In this instance Magellan alleges that it sent purchase orders to Salzgitter on February 15 that contained the material terms upon which the parties had agreed. Those terms included identification of the goods, quantity and price. Certainly an offer could be found consistently with those facts.

But Convention Art. 19(1) goes on to state that "[a] reply to an offer which purports to be an acceptance but contains additions, limitations or other modifications is a rejection of the offer and constitutes a counter-offer." That provision reflects[2] the common

---

2. Bad pun intended.

law's "mirror image" rule that the UCC has rejected (*see Filanto*, 789 F.Supp. at 1238). And Salzgitter's February 17 response to the purchase orders did propose price changes. Hence that response can be seen as a counteroffer that justified Magellan's belief that its acceptance of those new prices would form a contract.

Although that expectation was then frustrated by the later events in February and then in March, which in contract terms equated to further offers and counteroffers, the requisite contractual joinder could reasonably be viewed by a factfinder as having jelled on March 26. In that respect Convention Art. 18(a) requires an indication of assent to an offer (or counteroffer) to constitute its acceptance. Such an "indication" may occur through "a statement made by or other conduct of the offeree" (*id.*). And at the very least, a jury could find consistently with Magellan's allegations that the required indication of complete (mirrored) assent occurred when Magellan issued its LC on March 26. So much, then, for the first element of a contract: offer and acceptance.

Next, the second pleading requirement for a breach of contract claim—performance by plaintiff—was not only specifically addressed by Magellan ... but can also be inferred from the facts alleged in [the] Complaint ... and from Magellan's prayer for specific performance. Magellan's performance obligation as the buyer is simple: payment of the price for the goods. Magellan issued its LC in satisfaction of that obligation, later requesting the LC's cancellation only after Salzgitter's alleged breach.... Moreover, Magellan's request for specific performance implicitly confirms that it remains ready and willing to pay the price if such relief were granted. As for ... Salzgitter's breach ... [the] Complaint ... alleges:

> Salzgitter's March 30 letter ... demanding that [certain provisions] be removed from the letter of credit and threatening to cancel the contract constitutes an anticipatory repudiation and fundamental breach of the contract.

It would be difficult to imagine an allegation that more clearly fulfills the notice function of pleading.

Notes

2–5. The *Magellan* court says that "It is enough that Magellan has alleged facts that a factfinder could call an offer on the one hand and an acceptance on the other." But isn't the issue of what constitutes an offer a question of law, not fact? Is there a factual dispute between the parties? Compare the *Magellan* court's view with that expressed by the court in *Chateau des Charmes Wines*, *infra* at 29 ("[W]hether the parties agreed to a forum selection clause is a question of law that we review de novo"). Are these cases inconsistent?

2–6. In the *Magellan* court's view, when was the offer accepted? What is Salzgitter's view on this issue? Which do you find more persuasive?

2–7. In the next case, consider whether Sabaté France's conduct is any different from Salzgitter's. Is each of them simply trying to impose new terms on the other party to an existing contract? Compare the factual circumstances of the negotiations in each case, and consider whether either party—Salzgitter or Sabaté France—was more reasonable in seeking to have its disputed terms included.

CHATEAU DES CHARMES WINES LTD. v. SABATÉ USA INC.

328 F.3d 528 (9th Cir. 2003).

PER CURIAM.

Chateau des Charmes Wines, Ltd. ("Chateau des Charmes"), a Canadian company, appeals the dismissal of its action for breach of contract and related claims arising out of its purchase of wine corks from Sabaté, S.A. ("Sabaté France"), a French company, and Sabaté USA, Inc. ("Sabaté USA"), a wholly owned California subsidiary. The district court held that forum selection clauses in the invoices that Sabaté France sent to Chateau des Charmes were part of the contract between the parties and dismissed the case in favor of adjudication in France. Because we conclude that the forum selection clauses in question were not part of any agreement between the parties, we reverse.

FACTUAL BACKGROUND AND PROCEDURAL HISTORY

The material facts pertinent to this appeal are not disputed. Sabaté France manufactures and sells special wine corks that it claims will not cause wines to be spoiled by "cork taint," a distasteful flavor that some corks produce. It sells these corks through a wholly owned California subsidiary, Sabaté USA.

In February 2000, after some preliminary discussions about the characteristics of Sabaté's corks, Chateau des Charmes, a winery from Ontario, Canada, agreed by telephone with Sabaté USA to purchase a certain number of corks at a specific price. The parties agreed on payment and shipping terms. No other terms were discussed, nor did the parties have any history of prior dealings. Later that year, Chateau des Charmes placed a second telephone order for corks on the same terms. In total, Chateau des Charmes ordered 1.2 million corks.

Sabaté France shipped the corks to Canada in eleven shipments. For each shipment, Sabaté France also sent an invoice. Some of the invoices arrived before the shipments, some with the shipments, and some after the shipments. On the face of each invoice was a paragraph in French that specified that "Any dispute arising under the present contract is under the sole jurisdiction of the Court of Commerce of the City of Perpignan." On the back of each invoice a number of provisions were printed in French, including a clause that specified that "any disputes arising out of this agreement shall be brought before the court with jurisdiction to try the matter in the judicial district where Seller's registered office is located." Chateau des Charmes duly took delivery and paid for each shipment of corks. The corks were then used to bottle Chateau des Charmes' wines.

Chateau des Charmes claims that, in 2001, it noticed that the wine bottled with Sabaté's corks was tainted by cork flavors. Chateau des Charmes filed suit in federal district court in California against Sabaté France and Sabaté USA alleging claims for breach of contract, strict liability, breach of warranty, false advertising, and unfair competition. Sabaté France and Sabaté USA filed a motion to dismiss based on the forum selection clauses. The district court held that the forum selection clauses were valid and enforceable and dismissed the action. This appeal ensued.

DISCUSSION

I.

... [W]hether the parties agreed to a forum selection clause is a question of law that we review de novo. *Cf. Helash v. Ballard*, 638 F.2d 74, 75 (9th Cir.1980) (per curiam) (existence of contract based on undisputed facts is a question of law).

The question before us is whether the forum selection clauses in Sabaté France's invoices were part of any agreement between the parties. The disputes in this case arise out of an agreement for a sale of goods from a French party and a United States party to a Canadian party. Such international sales contracts are ordinarily governed by a multilateral treaty, the United Nations Convention on Contracts for the International Sale of Goods ("C.I.S.G."), which applies to "contracts of sale of goods between parties whose places of business are in different States ... when the States are Contracting States." C.I.S.G., art. 1(1)(a), 15 U.S.C.App., 52 Fed.Reg. 6262 (March 2, 1987). The United States, Canada, and France are all contracting states to the C.I.S.G.... [T]here is no doubt that the Convention is valid and binding federal law. Accordingly, the Convention governs the substantive question of contract formation as to the forum selection clauses.

Our conclusion that the C.I.S.G. governs the issues in this appeal is not in conflict with authority from our sister circuits that have applied state law. Both the Second Circuit and the First

Circuit have confronted the question of what law governs issues of contract formation that are antecedent to determining the validity of and enforcing forum selection clauses. In *Evolution Online Sys. Inc. v. Koninklijke PTT Nederland N.V., KPN*, 145 F.3d 505, 509 (2d Cir.1998), the Second Circuit applied New York law to a dispute between a Dutch company and a New York corporation regarding the production of computer software and the provision of technical services presumably because the Convention does not apply "to contracts in which the preponderant part of the obligations of the party who furnishes the goods consists in the supply of labor or other services." C.I.S.G., art. 3(2). The First Circuit's decision in *Lambert v. Kysar*, 983 F.2d 1110, 1119 (1st Cir.1993), involved the resolution of an interstate dispute that had no international dimension.

II.

Under the C.I.S.G., it is plain that the forum selection clauses were not part of any agreement between the parties. The Convention sets out a clear regime for analyzing international contracts for the sale of goods: "A contract of sale need not be concluded in or evidenced by writing and is not subject to any other requirement as to form." C.I.S.G., art. 11. A proposal is an offer if it is sufficiently definite to "indicate[ ] the goods and expressly or implicitly fix[ ] or make[ ] provision for determining the quantity and the price," *id.,* art. 14, and it demonstrates an intention by the offeror to be bound if the proposal is accepted. *Id.* In turn, an offer is accepted if the offeree makes a "statement ... or other conduct ... indicating assent to an offer." *Id.,* art. 18. Further, "A contract is concluded at the moment when an acceptance of an offer becomes effective." *Id.,* art. 23. Within such a framework, the oral agreements between Sabaté USA and Chateau des Charmes as to the kind of cork, the quantity, and the price were sufficient to create complete and binding contracts.

The terms of those agreements did not include any forum selection clause. Indeed, Sabaté France and Sabaté USA do not contend that a forum selection clause was part of their oral agreements, but merely that the clauses in the invoices became part of a binding agreement. The logic of this contention is defective. Under the Convention, a "contract may be modified or terminated by the mere agreement of the parties." *Id.,* art. 29(1). However, the Convention clearly states that "[a]dditional or different terms relating, among other things, to ... the settlement of disputes are considered to alter the terms of the offer materially." *Id.,* art. 19(3). There is no indication that Chateau des Charmes conducted itself in a manner that evidenced any affirmative assent to the forum selection clauses in the invoices. Rather, Chateau des Charmes merely performed its obligations under the oral contract.

Nothing in the Convention suggests that the failure to object to a party's unilateral attempt to alter materially the terms of an otherwise valid agreement is an "agreement" within the terms of Article 29. *Cf.* C.I.S.G., art. 8(3) ("In determining the intent of a party or the understanding a reasonable person would have had, due consideration is to be given to all relevant circumstances of the case including the negotiations, any practices which the parties have established between themselves, usages and any subsequent conduct of the parties."). Here, no circumstances exist to conclude that Chateau des Charmes's conduct evidenced an "agreement." We reject the contention that because Sabaté France sent multiple invoices it created an agreement as to the proper forum with Chateau des Charmes. The parties agreed in two telephone calls to a purchase of corks to be shipped in eleven batches. In such circumstances, a party's multiple attempts to alter an agreement unilaterally do not so effect. *See In re CFLC, Inc.*, 166 F.3d 1012, 1019 (9th Cir.1999).

B. FORMAL REQUIREMENTS AND CONTRACT FORMATION

As we have seen in the last section, if the CISG applies to a contract, the convention may have critical implications for formation issues. In *Chateau des Charmes Wines*, the court specifically noted that CISG art. 11 provides that a contract for the sale of goods "need not be concluded in or evidenced by writing and is not subject to any other requirement as to form." On the other hand, the CISG does not concern itself with issues of the *validity* of a contract. CISG art. 4(a). What about a writing requirement like the Statute of Frauds (*e.g.*, UCC § 2–201)? Does failure to comply with the statute render a contract invalid? Consider the *GPL* case which follows. The majority decision applied the "merchants' exception" (§ 2–201(2)) to the UCC statute of frauds writing requirement (§ 2–201(1)) rather than Article 11 of the CISG.[3] In fact, the only reference in *GPL* to the CISG is in a footnote at the end of the dissenting opinion. Should the court have applied CISG Article 11—

---

3. CISG art. 11 provides as follows:

A contract of sale need not be concluded in or evidenced by writing and is not subject to any other requirement as to form. It may be proved by any means, including witnesses.

Recall note 1–7, *supra*, discussing the preemption doctrine in federal constitutional law. In the contract formation context, the issue of whether to apply UCC § 2–201 or CISG Article 11 raises the constitutional conflict between a provision of a law like the UCC, enacted by a state, and a provision of a treaty duly ratified by the United States.

which abolishes the writing requirement—or UCC § 2–201, which retains the writing requirement?[4]

GPL TREATMENT, LTD. v. LOUISIANA– PACIFIC CORPORATION

133 Or.App. 633, 894 P.2d 470 (1995), *aff'd*, 323 Or. 116, 914 P.2d 682 (1996).

DE MUNIZ, JUDGE.

[Plaintiffs–Sellers, three separate wood products corporations owned and operated by the Clarke family in British Columbia, Canada, sued Louisiana–Pacific Corp. ("L–P"), an Oregon corporation operating in Oregon, USA, seeking to recover lost profits on an alleged oral agreement binding L–P to purchase 88 truckloads of cedar shakes from Plaintiffs. Plaintiffs–Sellers sent messages titled "Confirmation" of the oral agreement to Buyer calling on Buyer as the recipient to sign and return a copy of the "confirmation" to Seller. Defendant–Buyer never contacted Plaintiffs regarding receipt of these communications. The jury returned a verdict in favor of Plaintiffs. Defendant appealed.]

In its third assignment of error, L–P contends that the trial court erred in denying its motions *in limine* and for a directed verdict on the ground that the alleged contract for the sale of shakes fails for noncompliance with Oregon's Uniform Commercial Code Statute of Frauds. Specifically, the motions sought to exclude evidence of the written order confirmations that plaintiffs [Sellers] allegedly sent to L–P [Buyer].

ORS 72.2010 [the enacted version of UCC § 2–201] provides, in relevant part:

> (1) Except as otherwise provided in this section a contract for the sale of goods for the price of $500 or more is not enforceable by way of action or defense unless there is some writing sufficient to indicate that a contract for sale has been made between the parties and signed by the party against whom enforcement is sought or by the authorized agent or broker of the party. A writing is not insufficient because it omits or incorrectly states a term agreed upon but the contract is not enforceable under this subsection beyond the quantity of goods shown in such writing.

---

4. The comparative law student early on discovers that the meaning of identical words may not be identical as used in different legal systems. Civil law lawyers and many international documents use the term "article" for what the common law lawyer refers to as a "section." In addition, the Uniform Commercial Code uses "Article" to refer to its eleven major divisions (*i.e.*, Article 1 General Provisions, Article 2 Sales, Article 2A Leases, Article 3 Negotiable Instruments, etc.).

(2) Between merchants, if within a reasonable time *a writing in confirmation of the contract and sufficient against the sender* is received and the party receiving it has reason to know its contents, it satisfies the requirements of subsection (1) of this section against such party unless written notice of objection to its contents is given within 10 days after it is received. (Emphasis supplied.)

Under subsection (2), the "merchant's exception" to the Uniform Commercial Code Statute of Fraud writing requirement applies, when both parties to the transaction are merchants, if one merchant receives written confirmation of an oral contract from another merchant "sufficient against the sender," the contract becomes enforceable unless the recipient objects within 10 days. L–P argued to the trial court, and argues on appeal, that the "order confirmations" that Plaintiffs allegedly sent to L–P are inadmissible as proof of the agreements and in satisfaction of the Statute of Frauds, because, *as a matter of law*, they are insufficient under ORS 72.2010 to constitute written confirmations of the contracts. The trial court held, as a matter of the law, that the documents were confirmations. The court submitted to the jury the factual questions of whether the confirmations were received by L–P, whether L–P knew their contents and whether L–P sent written notice of objection to plaintiffs. The assignment of error relates only to the trial court's ruling concerning the legal effect of the documents, *i.e.*, that they are, as a matter of law, sufficient to constitute "confirmations" under ORS 72.2010.

The printed order confirmation forms consist of four pages, one original page and three copies. The original and first copy is sent to the buyer. Those two pages are, for the most part, identical. At the top left of both, in large print, is the name and address of the selling company. At the top right are boxes for the date and the seller's order number. Directly underneath those boxes, in large bold print, are the words "ORDER CONFIRMATION." The form contains two address blocks of three single-spaced lines each, encaptioned "SOLD TO" and "SHIP TO." Underneath those address blocks are three slim, long boxes of one line each for shipping instructions, terms of payment and the customer number. The largest part of the form, filling approximately one half the page, is for a description of the product, with a place to note FOB mill, freight and delivery price. At the bottom right of the form is the name of the selling company and underneath it a signature line following the word "BY." Underneath that line are the words "THANK YOU."

The original and first copy differs in one respect. At the bottom left of the original, in small print, are the words:

"CONDITIONS OF SALES; 'All orders accepted subject to strikes, labor troubles, car shortages or other contingencies beyond our power to control. Any freight rate increases, sales or use taxes is for buyers account.' "

Then, beneath that block, in smaller print but highlighted, are the words: "SIGN CONFIRMATION COPY AND RETURN." At the bottom left of the first copy, the "confirmation copy," in small print, are the words: "ORDER ACCEPTED BY:," followed by a line for firm name. Below that is a line for a signature and the title of the person signing, and the date.

L–P concedes that the documents contain all the elements necessary to confirm an order. However, L–P contends that, by instructing the buyer to sign the confirmation copy on the "order accepted by" line and return that copy to plaintiffs, plaintiffs have indicated an intention that the agreement is to become final only after L–P's approval of the quoted terms.

Considering the document in its entirety, we conclude that it cannot reasonably be read as L–P suggests. The form is captioned "ORDER CONFIRMATION," boldly and in large print. Unlike the forms involved in the cases relied on by the dissent, *see, e.g., Great Western Sugar Co. v. Lone Star Donut Co.*, 567 F. Supp. 340 (ND Tex), aff'd 721 F.2d 510 (5th Cir 1983); *Kline Iron & Steel Co., Inc. v. Gray Com. Consultants, Inc.*, 715 F. Supp. 135 (DSC 1989), there is no language on this form, either on the original or the first copy, indicating that the parties are in the course of negotiations, that plaintiffs are merely proposing terms or that L–P must approve the terms. Every feature of the form suggests that it is what it is labeled, a confirmation and not a mere offer. We conclude that the sign and return instruction does not alter the apparent purpose of the document, to confirm in writing a completed agreement for the sale of shakes.[4] The trial court did not err in denying L–P's motions *in limine* and for a directed verdict....

LEESON, J., dissenting. I disagree with the majority's conclusion that the documents allegedly sent by Plaintiffs to L–P were suffi-

---

4. If there is anything uniform about the way courts have decided the question presented here, it is that each document must be evaluated independently and in the light of its contents, and that there is no single correct answer to the question of the effect of a "sign and return" provision. Contrary to the view expressed by the dissent, our opinion is consistent with that analysis and does not create an Oregon exception.

The dissent disapprovingly suggests that our opinion holds that the form sent to L–P is a confirmation because it is labeled "ORDER CONFIRMATION." That certainly is one significant consideration. It is not the exclusive one, however, the primary inquiry being whether the contents of the form show that it is what it is labeled. It seems that the dissent would cast aside those considerations in favor of a rule that when a form contains a "sign and return" clause it cannot, as a matter of law, be an order confirmation. That is most clearly wrong.

cient to satisfy the UCC Statute of Frauds. The majority's opinion is at odds with courts from other jurisdictions that have ruled on facts similar to those in this case. Regrettably, it creates an "Oregon exception" to the uniformity that is one of the underlying purposes of the UCC. *See* ORS 71.1020(2)(c).

According to the majority, the forms sent by plaintiffs to L–P are writings in confirmation of a contract because they are labeled "ORDER CONFIRMATION" and because neither "the original" nor "first copy" contains any language "indicating that the parties are in the course of negotiations, that plaintiffs are merely proposing terms or that L–P must approve the terms." . . . The majority goes to great lengths to describe the layout of those documents. Unfortunately, it does not analyze the import of the words used in them.

The majority's analysis begins incorrectly by characterizing the two parts of each form sent by plaintiffs to L–P as "the *original* and first *copy*." . . . (Emphasis supplied.) All pages of the multicopy form do not contain the same information. The top page plainly informs the prospective buyer that "all orders accepted subject to strikes * * * [and] other contingencies beyond our power to control" and instructs the buyer to "SIGN CONFIRMATION COPY AND RETURN." The confirmation copy (second page) provides a signature block for the recipient to comply with the instruction on the top copy:

"ORDER ACCEPTED BY: _____

FIRM NAME

SIGNATURE AND TITLE

DATE" _____

Neither page is an "original." Neither is a "copy" of the other.

ORS 72.2010 is a verbatim enactment of the Statute of Frauds in Article 2 of the UCC. The official commentary to UCC 2–201 indicates that the writing need not be a complete memorial of the contract, as long as it affords a sufficient basis for believing that a contract has been made. *Tripp v. Pay 'N Pak Stores, Inc.*, 268 Ore. 1, 5, 518 P.2d 1298 (1974). ORS 72.2010(2) eliminates the signature requirement when both parties are "merchants."[1] The official commentary explains that failure to answer a written confirmation within 10 days makes the writing sufficient against both parties under subsection (1). Under both subsections (1) and (2) the writing must evidence the existence of an agreement between the

---

1. There is no dispute that all parties are "merchants" under the code. ORS 72.1040(1).

parties. Failure to respond to a merchant's confirming memorandum takes away from the nonresponding merchant the Statute of Frauds defense. To ultimately prevail, however, the sender still must show that an oral contract was in fact made prior to the confirming memorandum. Here, it is not necessary to reach the issue of whether an oral contract was formed between the parties, because that contract would be unenforceable absent satisfaction of the Statute of Frauds. UCC § 2–201, comment 3.

The question of whether a writing satisfies the Statute of Frauds is a matter of law, to be determined from an examination of the writing itself.[2] *R.S. Bennett & Co. v. Economy Mech. Industries*, 606 F.2d 182, 186 n 4 (7th Cir 1979); *Howard Const. Co. v. Jeff–Cole Quarries, Inc.*, 669 S.W.2d 221, 230 (Mo App 1983); *Bazak Intl Corp v. Mast Indus*, 73 N.Y.2d 113, 118, 535 N.E.2d 633, 635, 538 N.Y.S.2d 503 (1989); *Adams v. Petrade Intern., Inc.*, 754 S.W.2d 696, 705 (Tex App 1988). That a writing labels itself a "confirmation" is not determinative of whether it satisfies the merchants' exception. *Adams*, 754 S.W.2d at 706. Cases from other jurisdictions have directly addressed the use of a sign-and-return clause in a document that purports to be a "confirmation" under UCC section 2–201(2). In *Great Western Sugar Co. v. Lone Star Donut Co.*, 567 F. Supp. 340 (ND Tex), *aff'd* 721 F.2d 510 (5th Cir 1983), for example, a sugar merchant brought a breach of contract action, claiming that a writing sent to the buyer, and denominated a "written confirmation," operated to take the alleged oral contract out of the UCC Statute of Frauds. The writing stated:

> "This letter is a written confirmation of our agreement. Please sign and return to me the enclosed counterpart of this letter signaling your acceptance of the above agreement." 567 F. Supp. at 342.

That trial court explained that the sugar merchant's argument concerning the merchants' exception:

> "is at odds with elementary principles of contract law. By requiring the buyer to take further action in order to signal acceptance (signing and returning a copy of the letter agreement), [the seller] indicated to the buyer * * * that the terms quoted were still subject to acceptance or rejection rather than

---

2. Plaintiffs contend that the forms satisfy the "merchants' exception," because the "sign and return" clause is "spurious language mostly ignored in the industry" and "absolutely irrelevant to the dealings between the parties." I would reject plaintiffs' attempts to explain the meaning of the forms with extrinsic evidence. Permitting parol evidence on this issue undermines the Statute of Frauds by allowing proof of an oral contract to explain a writing that itself is required to prove the existence of the oral contract. *Howard Const. Co. v. Jeff–Cole Quarries, Inc.*, 669 S.W.2d 221, 230 (Mo App 1983); *R.S. Bennett & Co. v. Economy Mech. Industries*, 606 F.2d 182, 186 n 4 (7th Cir 1979).

representing a memorialization of an oral contract. *A true confirmation requires no response.*" *Id.* (Emphasis supplied.)

The court held that, as a matter of law, the writing was not a "writing in confirmation" under UCC section 2–201(2). *Id.* at 342–43. The court of appeals affirmed:

> "While a mere confirmation without timely objection might have been sufficient under the 'merchants exception,' the trial court correctly concluded that, as the master of its offer, [seller,] *the sender, had the power to require written acceptance as a prerequisite to the formation of a contract. Since it did, and since none was given, no contract arose.*" 721 F.2d at 510–11. (Emphasis supplied.)

Courts in other jurisdictions have cited *Great Western Sugar* for the rule that a writing requiring the recipient to take further action by signing and returning a copy to the sender is merely an offer and, therefore, is not a confirmation of a prior oral contract under UCC section 2–201(2). *Kline Iron & Steel v. Gray Com. Consultants, Inc.*, 715 F. Supp. 135, 142 (DSC 1989); *Adams*, 754 S.W.2d at 706; *see also R.S. Bennett & Co.*, 606 F.2d at 185–86; *Perdue Farms Inc. v. Motts, Inc. of Mississippi*, 459 F. Supp. 7, 15–17 (ND Miss 1978); *Howard Const. Co.*, 669 S.W.2d at 227; *Trilco Terminal v. Prebilt Corp.*, 167 N.J. Super. 449, 454–55, 400 A.2d 1237, 1240 (Law Division 1979).[3]

Despite being labeled "ORDER CONFIRMATION," plaintiffs' forms unambiguously require L–P to sign and return a "confirmation copy" on which it has signified its acceptance. That language indicates that plaintiffs' were seeking agreement *from* L–P in order to form a contract, rather than merely providing confirmation to L–P of a previously concluded oral agreement. The forms require further action by L–P. Consistent with the rule in *Great Western Sugar*, I would hold that the writings offered by plaintiffs were merely offers to L–P to enter into a contract, and not a confirmation of a prior oral contract between them.

---

3. Plaintiffs cite *Bazak Intl Corp* for its holding that a buyer's written confirmation indicating that it was "ONLY AN OFFER AND NOT A CONTRACT UNLESS ACCEPTED IN WRITING BY THE SELLER" was, nevertheless, a writing in confirmation of an oral agreement within UCC section 2–201(2). However, that court acknowledged the general rule and distinguished the case on its peculiar facts. *Id.* at 123–24, 535 N.E.2d at 638. Plaintiffs also cite *Busby, Inc. v. Smoky Valley Bean, Inc.*, 767 F. Supp. 235 (D Kan 1991), for the proposition that highlighting of a "please sign and return" clause by the sender of a writing was insufficient to turn a written confirmation into an offer. In that case, however, the sender's written confirmation expressly stated that "receipt of this contract by the seller without written notice to us of objection or error within ten days is an acknowledgment of acceptance." *Id.* at 236. The court distinguished both *Great Western Sugar* and *Adams*, in which the recipients were required to take further action. A thorough survey of relevant case law appears in Annot., 82 ALR 4th 709 (1990), including Supp 10–14 (1994).

I would reverse the trial court's ruling that plaintiffs' forms constitute "writings in confirmation of a contract" under ORS 72.2010(2)....[4]

Notes

2–8. Is there any doubt that the CISG applied in this case? Were the Seller and the Buyer persons with places of business in "different Contracting States"? (See CISG Article 1(1)(a).)

2–9. Fortuitously for plaintiffs, despite its decision not to apply the CISG the majority opinion in *GPL* reached a correct result, based on its conclusion that the communication sent by Seller to Buyer qualified as a UCC 2–201(2) "confirmation" that could be used to enforce the oral contract by Seller against the Buyer who had failed to object to its contents within 10 days of its receipt. The court therefore reached the same result it would have reached if it had applied the CISG Article 11 rather than the UCC § 2–201(2) "merchants exception" as the basis for concluding that the oral contract was enforceable. Would application of the CISG to this case, rather than the UCC, have made any practical difference in the case?

2–10. If the CISG was clearly applicable, should counsel for plaintiffs be liable for additional costs plaintiffs incurred in having a full trial and appeal of the case, in lieu of a prompt disposition at the trial level based on grant of a summary judgment in favor of plaintiffs?[5] Using this approach, the plaintiff-seller would not be trying to obtain a "lost recovery," but instead trying to obtain disgorgement of attorney's fees and related costs which it incurred unnecessarily because of the failure of counsel to recognize the applicability of the CISG and its elimination of the writing requirement.

2–11. Contrast the decision in the *GPL* case with *Calzaturificio Claudia,* the next case in this chapter. Does the *Calzaturificio* court do a better job of sorting out the UCC and CISG?

CALZATURIFICIO CLAUDIA S.N.C. v. OLIVIERI FOOTWEAR LTD.

1998 WL 164824 (S.D.N.Y. 1998).

Katz, Magistrate J.

[A foreign seller brought an action against U.S. buyer to recover payment for shoes manufactured by seller and delivered to

---

4. I would, however, address plaintiffs' cross-assignment that the trial court erred in refusing to apply the United Nations Convention on Contracts for the International Sale of Goods (CISG), 15 USCA App. (Supp 1994), instead of the UCC. Article 11 of the CISG does not require a contract to be "evidenced by writing" and, thus, would defeat L–P's statute of frauds defense if the trial court abused its discretion ... in ruling that plaintiffs' attempt to raise the CISG was untimely and that they had waived reliance on that theory.

5. *See* Ronald Brand, *Professional Responsibility in a Transnational Transactions Practice: Must a Lawyer Involved in a Negotiation or Litigation of a Contract Matter Be Aware of the Sales Convention?*, 17 J.L. & Com. 301, 335–36 (1998) (discussing potential liability of counsel).

buyer at seller's factory. Buyer counterclaimed for breach of contract, claiming that seller failed to deliver certain goods, and that the goods that were delivered were either late or nonconforming, but also questioned the existence of a contractual relationship with seller—since there was never a formal written agreement between the parties—or that it ever agreed to delivery at seller's factory. The seller moved for summary judgment based on its breach of contract claim. The court denied the motion.]

Plaintiff, Calzaturificio Claudia s.n.c. ("Claudia") brought this action against defendant Olivieri Footwear Ltd. ("Olivieri"), to recover payment for shoes manufactured by plaintiff and delivered to defendant. Defendant counterclaimed for breach of contract, claiming that plaintiff failed to deliver certain goods, and that the goods that were delivered were either late or nonconforming. The parties consented to trial before a United States Magistrate Judge.... Currently before the Court is plaintiff's Motion for Summary Judgment based on its breach of contract claim. For the reasons that follow, the motion is denied.

BACKGROUND

Plaintiff is a shoe manufacturer organized under the laws of the Republic of Italy, with its principal place of business in Italy.... Defendant is a corporation organized under the laws of the State of New York, with its principal place of business in New York.... Plaintiff contends that its business relationship with Olivieri first began in the Spring of 1993, when defendant approached plaintiff to negotiate the purchase of shoes.... During the course of the parties' relationship, Claudia alleges that it engaged in thirteen transactions with Olivieri, in which plaintiff manufactured and delivered shoes to Olivieri in accordance with the terms set forth in the respective invoices detailing each order.... The present dispute arises from Olivieri's failure to pay for the goods reflected in four invoices. Claudia claims that it is entitled to payment in the approximate amount of LIT (Italian Lira) 131,597,820 ($80,000), plus interest, for the shoes identified in the four unpaid invoices and the value added tax ("V.A.T.") on certain of the goods.

It is undisputed that there is no formal written contract defining the terms of the four disputed transactions that gave rise to this litigation. Rather, plaintiff relies upon its invoices as evidencing the terms of Claudia and Olivieri's agreement.... Plaintiff contends that the shipments covered by the invoices were made available to Olivieri in accordance with the delivery terms reflected in the invoices, were picked up by Olivieri's agents at Claudia's factory, and were accepted by Olivieri.... Plaintiff thus contends that Olivieri's failure to pay for the invoiced goods constitutes a breach of their contractual agreement.

In support of its breach of contract claim, plaintiff submitted the following four invoices: (1) no. 336, dated November 16, 1993, for shoes valued at LIT 38,250,000; (2) no. 372, dated December14, 1993, for shoes valued at LIT 14,364,000; (3) no. 383, dated December 29, 1993, for shoes valued at LIT 77,418,000; and (4) no. 5, dated January 14, 1994, for shoes valued at LIT 36,696,000.... Each of these invoices was marked "Merce Resa Ex Factory," which is literally translated as "Merchandise delivery ex works (or ex factory)." ... "Ex works" or "ex factory" means that the seller's delivery obligation is merely to deliver the goods to the buyer at the seller's factory.[2]

Claudia argues that the inclusion of the term "ex works" in the invoices demonstrates that its obligations to Olivieri ended when Claudia made the shipments of shoes available for pick-up at its factory, and that Olivieri bore the responsibility for shipping the shoes.... Moreover, plaintiff asserts that the shippers to whom delivery was made were agents of Olivieri, and that it, Claudia, bore no responsibility for any late or incomplete deliveries. In support of this proposition, and in response to the Court's inquiry at oral argument, plaintiff submitted an affidavit attesting that defendant "always ... paid the shipper for its services, and the shipper always acted as Olivieri's agent in the transactions." ...

As evidence of plaintiff's performance, and in response to defendant's counterclaim that defendant never received the goods at issue, plaintiff submitted bills of lading which allegedly demonstrate that a shipper accepted and picked up each disputed invoice shipment. Each invoice references a corresponding bill of lading by number, and each referenced bill of lading bears the name and signature of the shipper, the exact time and date of pick-up, and a customs stamp, indicating that the shipment left Italy.... The bills of lading bear the same date as the corresponding invoices. Further, plaintiff has submitted a letter from the shipper Matricardi stating that it delivered the goods reflected in invoice nos. 383 and 5 to Olivieri in New York....

---

2. "Ex works" assigns a minimum obligation to the seller. *See Incoterms* 1990, an International Chamber of Commerce publication.... "Ex works" indicates that "the seller fulfils [sic] his obligation to deliver when he has made the goods available at his premises (*i.e.* works, factory, warehouse, etc.) to the buyer.... The buyer bears all costs and risks involved in taking the goods from the seller's premises to the desired destination." ...

Defendant does not dispute that the term "ex works" appears on all of the contested invoices, nor does it dispute that "ex works" means "delivery at seller's factory." Nevertheless, defendant opposes this summary judgment motion, claiming that there remain disputed issues of material fact. Specifically, Olivieri contests (1) the existence of a contractual relationship with Claudia; (2) that it agreed to delivery "ex works;" and (3) that it received the goods at issue. It further argues that any goods received were either late or nonconforming, thus resulting in a breach by plaintiff. . . .

In support of its position, defendant submitted several facsimiles ("faxes"), all of which plaintiff contends are not authentic and were never received by plaintiff. In a fax dated November 29, 1993, defendant complained of plaintiff's marking all invoices with "Franco Fabrica" ("ex works") because it was not consistent with the "original agreement," which instead allegedly provided defendant with an opportunity to inspect and accept the merchandise first. . . . Defendant also reminded plaintiff in that fax that the parties had agreed not to use the shipper Matricardi, because defendant did not want to be responsible for that shipper's unreliability. . . .

In another fax, dated November 26, 1993, which specifically addressed invoice no. 336, defendant emphasized that its agent must inspect the goods and approve them prior to shipping. . . . Defendant further demanded a bill of lading to document plaintiff's "release of goods." . . .

In faxes dated December 24, 1993 and January 10, 1994, defendant demanded proof of delivery for the goods listed in invoice no. 372. . . . In a fax dated January 11, 1994, defendant demanded proof of delivery for the goods listed in invoice no. 383, claiming that the delivery was late. . . . Defendant further stated that it only accepted merchandise totaling LIT 10,764,000 and not LIT 77,418,-000, as indicated in invoice no. 383. . . .

Finally, in a fax dated June 28, 1994, defendant objected to plaintiff's inclusion of the term "Franco Fabrica" on invoice no. 5. . . . Defendant stated in the fax that it did not agree to that term and that the "agreement was that instead of sitting on this (*sic*) shoes in your warehouse you use our services to sell them here in [the] states." . . . Defendant also asserted that it rejected 528 pairs of shoes, valued at LIT 12,936,000, that were reflected in invoice no. 5. . . . Plaintiff's bill of lading, bearing the name and signature of the shipper, noted defendant's rejection of 528 pairs of shoes. . . . Plaintiff does not dispute that these goods were rejected and points to the credit in invoice no. 13 for that exact amount. . . .

In addition, defendant submitted an affidavit of Michail [*sic*] Litvin, the principal owner of Olivieri, contesting factual allegations made by plaintiff.... In his affidavit, Litvin denies that any agreement existed between Olivieri and Claudia.... Litvin also states that Olivieri did not receive any of the goods at issue and that the "ex works" provision on the contested invoices was not agreed to by Olivieri.... Litvin further claims that Olivieri's faxes requesting proof of delivery serve as evidence of nondelivery of the goods at issue....

Defendant thus argues that its faxes and affidavit place in dispute material issues of fact and that summary judgment should be denied....

DISCUSSION

I. Summary Judgment Standards ...

In order to prevail on this motion, plaintiff must demonstrate that there are no genuine issues of material fact as to the terms of the parties' agreement, whether the parties agreed to be bound by the terms of the invoices, and whether plaintiff fulfilled all of its obligations under the parties' agreement.

II. Legal Principles Governing the Construction of the Parties' Agreement

The transactions in the instant case are governed by the United Nations Convention on Contracts for the International Sale of Goods ("CISG"), codified at 15 U.S.C.A. Appendix (West 1998). When two foreign nations are signatories to this Convention, as are the United States and Italy, the Convention governs contracts for the sale of goods between parties whose places of business are in these different nations, absent a choice-of-law provision to the contrary. *See* CISG, Article 1(1)(a); *see also Delchi Carrier SpA v. Rotorex Corp.,* 71 F.3d 1024, 1027–28 (2d Cir.1995) (applying CISG in contract dispute between Italian manufacturer and a New York corporation); *Filanto, S.p.A. v. Chilewich Int'l Corp.,* 789 F.Supp. 1229, 1237 (S.D.N.Y.1992) (applying CISG in a contract dispute between an Italian footwear manufacturer and New York export-import company), *appeal dismissed,* 984 F.2d 58, 61 (2d Cir.1993); *Helen Kaminski Pty., Ltd. v. Marketing Australian Products,* Nos. M–47 (DLC), 96B46519–97–8072A, 1997 WL 414137, at *2 (S.D.N.Y. July 23, 1997). As the contractual relationship between plaintiff Claudia, an Italian shoe manufacturer, and defendant Olivieri, a United States corporation, did not provide for a choice of law, the CISG controls.

The caselaw interpreting and applying the CISG is sparse. *See, e.g., Helen Kaminski Pty., Ltd.,* 1997 WL 414137, at *3 (stating that there is "little to no case law on the CISG in general"); *Filanto, S.p.A.,* 789 F.Supp. at 1237 (acknowledging that there is virtually no United States caselaw interpreting the CISG). Thus, the Court must "look to its language and 'to the general principles' upon which it is based." *Delchi Carrier SpA,* 71 F.3d at 1027 (citing CISG Art. 7(2)). Caselaw interpreting Article 2 of the Uniform Commercial Code ("UCC") may also be used to interpret the CISG where the provisions in each statute contain similar language. *See Delchi Carrier SpA,* 71 F.3d at 1027. However, the Second Circuit has cautioned that caselaw interpreting UCC provisions is not "per se applicable." *Id.; see also Orbisphere Corp. v. United States,* 726 F.Supp. 1344, 1355 n. 7 (Ct. Int'l Trade 1989). Although the CISG is similar to the UCC with respect to certain provisions, it differs from the UCC with respect to others, including the UCC's writing requirement for a transaction for the sale of goods and parol evidence rule. Where controlling provisions are inconsistent, it would be inappropriate to apply UCC caselaw in construing contracts under the CISG.

In the instant case, there is no formal written contract and there are no purchase orders setting forth the terms of the parties' sales transactions.[3] While an oral agreement may be enforceable under the CISG, . . . neither party has offered any evidence regarding their oral communications, although it is apparent that the parties had oral communications regarding the purchase and sale of shoes between August 1993 and March 1994, the time period relevant to the disputed invoices. Plaintiff relies on its invoices and bills of lading as evidence of the agreement between Claudia and Olivieri. Plaintiff argues that the invoices are unambiguous, that they constituted the final expression of the parties' agreement, and that the parol evidence rule bars the Court from considering any extrinsic evidence (*i.e.,* the faxes and prior oral communications) regarding the parties' intentions or understanding. . . .

Under certain circumstances, invoices may be viewed as contracts and, in such cases, under the UCC, the parol evidence rule prohibits evidence of contradictory oral agreements that were made prior to the receipt of the invoice. . . . *See Polygram, S.A., v. Enterprises, Inc.,* 697 F.Supp. 132, 135 (E.D.N.Y.1988) (holding that invoices containing express "terms of sale" provisions were the final expression of the parties' agreement and could not be contradicted by evidence of a prior agreement); *Battista v. Radesi,* 112 A.D.2d 42, 491 N.Y.S.2d 81, 81 (4th Dep't 1985) (holding that an invoice including names and addresses of the parties, the date and payment terms, a description, and the price for the goods, was intended to be the final expression of the parties' agreement and

3. Defendant argues that the absence of purchase orders demonstrates that defendant never entered into any agreement for the purchase of shoes manufactured by plaintiff. . . . There is no basis in law for this contention and defendant cites none. Indeed, it is undisputed that the plaintiff and defendant had agreed upon and conducted several successful transactions for the sale of shoes, none of which are at issue in this suit, without the use of purchase orders.

could not be contradicted by evidence of a prior oral agreement); *Matthew Bender, & Co., Inc. v. Jaiswal,* 93 A.D.2d 969, 463 N.Y.S.2d 78, 78 (3rd Dep't 1983) (holding that invoices containing names and addresses of the parties, the date, payment and refund terms, and the price and description of goods, represented a final written expression of the parties' agreement and could not be contradicted by evidence of a prior agreement). *But see Getz v. Eichner,* No. 96 Civ. 8304(LBS) (AGS), 1997 WL 362318, at *3–4 (S.D.N.Y. July 1, 1997) (summary judgment denied on breach of contract claim where only written evidence of oral agreement was an unsigned invoice, which defendant denied receiving and which contained disputed terms). Accordingly, in cases governed by the UCC, where written documents evidencing the parties' agreement are unambiguous, summary judgment may be appropriate. *See L.B. Foster Co. v. America Piles, Inc., et al.,* 138 F.3d 81, 1998 WL 88873, at *6 (2d Cir. Feb.26, 1998); *Schiavone v. Pearce,* 79 F.3d 248, 252 (2d Cir.1996) (summary judgment appropriate only where language of the contract is "wholly unambiguous"); *accord John Hancock Mut. Life Ins. Co. v. Amerford Int'l Corp.,* 22 F.3d 458, 461 (2d Cir.1994).

Unlike the UCC, under the CISG a contract need not be evidenced by a writing.[4] *See* CISG, Art. 11 ("A contract of sale need not be ... evidenced by a writing and is not subject to any other requirement as to form."). According to the CISG, a contract "may be proved by any means ..." and "any evidence that may bear on the issue of formation is admissible." *Id.* Such evidence may include oral statements made prior to a writing. Larry A. Dimatteo, *An International Contract Law Formula: The Informality of International Business Transactions Plus the Internationalization of Contract Law Equals Unexpected Contractual Liability,* 23 SYRACUSE J. INT'L L. & COM. 67, at 103 (1997). Under the CISG, "prior oral representations regarding the quality and performance would be enforceable." *Id.* Thus, contracts governed by the CISG are freed from the limits of the parol evidence rule and there is a wider spectrum of admissible evidence to consider in construing the terms of the parties' agreement. Larry A. Dimatteo, *The CISG and the Presumption of Enforceability: Unintended Contractual Liability in International Business Dealings,* 22 YALE J. INT'L L. 111, at 127 (1997). The CISG's "lack of a writing requirement allows all relevant information into evidence even if it contradicts the written

---

4. The UCC requires that a sale of goods must be evidenced by a writing sufficient to indicate that a contract of sale has been made and must be signed by the party against whom enforcement is sought. UCC § 2–201(1). The writing may be a one-sided instrument, however, under the written confirmation rule. According to this rule, a merchant may legally confirm an oral agreement in writing. If the receiving party fails to object within a reasonable time, then she has waived her statute of frauds defense.

documentation." *Id.* at *108. Under the CISG, "any relevant statement made in negotiations prior to the signing of the contract are [sic] admissible into evidence." *Id.* at *103 *citing* John E. Murray, Jr., *Different Laws Might Apply to Foreign Buys Under the UN Convention for the International Sale of Goods,* 119 PURCHASING 30 (Oct. 19, 1995).

Consequently, the standard UCC inquiry regarding whether a writing is fully or partially integrated has little meaning under the CISG and courts are therefore less constrained by the "four corners" of the instrument in construing the terms of the contract. 23 Syracuse J. Int'l L. & Com. 67, at *108. Evidence concerning any negotiations, agreements, or statements made prior to the issuance of the invoices in issue may be considered in determining the scope of the parties' agreement. Further, Article 9 of the CISG provides that "the parties are bound by any usage to which they have agreed and by any practices which they have established." CISG, Article 9(1).

III. DISPUTED ISSUES

Plaintiff argues that the invoice terms are unambiguous. At first glance, that appears to be true in that they provide the names and addresses of the parties, the date, a description of the items, the price for the goods, the terms for payment, and a method of delivery. Nevertheless, any inquiry regarding ambiguous/unambiguous contractual language is not very instructive in this case, where (1) there is no formal written contract, (2) plaintiff relies on invoices which it prepared unilaterally and which do not contain language evidencing, either explicitly or implicitly, that the invoices reflect the parties' final agreement, and (3) the CISG allows for the use of extrinsic evidence in determining the parties' agreement and intent. The record also contains faxes from the defendant disavowing certain provisions in the invoices and/or questioning whether there was proper performance under the parties' agreement. This case is therefore distinguishable from others in which invoices were found to be unambiguous, binding contracts. *Compare Data Research Assocs., Inc. v. Computer Center, Inc.,* No. 84 Civ. 8334(JFK), 1988 WL 140864, at *3 (S.D.N.Y. Dec.21, 1988) (parties' intent to be bound by invoice terms was evidenced by invoice provision specifically stating that the invoice "will be forwarded to an attorney for collection" if goods not paid for in accordance with invoice terms); *Polygram, S.A.,* 697 F.Supp. at 133 (defendant failed to make any written or oral objection to the terms of sale explicitly stated in the invoice until after the action was commenced); *Community Bank v. Newmark & Lewis, Inc.,* 534 F.Supp. 456, 458–59 (E.D.N.Y.1982) (invoices stated "acceptance of merchandise covered by this invoice represents buyer's agreement to meet the current terms and conditions of sale under which the order was entered.

Title passes from buyer to seller upon seller's delivery to carrier ... "; defendant admitted that it received the invoiced goods; and defendant did not produce any evidence that it proposed different terms or that it timely objected to the terms set forth in the invoices); *Orbisphere Corp.*, 726 F.Supp. at 1345 (invoice contained express provisions stating that "title and risk of loss passes (*sic*) from the seller to the buyer on delivery of the merchandise to the carrier at the F.O.B. point indicated in the invoice"; "All prices are F.O.B. Haworth, N.J."; and "Orders are subject to acceptance only at seller's office in Haworth, N.J."); *Battista,* 491 N.Y.S.2d at 81 (defendant signed the invoice containing the payment terms and did not dispute that it received the invoiced goods); *General Motors Acceptance Corp. v. Fairway Dodge Sales, Inc.,* 80 A.D.2d 740, 437 N.Y.S.2d 171, 173 (sales contract explicitly stated that the writing "comprised the complete and exclusive statement of the terms of the agreement.").

A. *Whether the parties agreed to delivery "ex works"*

Plaintiff claims that "the parties agreed, and the invoices reflect, the place of delivery for all sales to Olivieri was ... Claudia's factory." ... Plaintiff claims that according to the delivery term "ex works," explicitly set forth in each of the invoices, it never assumed any responsibility for shipping the shoes and that defendant Olivieri "bore all risk of loss or damage in moving the goods from Claudia's factory to defendant's chosen destination." ... Plaintiff further contends that the sales invoices reflect the amount due for shoes that were "delivered to Olivieri, picked up by its agents at the Claudia factory, and accepted." ... Moreover, Claudia contends that it never received any communication or complaint from defendant objecting to the delivery terms....

Defendant denies that the place of delivery was Claudia's factory and that Claudia never assumed responsibility for shipping.... Defendant further disputes that the phrase "ex works," which is contained in each of the invoices at issue, represented any agreement to accept delivery of goods at Claudia's factory.... In support of its contention, defendant submitted a fax, dated November 29, 1993, in which defendant timely objected to the invoice term "Franco Fabrica" (translated as Merchandise Delivery Ex Factory) and requested that the invoices be marked in accordance with "the way we agreed." ... According to defendant, the parties' agreement was that the goods were to be inspected and accepted by defendant prior to shipment and that plaintiff was to comply with delivery dates.[5] ... Defendant submitted another fax dated June 28, 1994, in which defendant again objected to the term "Franco Fabrica," stating "it was not our agreement." ... While it does not

---

5. Defendant's fax states that plaintiff failed to comply with the terms of their "original October agreement" by (1) using Matricardi to ship defendant's

appear to the Court that the defendant's characterization of its "agreement" with plaintiff is necessarily inconsistent with the delivery term "ex works," on their face the faxes explicitly object to the inclusion of such terms in the invoices.[6] Because defendant objected to the delivery terms, for purposes of the instant motion plaintiff's invoices alone cannot be viewed as the unambiguous embodiment of the agreement between the parties.[7] Moreover, any inquiry into the parties' intentions must be reserved for trial. *See Ronan Assocs., Inc. v. Local 94–94A–94B, Int'l Union of Operating Eng'rs*, 24 F.3d 447, 449 (2d Cir.1994) ("Under traditional principles of contract law, questions as to what the parties said, what they intended, and how a statement by one party was understood by the other are questions of fact . . .").

Viewing the record in a light most favorable to the defendant, the non-moving party, the Court is unable to conclude as a matter of law that defendant agreed to or intended to be bound by the invoice terms. *See* CISG, Art. 8(3) ("In determining the intent of a party . . . due consideration is to be given to all relevant circumstances of the case . . .").

B. Whether the terms of the parties' agreement can be gleaned from their prior practices

Plaintiff also asserts that it had an ongoing contractual relationship with defendant whereby Claudia would deliver goods "ex

purchased goods, and (2) marking the invoices "Franco Fabrica." Thus, defendant acknowledges an earlier purchase and sale agreement between the parties. However, there is no evidence in the record regarding the terms of this October agreement. The Court further notes that defendant has never explicitly stated its understanding of the parties' agreement as to which party bore the responsibility for delivery and shipment of the goods.

6. Plaintiff has argued that the faxes were fabricated and that defendant's objection to "ex works" delivery and complaints about late deliveries and nonconforming goods were never communicated to Claudia. . . . In light of the arguments set forth by plaintiff, the Court seriously questions the validity of the faxes. Nevertheless, it is not for the Court to weigh credibility on a summary judgment motion and the resolution of this issue must await trial.

7. We do not know what the terms of the oral offer and acceptance were or whether plaintiff's invoices modified the terms orally agreed upon. Under the CISG, "all material terms of [an] acceptance should mirror the offer." 23 SYRACUSE J. INT'L L. & COM. at *108. Article 19 of the CISG provides that "a reply to an offer which purports to be an acceptance but contains additions . . . or other modifications is a rejection of the offer and constitutes a counter-offer" if the modification materially alters the terms of the offer. CISG, Article 19(1). Material modifications, including the alteration of delivery terms, often occur in "the routine exchange of the buyer's printed purchase order and the seller's printed acknowledgment of sale form." *See Legal Analysis of the United Nations Convention on Contracts for the International Sale of Goods*, (1980), commentary on Article 19, "Acceptance with Modifications," attached to the CISG. Under the CISG, "no contract results from such an exchange if the purported acceptance contains additional or different terms that materially alter the offer." *Id.*

works" and defendant would pick them up at Claudia's factory. Plaintiff contends that between August 1993 and March 1994, Olivieri placed thirteen orders with Claudia, only four of which are in dispute in this action.... In each of the non-disputed transactions between Claudia and Olivieri, Claudia asserts that "Olivieri contracted for [shipping] services separately and paid Claudia only to manufacture the shoes." ...

In support of its assertion, plaintiff submitted invoice no. 236, which reflected the first order Olivieri placed with Claudia. Invoice no. 236, which was paid in full and is not contested in this action, contained the term "ex works." Plaintiff notes that defendant performed without objection according to this term, *i.e.*, defendant picked up the goods at Claudia's factory and paid the invoice price in full. Plaintiff points out that all of the subsequent sales invoices, with the exception of one invoice which was silent as to delivery, contained the same delivery term: merchandise delivery ex works (or ex factory).... Claudia argues that this delivery term, which was established at the time of Olivieri's initial order and was explicitly contained in the invoices thereafter, continued to govern the parties' future dealings.... Thus, plaintiff argues that Olivieri should be bound by the terms established in the parties' successful transactions....

Although Claudia alleges that it engaged in nine successful transactions with Olivieri, where goods were delivered "ex works," plaintiff has provided virtually no documentation with regard to the terms of these other transactions and defendant disputes that these transactions occurred.... The only evidence submitted by Claudia in support of its course of dealing argument is invoice no. 236. Plaintiff failed to submit evidence as to the other "successful" transactions that Olivieri and Claudia allegedly engaged in between August 1993 and March 1994. Thus, even if defendant accepted the terms of invoice no. 236, it is questionable whether this one transaction is enough to establish a course of dealing. Plaintiff has simply not submitted sufficient evidence to demonstrate conclusively the parties' prior practices, and questions of fact remain as to the agreed upon terms of their earlier transactions.

C. Whether Olivieri communicated its dissatisfaction with the goods to Claudia

Defendant disputes plaintiff's contention that defendant (1) never communicated to plaintiff that the invoiced goods were either not delivered or were delivered late, and (2) never indicated that it was dissatisfied with the quality of the invoiced goods.[8] ... In

---

8. Zamboni's statements, in his affidavit, that Olivieri (1) never complained that any goods were not delivered, (2) never complained about the quality of

support of its contention, defendant submitted several faxes, allegedly sent to plaintiff, that complained of the plaintiff's failure to provide defendant with proof of delivery for the invoiced goods.... Moreover, three faxes indicated that the invoiced goods were late and at least one fax complained that the merchandise was of "inferior quality and contain[ed] obvious damages." ... There is no evidence in the record regarding the time frame agreed upon for the delivery of goods. Thus, the Court cannot determine, as a matter of law, whether Claudia's delivery of goods was timely under the parties' agreements.

D. Conflicting evidence regarding goods "delivered" in invoice nos. 383 and 5

Reviewing the record, the Court finds that there remain genuine issues of fact with regard to whether defendant received all of the goods in question and whether defendant took delivery "ex works" of the goods reflected in invoice nos. 383 and 5. Plaintiff's conflicting submissions call into question the facts surrounding the delivery of goods.

Plaintiff claims that goods valued at LIT 77,418,000, reflected in invoice no. 383, were delivered to and accepted by Olivieri.[9] ... Nevertheless, the record is unclear with regard to what portion of the goods reflected in invoice no. 383 were actually delivered and accepted by Olivieri. Plaintiff alleged in its Complaint that it properly "sold and delivered" the invoiced goods to Olivieri, but that Olivieri, "failed to remove" goods valued at LIT 66,654,000 from Claudia's factory.[10] ...

Olivieri argues that, with respect to the goods identified on invoice no. 383, it only received and accepted goods valued at LIT 10,764,000.... In support of its position, Olivieri submitted a fax dated December 29, 1993, in which it explicitly stated: "We have accepted merchandise only for lire 10,764,000 but you are billing us for lire 77,418,000." ... In this fax, Olivieri specifically requested proof of delivery for the "full amount of goods." ... As of August 1997, the date of Mr. Litvin's affidavit, Olivieri claimed that it had not been furnished with such proof of delivery.... Further, plaintiff submitted a letter by the shipper Matricardi, which could be viewed as casting doubt on plaintiff's allegation that Olivieri, or its agent, was responsible for failing to remove the goods from plain-

---

any goods, and (3) never attempted to return any goods, ... are inconsistent with plaintiff's acknowledgment that Olivieri rejected and returned certain goods reflected in invoice no. 5....

9. According to plaintiff, LIT 43,-470,000 remain due and unpaid out of LIT 77,418,000....

10. Plaintiff also submitted invoice no. 75 to recover LIT 8,665,020, reflecting the V.A.T. on LIT 66,654,000, for the shoes on invoice no. 383. Plaintiff claims that defendant left these shoes in Claudia's factory....

tiff's factory. The shipper's letter stated that the goods "given to us have been sent to ... Olivieri ... in New York." ... Based on this letter, it appears that the shipper delivered the goods that it received from Claudia. Thus, if any goods remained in Claudia's factory, a trier of fact could infer that Claudia failed to deliver these goods. The Matricardi letter seemingly contradicts Claudia's assertion that it delivered the full amount of the invoiced goods to Olivieri, but that Olivieri "failed to remove" the majority of the goods from the factory.[11]

Based upon the record as it now stands, the Court is unable to determine exactly what happened with regard to this shipment. Thus, genuine issues of material fact exist with regard to the delivery and acceptance of the invoiced goods.

Issues of fact exist with respect to other invoices as well....

Plaintiff's allegations and evidence offered in support of its claims on invoice no. 5 are at times inconsistent, and raise issues of fact concerning delivery and acceptance. For example, plaintiff notes that invoice no. 5 "bears the Customs stamp of the City of Milan, as well as the shipper's agent's receipt for the goods." ... According to plaintiff, the invoice evidences that the goods in question were picked up at Claudia's factory by defendant's shipper and delivered outside of Italy. In addition, plaintiff notes that invoice no. 5 references bill of lading 17994, dated January 14, 1994.... Plaintiff further notes that bill of lading no. 17994 contains the signature of shipper Matricardi and the date and time that the shipper picked up the shoes reflected in invoice no. 5 from Claudia's factory.... Nevertheless, the invoice and bill of lading, which presumably demonstrate that the goods left Italy, contradict plaintiff's assertion that the goods remained in plaintiff's factory and were subject to a value added tax, itemized in invoice no. 97. Again, Matricardi's letter, discussed above, also noted that it delivered all of the goods "given to us" as reflected in invoice no. 5.... The letter casts doubt on plaintiff's assertion that defendant failed to remove goods from plaintiff's factory.

The evidence is thus ambiguous with regard to whether all of the goods covered by invoice no. 5 were picked up from Claudia's factory and were delivered to New York. There are genuine issues of material fact regarding the acceptance and delivery of this specific shipment, the meaning to be afforded to the shipper's letter, the significance and interpretation of the shipper's signature and customs stamp on the invoice, the meaning and interpretation

---

11. Although plaintiff submitted invoice no. 383 and bill of lading no. 17947, evidencing that goods valued at LIT 10,764,000 left the country, ... neither document sheds any light on whether the non-exported goods that remained in plaintiff's factory were made available to the defendant for pick up.

of the shipper's signature on the bill of lading, and whether the terms of the parties' agreement were complied with. The resolution of these factual issues must be reserved for trial. . . .

CONCLUSION

Given the factual disputes as to whether "ex works" was an agreed upon term of the contract, whether the parties' agreement was accurately reflected in the invoices, whether delivery was satisfactorily performed, and whether the shippers were in all cases defendant's agents, summary judgment is inappropriate and plaintiff's motion is denied. This ruling is obviously not intended to suggest that plaintiff's claims lack merit. Indeed, a number of the assertions made in defendant's motion papers are highly dubious and there has been a strong suggestion that evidence offered by defendant has been contrived. These issues can only be resolved at trial.

Notes

2–12. Based on the facts and evidence available, what do you think actually happened between these two parties? If no other relevant facts or other evidence is adduced at trial, who should win this contract dispute?

2–13. Would this dispute have been resolved more easily if it had been subject to the UCC rather than the CISG?

2–14. Since the CISG does not require a "writing" in order for a contract to be recognized, on what basis is a contract identified, and how is it to be interpreted and enforced?

2–15. Notice the court's position on the issue of the relevance of UCC provisions where the CISG is silent or otherwise unhelpful as a guide to decision. Do you think the court's approach is correct? (Keep *Calzaturificio Claudia* in mind when you consider note 2–31, *infra*.)

2–16. Review note 1 in *Calzaturificio Claudia, supra*. The court assumes that the term "ex works" is to be interpreted in accordance with the *Incoterms* 1990, an International Chamber of Commerce publication. Is that conclusion consistent with the CISG? Supplementing the CISG are standard agreement forms, developed by the Paris-based International Chamber of Commerce and now called "Incoterms." These terms permit easy referencing of detailed arrangements for a sale. There are a variety of available arrangements for different allocations of obligations, such as those for paying freight and insurance.

2–17. Despite the drive towards uniformity in international commercial practice that seems to lie behind the provisions of CISG, contract formation issues remain an important area for comparative analysis, for several reasons. First of all, many states are still not signatories to the convention—including significant commercial jurisdictions like the United Kingdom—and so individual state approaches to formal requirements in contract law must be kept in mind. Second, even for CISG signatories, certain formation issues are explicitly outside the scope of the convention,[6] which itself only applies to sales of goods in *commercial* settings.[7] Third, there is always the possibility that local courts (or counsel) may be reluctant to re-think their approaches to basic contract law in light of the CISG. The *GPL-Calzaturificio* sequence of cases illustrates the fact that "[s]ome delay and resistance in applying norms of a new legal order transplanted into a dissimilar legal order is a predictable [phenomenon] recognized by comparative lawyers.... Comfort can be taken from the fact that in many instances subsequent decisions of courts from the same country have properly applied the CISG norm in question."[8]

2–18. A fourth reason for continued attention to comparative analysis is rooted in the text of the CISG itself. For example, Article 96 of the CISG in part provides:

> A Contracting State whose legislation requires contracts of sale to be concluded in or evidenced by writing may at any time make a declaration ... that any provision of Article 11 ... that allows a contract of sale ... to be made in any form other than in writing, *does not apply where any party has his place of business in that State.* (Emphasis supplied.)

During the drafting of the CISG, some countries insisted on retaining their writing requirements for contracts for sale of goods on grounds that such documentation was indispensable to successful operation of their economies.[9] The United States has not exercised its Article 96 right to exclude itself from application of Article 11, but opinion in the

---

6. *See, e.g.*, CISG art. 4(a), which provides in pertinent part: "[E]xcept as otherwise expressly provided in this Convention, it is not concerned with ... [t]he validity of the contract or of any of its provisions or of any usage...." Case law exists characterizing *consideration* as an issue of validity (thus covered by individual state law, not preempted by the CISG), rather than formation. *See, e.g., Geneva Pharmaceuticals Technology Corp. v. Barr Laboratories, Inc.*, 201 F. Supp. 2d 236, 283–284 (S.D.N.Y. 2002), *aff'd in part, rev'd in part and remanded on other grounds*, 386 F.3d 485 (2d Cir. 2004) (treating question of consideration as state law issue).

7. *Id.* art. 2(a), which provides: "This Convention does not apply to sales ... [o]f goods bought for personal, family or household use, unless the seller, at any time before or at the conclusion of the contract, neither knows nor

ought to have known that the goods were bought for any such use...."

8. Louis F. Del Duca, *Implementation of Contract Formation Statute of Frauds, Parol Evidence, and Battle of Forms CISG Provisions in Civil and Common Law Countries*, 25 J.L. & Com. 133, 133 (2005).

9. Argentina, Belarus, Chile, Hungary, Latvia, Lithuania, The Russian Federation and the Ukraine have all made Article 96 reservations. Estonia had previously made an Article 96 reservation, but withdrew that reservation on March 9, 2004. The People's Republic of China has also declared that "it did not consider itself bound by...Article 11..." United Nations Commission on International Trade Law, *Status of Conventions and Model Laws*, 38th Sess., U.N. Doc. A/CN.9/583 [hereinafter *Status of Conventions*], available at www.unictral.org/en/commissions/session/34th.html.

United States was and continues to be divided on the desirability of retaining the Statute of Frauds for sales of goods. This results potentially in three different sets of rules for U.S. buyers and sellers—domestic sales transactions subject to UCC § 2–201, transnational sales transactions covered by the CISG, not subject to any formal writing requirement,[10] and transnational sales transactions with a party who is a national of a state that is either not a CISG signatory or that has exercised its Article 96 right.

C. AMBIGUITY OF TERMS, THE PAROL EVIDENCE RULE, AND CISG ARTICLE 8

In *Calzaturificio Claudia, supra* at 43, the court referred to the *parol evidence rule*, as it attempted to reconstruct the terms of the parties' contract where they had not reduced it to a "formal written contract." More broadly, however, the rule comes into play whenever a court must interpret ambiguous contract language—whether or not the contract is formalized in a written contract. The materials that follow discuss the appropriate sources that a court may consult in trying to understand ambiguous contract terms.

MITCHELL AIRCRAFT SPARES, INC. v. EUROPEAN AIRCRAFT SERVICE AB

23 F.Supp.2d 915 (N.D.Ill. 1998).

ALESIA, DISTRICT JUDGE.

[Mitchell, a U.S. buyer, brought suit against EAS, a foreign seller of aircraft parts, for breach of contract and breach of warranty. In denying the parties' cross-motions for summary judgment, the district court held, *inter* alia, that it could consider parol evidence in resolving a contract dispute governed by the CISG.]

I. BACKGROUND

Plaintiff Mitchell Aircraft Spares, Inc. ("Mitchell") has filed suit against defendant European Aircraft Service AB ("EAS") in this court, asserting claims for breach of contract and breach of warranty. Mitchell is an Illinois corporation with its principal place of business in Illinois. Mitchell acts as a speculator and broker in the market for surplus commercial aircraft parts. Greg Fletcher ("Fletcher") is a vice president and part owner of Mitchell.

---

10. *See* Louis Del Duca & Patrick Del Duca, *Selected Topics Under the Convention on International Sale of Goods (CISG),* 106 Dick. L. Rev. 205, 207–218 (2001) (discussing "places of business in different contracting states" basis for applying CISG, as well as three additional basis for CISG application—"private international law—conflict of laws," opting in, and *Lex Mercatoria*).

EAS is a Swedish corporation with its principal place of business in Sweden. EAS buys parts from companies in Western Europe and the United States and sells these parts to airlines, overhaul shops, brokers, and companies like itself. Leif Headberg [*sic*] ("Hedberg") is a vice president and part owner of EAS. Hedberg's main responsibilities at EAS are purchasing and sales.

The dispute between these parties arises from an agreement between the parties that EAS would sell certain aircraft parts, specifically integrated drive generators ("IDGs"), to Mitchell. An IDG is an aircraft part used on L–1011 aircraft and is composed of two parts: a constant speed drive or transmission and a generator. In June of 1996, EAS had three IDGs available for purchase. EAS listed these IDGs on the Inventory Locator Database ("ILD"), which is an international database that contains listings of surplus aircraft parts available for purchase. The parties dispute exactly how EAS listed these parts: Mitchell claims that EAS listed the parts as three number 729640 IDGs; EAS claims that it listed the parts with two or three alternative part numbers, one of which was 729640....

On or about June 30, 1996, Fletcher contacted Hedberg about the three IDGs that EAS had listed on the ILD. One of Fletcher's sub-specialties within the Mitchell organization is buying and selling L–1011 IDGs. Fletcher, who considers himself to be an expert with respect to the buying and selling of IDGs, told Hedberg that he had experience in dealing with IDGs. Fletcher asked Hedberg about the availability, the condition, and the price of the three IDGs and about how soon EAS could ship the parts. Hedberg told Fletcher that EAS had three IDGs for the L–1011 available and that they were in "as removed" condition. At his deposition, Fletcher testified that he also asked Hedberg if EAS had any IDGs part number 729640 and Hedberg responded "Yes." ... At Hedberg's deposition, Hedberg testified that he and Fletcher did not discuss the part number of the IDGs in that first conversation....

Fletcher and Hedberg then began negotiations over the IDGs. Hedberg testified that he told Fletcher that EAS could not determine the exact part number of the IDGs available for sale....

Fletcher then requested information about the IDGs "to try to confirm the part number of the units that [EAS] wished to sell and that [Mitchell] wished to buy." ... In response, Hedberg sent Fletcher a fax dated July 3, 1996. In the fax, Hedberg listed the information off of the data plates on the three IDGs. The information was given to Hedberg by Mr. Goran at Mondair. The July 3 fax did not expressly state that the IDGs were part number 729640; rather, the fax gave the part numbers for the generators and transmissions that went together to form the IDG. Hedberg testified that he "made it clear" to Fletcher that he did not have the information necessary to determine whether the part number of the IDGs was 729640.... Fletcher testified that he could not remember if Hedberg told him that EAS could not determine the part number of the IDGs.... Hedberg testified that he sent Fletcher the July 3 fax "so that [Mitchell] might make a determination" of the part number of the IDGs and that Fletcher told him that he was going to contact Sundstrand Aerospace, the original manufacturer of the IDGs.... Fletcher testified that he did not tell Hedberg that he was going to call Sundstrand concerning the information contained in the July 3 fax.... Fletcher further testified that both EAS and Mitchell knew that Mitchell was only interested in purchasing IDGs with part number 729640 at the time that the July 3 fax was sent....

Fletcher did not contact Sundstrand immediately. Rather, Fletcher determined from the information contained in the July 3 fax that the parts available for sale were part number 729640. Fletcher then called Hedberg and said: "It appears that all three IDGs are what we want, part number 729640. Let's negotiate a price." ... Hedberg testified that he relied on the information Fletcher told him regarding the IDGs because Fletcher "had been dealing with IDGs for years and is very knowledgeable about them" and because Fletcher "had been talking with Sundstrand about the IDGs." ... Fletcher and Hedberg agreed upon a price of $50,000 per IDG.

Mitchell then issued a purchase order for the IDGs. The purchase order describes the IDGs as part number 729640. The purchase order also states that the "UNITS ARE TO BE AS DESCRIBED IN TELEFAX OF JUL 3, 1996 FROM LEIF TO GREG: UNIT #1: CSD SN 5201 / GEN SN 2370; UNIT #2: CSD SN 1692 / GEN SN 180; UNIT #3; CSD SN 233 / GEN SN 432C." EAS then prepared an invoice which describes the parts as "729640 IDG." The invoice also references Mitchell's purchase order. EAS also provided Mitchell with a "Material Certification Form," which describes the parts as 729640 IDGs and references Mitchell's purchase order.

EAS then shipped the IDGs to Mitchell. Mitchell then forwarded the IDGs to Sundstrand for overhaul. After working on the parts, Sundstrand informed Mitchell that all three of the IDGs were part number 708524 and not part number 729640. At Hedberg's request, Mitchell sent the IDGs with serial numbers 233 and 1692 to Nortek in Miami Florida. Nortek confirmed that those IDGs were part number 708524. Mitchell claims that it has suffered damages in the amount of $120,000 as a result of having received IDGs that were part number 708524 instead of part number 729640.

Unable to resolve the dispute, Mitchell filed suit in this court for breach of contract and breach of warranty.... On August 13, 1998, the court issued an order, ruling that the applicable law is the United Nations Convention on Contracts for the International Sale of Goods ("CISG"), 15 U.S.C. app. (West 1998)....

II. Discussion ...

C. *Mitchell's breach-of-contract claim*

Both parties argue that they are entitled to summary judgment on Mitchell's breach-of-contract claim. Mitchell argues that the parties contracted for EAS to sell Mitchell three IDGs part number 729640 and that EAS breached the contract when it sold Mitchell IDGs which were not part number 729640. EAS argues that the parties contracted for EAS to sell Mitchell the three IDGs that EAS had available for sale and not for EAS to sell IDGs part number 729640. EAS further argues that Mitchell assumed the risk that the IDGs would not be part number 729640 and that Mitchell's decision to purchase the IDGs was the direct result of Mitchell's unilateral mistake in interpreting the information that EAS provided.

Under the CISG, "[t]he seller must deliver goods which are of the quantity, quality and description required by the contract." CISG art. 35. The seller is liable in accordance with the contract and this Convention for any lack of conformity. CISG art. 36. Therefore, the issue is what specific goods the parties contracted for EAS to sell Mitchell.

1. *Parol evidence and the CISG*

Before analyzing the evidence submitted by the parties, the court must determine whether it can consider parol evidence in deciding the parties' dispute. Mitchell argues that the court cannot because the contract, *i.e.,* the purchase order, is clear and unambiguous. EAS argues that the court can because the contract is patently ambiguous. Neither Mitchell nor EAS addressed whether parol evidence is admissible under the relevant provisions of the CISG.

This court was unable to find any case from the Seventh Circuit or a district court in the Seventh Circuit which has addressed the issue of whether a court can consider parol evidence in a contract dispute governed by the CISG. This is not surprising because "there is virtually no case law under the Convention." *Delchi Carrier SpA v. Rotorex Corp.,* 71 F.3d 1024, 1028 (2d Cir.1995). Thus, the issue of whether the court can consider parol evidence in a contract dispute governed by the CISG is an issue of first impression for this court.

The Eleventh Circuit addressed this issue in its highly per[?]sive opinion in the case of *MCC-Marble Ceramic Center, Inc.[?] Ceramica Nuova d'Agostino,* 144 F.3d 1384, 1389–90 (11th Cir[?] 1998). . . .

This court agrees with the Eleventh Circuit that article 8 of the CISG requires the court to consider parol evidence inasmuch as that evidence is probative of the subjective intent of the parties. This conclusion is in accord with the great weight of persuasive authority on the issue. *See MCC–Marble,* 144 F.3d at 1390 & n. 17 (citations omitted); *Claudia v. Olivieri Footwear Ltd.,* No. 96 Civ. 8052, 1998 WL 164824, at *5–6 (S.D.N.Y. Apr.1, 1998) (stating that "contracts governed by the CISG are freed from the limits of the parol evidence rule and there is a wider spectrum of admissible evidence to consider in construing the terms of the parties' agreement"); *see also Filanto v. Chilewich Int'l Corp.,* 789 F.Supp. 1229, 1238, n. 7 (S.D.N.Y.1992).[3] Accordingly, the court finds that it must consider any evidence concerning any negotiations, agreements, or statements made prior to the issuance of the purchase order in this case in determining whether the parties contracted for EAS to sell Mitchell three IDGs part number 729640 or, alternatively, to sell Mitchell the three IDGs that EAS had available for purchase.

One might argue that Illinois law, not the CISG, governs the parol evidence issue in this case because the parol evidence rule is a rule of contract formation and, as discussed above, Illinois law governs contract formation issues in this case. *Mohr v. Metro East Mfg. Co.,* 711 F.2d 69, 71 (7th Cir.1983). However, the issue of parol evidence is addressed in article 8 of the CISG, which is in Part I of the CISG. CISG art. 8. Neither Sweden nor the United States declared that it would not be bound by Part I of the CISG. *See* CISG Parties to the Convention nn. 16 & 19. Thus, the court finds that the CISG, not Illinois law, governs the parol evidence issue in this contract dispute.

Assuming that Illinois law would govern the parol evidence issue, however, parol evidence would still be admissible in this case. In Illinois, parol evidence is admissible when the contract is ambiguous. *Foxfield Realty Inc. v. Kubala,* 287 Ill.App.3d 519, 223 Ill.Dec. 52, 678 N.E.2d 1060, 1063 (Ill.App.Ct.1997). Whether an ambiguity exists is a question of law for the court to decide. *Id.* (citing *Hammel v. Ruby,* 139 Ill.App.3d 241, 93 Ill.Dec. 742, 487 N.E.2d 409 (1985)).

---

3. In *Beijing Metals & Minerals Import/Export Corp. v. American Bus. Ctr.,* 993 F.2d 1178 (5th Cir.1993), the Fifth Circuit reached an opposite conclusion. However, the court did not conduct any analysis of the CISG to support its conclusion. Thus, the court finds that the *Beijing Metals* opinion is not persuasive on this issue. *See MCC–Marble,* 144 F.3d at 1389–90 (stating that the *Beijing Metals* opinion was "not particularly persuasive").

the purchase order is ambiguous. Although the
describes the goods as IDGs part number 729640, it
at the "UNITS ARE TO BE AS DESCRIBED IN
OF JUL 3." The July 3 fax never describes the IDGs as
ber 729640; rather, the fax gives the part numbers for the
ors and transmissions. EAS has submitted evidence that the
numbers given for the transmissions and the generators could
er go together to form an IDG part number 729640. Therefore,
the contract is ambiguous as to whether the parties contracted for
EAS to sell Mitchell IDG's part number 729640 or the three IDGs
with the generator and transmission parts described in the July 3
fax, which were not IDG's part number 729640. Because the
contract contains such an ambiguity, Illinois law allows the court to
consider parol evidence in interpreting the contract.

2. The evidence in this case

Having determined that the CISG requires the court to consider the contract along with any evidence concerning any negotiations, agreements, or statements made prior to the issuance of the purchase order in this case, the court must now determine whether there is a genuine issue of fact as to whether the parties contracted for EAS to sell Mitchell three IDGs part number 729640 or, alternatively, to sell Mitchell the three IDGs that EAS had available for purchase. The court finds that there is.

On the one hand there is evidence that the parties contracted for EAS to sell Mitchell IDGs part number 729640. First the purchase order, invoice, and material certification all state that EAS is selling Mitchell three IDGs part number 729640. Second, there is evidence that the information contained in the July 3 fax indicated that the part number of the IDGs was 729640. Finally, there is Fletcher's testimony that (1) the parts were listed on the ILD as three number 729640 IDGs; (2) at the time that the July 3 fax was sent, both EAS and Mitchell knew that Mitchell was only interested in purchasing IDGs with part number 729640; and (3) Fletcher asked Hedberg if EAS had any IDGs part number 729640 and Hedberg responded "Yes."

On the other hand, there is evidence that the parties contracted for EAS to sell the IDGs it had available for purchase, which were not part number 729640. First, the July 3 fax never identified the IDGs as part number 729640; rather, it simply listed the part numbers of the transmissions and the generators which went together to form the IDG. Second, the purchase order states that it is for the units described in the July 3 fax, which are the units EAS had available for purchase. Finally, there is Hedberg's testimony that (1) the parts were listed on the ILD with two or three alternative part numbers and not just part number 729640; (2) he and Fletcher did not discuss the part number of the IDGs in that first conversation; (3) he relied on Fletcher's expertise in IDGs in the negotiations; (4) he told Fletcher that EAS could not determine the exact part number of the IDGs available for sale and "made it clear" to Fletcher that he did not have the information necessary to determine whether the part number of the IDGs was 729640; (5) Fletcher requested information about the IDGs "to try to confirm the part number of the units that [EAS] wished to sell and that [Mitchell] wished to buy"; (6) Hedberg sent Fletcher the July 3 fax "so that [Mitchell] might make a determination" of the part number of the IDGs; and (7) Fletcher decided to buy the IDGs available after determining for himself that the IDGs were part number 729640.

Based on the above evidence, the court finds that there is a genuine issue of material fact which precludes summary judgment. There is evidence that the parties contracted for EAS to sell IDGs part number 729640. There is also evidence that the parties contracted for EAS to sell Mitchell the IDGs that EAS had available for purchase. Accordingly, neither party is entitled to summary judgment on this issue.

EAS also argues that it is entitled to summary judgment because Mitchell assumed the risk that the IDGs were not part number 729640 and made a unilateral mistake in determining that the IDGs were part number 729640. There is a genuine issue of fact, however, as to whether Mitchell assumed the risk and whether the mistake was unilateral or bilateral.

As a preliminary matter, the court notes that these issues are moot if the parties contracted for EAS to sell Mitchell the IDGs that EAS had available for purchase. If that is all that the parties agreed on, then the goods which EAS sent to Mitchell would not be nonconforming and EAS would not be liable for breach of contract. Thus, these issues as to the assumption of risk and mistake are only issues if the parties contracted for EAS to sell Mitchell IDGs part number 729640.

As to the assumption of risk issue, however, there is a genuine issue of fact as to whether Mitchell assumed the risk. On the one hand, EAS submitted evidence that (1) the parts were listed on the ILD as three number 729640 IDGs; (2) Fletcher asked Hedberg if EAS had any IDGs part number 729640 and Hedberg responded "Yes"; and (3) one could tell from an external examination whether the IDGs were part number 729640 or 708524. This evidence would tend to show that Mitchell did not assume the risk. On the other hand, there is evidence that (1) Hedberg relied on ... Fletcher's determination that the IDGs were part number 729640 and (2) Fletcher knew that Hedberg/EAS did not and could not determine the IDGs part number. This evidence tends to show that Mitchell did assume the risk. Accordingly, neither party is entitled to summary judgment on this issue. . . .

Notes

2–19. Why does the court waffle so much on the issue of the role of the CISG with respect to the parol evidence issue in the case? Recall that the court also had similar difficulty determining the role of the CISG as to subject matter jurisdiction in the case. *See* note 1–14, *supra* (discussing subject matter jurisdiction in *Mitchell Aircraft*).

2–20. As to ambiguous terms, what is the role of parol evidence under the CISG, according to *Mitchell Aircraft*? Is the court correct in
its conclusion that the parol evidence can be invoked under the CISG?

2–21. *Mitchell Aircraft* says that it relies on
MCC-Marble, infra.

Reconsider *Mitchell Aircraft* in light of the following excerpt from
MCC-Marble to decide whether *Mitchell Aircraft*
 is reading the precedents accurately.

MCC–MARBLE CERAMIC CENTER, INC. v. CERAMICA NUOVA d'AGOSTINO, S.p.A.
144 F.3d 1384 (11th Cir. 1998).

Birch, Circuit Judge.

[A U.S. purchaser of ceramic tiles for resale brought a breach of contract action against the foreign seller of tiles, and the seller brought counterclaims seeking damages for nonpayment. The District Court granted summary judgment for the seller, and the purchaser appealed. The Eleventh Circuit reversed and remanded, holding that: (*i*) the district court was required, under the CISG, to consider evidence of the parties' subjective intent that certain terms of their written agreement were not applicable; (*ii*) the parol evidence rule did not apply in actions involving the CISG; and, (*iii*) factual issues precluded summary judgment in this case.]

This case requires us to determine whether a court must consider parol evidence in a contract dispute governed by the United Nations Convention on Contracts for the International Sale of Goods ("CISG"). The district court granted summary judgment on behalf of the defendant-appellee, relying on certain terms and provisions that appeared on the reverse of a pre-printed form contract for the sale of ceramic tiles. The plaintiff-appellant sought to rely on a number of affidavits that tended to show both that the parties had arrived at an oral contract before memorializing their agreement in writing and that they subjectively intended not to apply the terms on the reverse of the contract to their agreements.

The magistrate judge held that the affidavits did not raise an issue of material fact and recommended that the district court grant summary judgment based on the terms of the contract. The district court agreed with the magistrate judge's reasoning and entered summary judgment in the defendant-appellee's favor. . . .

BACKGROUND

The plaintiff-appellant, MCC–Marble Ceramic, Inc. ("MCC"), is a Florida corporation engaged in the retail sale of tiles, and the defendant-appellee, Ceramica Nuova d'Agostino S.p.A. ("D'Agostino") is an Italian corporation engaged in the manufacture of ceramic tiles. In October 1990, MCC's president, Juan Carlos Mozon [*sic*], met representatives of D'Agostino at a trade fair in Bologna, Italy and negotiated an agreement to purchase ceramic tiles from D'Agostino based on samples he examined at the trade fair. Monzon, who spoke no Italian, communicated with Gianni Silingardi, then D'Agostino's commercial director, through a translator, Gianfranco Copelli, who was himself an agent of D'Agostino. The parties apparently arrived at an oral agreement on the crucial terms of price, quality, quantity, delivery and payment. The parties then recorded these terms on one of D'Agostino's standard, pre-printed order forms and Monzon signed the contract on MCC's behalf. According to MCC, the parties also entered into a requirements contract in February 1991, subject to which D'Agostino agreed to supply MCC with high grade ceramic tile at specific discounts as long as MCC purchased sufficient quantities of tile. MCC completed a number of additional order forms requesting tile deliveries pursuant to that agreement.

MCC brought suit against D'Agostino claiming a breach of the February 1991 requirements contract when D'Agostino failed to satisfy orders in April, May, and August of 1991. In addition to other defenses, D'Agostino responded that it was under no obligation to fill MCC's orders because MCC had defaulted on payment for previous shipments. In support of its position, D'Agostino relied on the pre-printed terms of the contracts that MCC had executed. The executed forms were printed in Italian and contained terms and conditions on both the front and reverse. According to an English translation of the October 1990 contract, the front of the order form contained the following language directly beneath Monzon's signature:

> [T]he buyer hereby states that he is aware of the sales conditions stated on the reverse and that he expressly approves of them with special reference to those numbered 1–2–3–4–5–6–7–8.

... Clause 6(b), printed on the back of the form states:

> [D]efault or delay in payment within the time agreed upon gives D'Agostino the right to ... suspend or cancel the contract itself and to cancel possible other pending contracts and the buyer does not have the right to indemnification or damages....

D'Agostino also brought a number of counterclaims against MCC, seeking damages for MCC's alleged nonpayment for deliveries of tile that D'Agostino had made between February 28, 1991 and July 4, 1991. MCC responded that the tile it had received was of a lower quality than contracted for, and that, pursuant to the CISG, MCC was entitled to reduce payment in proportion to the defects.[4] D'Agostino, however, noted that clause 4 on the reverse of the contract states, in pertinent part:

> Possible complaints for defects of the merchandise must be made in writing by means of a certified letter within and not later than 10 days after receipt of the merchandise....

... Although there is evidence to support MCC's claims that it complained about the quality of the deliveries it received, MCC never submitted any written complaints.

MCC did not dispute these underlying facts before the district court, but argued that the parties never intended the terms and conditions printed on the reverse of the order form to apply to their agreements. As evidence for this assertion, MCC submitted Monzon's affidavit, which claims that MCC had no subjective intent to be bound by those terms and that D'Agostino was aware of this intent. MCC also filed affidavits from Silingardi and Copelli, D'Agostino's representatives at the trade fair, which support Monzon's claim that the parties subjectively intended not to be bound by the terms on the reverse of the order form. The magistrate judge held that the affidavits, even if true, did not raise an issue of material fact regarding the interpretation or applicability of the terms of the written contracts and the district court accepted his recommendation to award summary judgment in D'Agostino's favor....

DISCUSSION ...

The parties to this case agree that the CISG governs their dispute because the United States, where MCC has its place of business, and Italy, where D'Agostino has its place of business, are both States Party to the Convention.[5] *See* CISG, art. 1. Article 8 of

---

4. Article 50 of the CISG permits a buyer to reduce payment for nonconforming goods in proportion to the nonconformity under certain conditions. See CISG, art. 50.

5. The United States Senate ratified the CISG in 1986, and the United States deposited its instrument of ratification at the United Nations Headquarters in New York on December 11, 1986. *See*

the CISG governs the interpretation of international contracts for the sale of goods and forms the basis of MCC's appeal from the district court's grant of summary judgment in D'Agostino's favor.[7] MCC argues that the magistrate judge and the district court improperly ignored evidence that MCC submitted regarding the parties' subjective intent when they memorialized the terms of their agreement on D'Agostino's pre-printed form contract, and that the magistrate judge erred by applying the parol evidence rule in derogation of the CISG.

I. Subjective Intent Under the CISG

Contrary to what is familiar practice in United States courts, the CISG appears to permit a substantial inquiry into the parties' subjective intent, even if the parties did not engage in any objectively ascertainable means of registering this intent.[8] Article 8(1) of the CISG instructs courts to interpret the "statements . . . and other conduct of a party . . . according to his intent" as long as the other party "knew or could not have been unaware" of that intent. The plain language of the Convention, therefore, requires an inqui-

---

Preface to Convention, reprinted at 15 U.S.C. app. 52 (1997). The Convention entered into force between the United States and the other States Parties, including Italy, on January 1, 1988. *See id.; Filanto S.p.A. v. Chilewich Int'l Corp.,* 789 F.Supp. 1229, 1237 (S.D.N.Y. 1992).

7. Article 8 provides:

(1) For the purposes of this Convention statements made by and other conduct of a party are to be interpreted according to his intent where the other party knew or could not have been unaware what that intent was.

(2) If the preceding paragraph is not applicable, statements made by and conduct of a party are to be interpreted according to the understanding a reasonable person of the same kind as the other party would have had in the same circumstances.

(3) In determining the intent of a party or the understanding a reasonable person would have had, due consideration is to be given to all relevant circumstances of the case including the negotiations, any practices which the parties have established between themselves, usages and any subsequent conduct of the parties.

CISG, art. 8.

8. In the United States, the legislatures, courts, and the legal academy have voiced a preference for relying on objective manifestations of the parties' intentions. For example, Article Two of the Uniform Commercial Code, which most states have enacted in some form or another to govern contracts for the sale of goods, is replete with references to standards of commercial reasonableness. *See e.g.,* U.C.C. § 2–206 (referring to reasonable means of accepting an offer); *see also Lucy v. Zehmer,* 196 Va. 493, 503, 84 S.E.2d 516, 522 (1954) ("Whether the writing signed . . . was the result of a serious offer . . . and a serious acceptance . . . , or was a serious offer . . . and an acceptance in secret jest . . . , in either event it constituted a binding contract of sale between the parties."). Justice Holmes expressed the philosophy behind this focus on the objective in forceful terms: "The law has nothing to do with the actual state of the parties' minds. In contract, as elsewhere, it must go by externals, and judge parties by their conduct." Oliver W. Holmes, *The Common Law* 242 (Howe ed.1963) *quoted in* John O. Honnold, *Uniform Law for International Sales under the 1980 United Nations*

ry into a party's subjective intent as long as the other party to the contract was aware of that intent.

In this case, MCC has submitted three affidavits that discuss the purported subjective intent of the parties to the initial agreement concluded between MCC and D'Agostino in October 1990. All three affidavits discuss the preliminary negotiations and report that the parties arrived at an oral agreement for D'Agostino to supply quantities of a specific grade of ceramic tile to MCC at an agreed upon price. The affidavits state that the "oral agreement established the essential terms of quality, quantity, description of goods, delivery, price and payment." ... The affidavits also note that the parties memorialized the terms of their oral agreement on a standard D'Agostino order form, but all three affiants contend that the parties *subjectively* intended not to be bound by the terms on the reverse of that form despite a provision directly below the signature line that expressly and specifically incorporated those terms.[9]

The terms on the reverse of the contract give D'Agostino the right to suspend or cancel all contracts in the event of a buyer's non-payment and require a buyer to make a written report of all defects within ten days. As the magistrate judge's report and recommendation makes clear, if these terms applied to the agreements between MCC and D'Agostino, summary judgment would be appropriate because MCC failed to make any written complaints about the quality of tile it received and D'Agostino has established MCC's non-payment of a number of invoices amounting to $108,389.40 and 102,053,846.00 Italian lira.

Article 8(1) of the CISG requires a court to consider this evidence of the parties' subjective intent. Contrary to the magistrate judge's report, which the district court endorsed and adopted, article 8(1) does not focus on interpreting the parties' statements alone. Although we agree with the magistrate judge's conclusion that no "interpretation" of the contract's *terms* could support

---

Convention § 107 at 164 (2d ed.1991) (hereinafter Honnold, *Uniform* Law).

9. MCC makes much of the fact that the written order form is entirely in Italian and that Monzon, who signed the contract on MCC's behalf directly below this provision incorporating the terms on the reverse of the form, neither spoke nor read Italian. This fact is of no assistance to MCC's position. We find it nothing short of astounding that an individual, purportedly experienced in commercial matters, would sign a contract in a foreign language and expect not to be bound simply because he could

not comprehend its terms. We find nothing in the CISG that might counsel this type of reckless behavior and nothing that signals any retreat from the proposition that parties who sign contracts will be bound by them regardless of whether they have read them or understood them. *See e.g., Samson Plastic Conduit and Pipe Corp. v. Battenfeld Extrusionstechnik GMBH,* 718 F.Supp. 886, 890 (M.D.Ala.1989) ("A good and recurring illustration of the problem ... involves a person who is ... unfamiliar with the language in which a contract is written and who has signed a document which was not read to him. There is all

MCC's position,[10] article 8(1) also requires a court to consider subjective intent while interpreting the *conduct* of the parties. The CISG's language, therefore, requires courts to consider evidence of a party's subjective intent when signing a contract if the other party to the contract was aware of that intent at the time. This is precisely the type of evidence that MCC has provided through the Silingardi, Copelli, and Monzon affidavits, which discuss not only Monzon's intent as MCC's representative but also discuss the intent of D'Agostino's representatives and their knowledge that Monzon did not intend to agree to the terms on the reverse of the form contract. This acknowledgment that D'Agostino's representatives were aware of Monzon's subjective intent puts this case squarely within article 8(1) of the CISG, and therefore requires the court to consider MCC's evidence as it interprets the parties' conduct.[11]

II. PAROL EVIDENCE AND THE CISG

Given our determination that the magistrate judge and the district court should have considered MCC's affidavits regarding the parties' subjective intentions, we must address a question of first impression in this circuit: whether the parol evidence rule, which bars evidence of an earlier oral contract that contradicts or varies the terms of a subsequent or contemporaneous written contract,[12] plays any role in cases involving the CISG. We begin by observing that the parol evidence rule, contrary to its title, is a substantive rule of law, not a rule of evidence. *See* II E. Allen Farnsworth, *Farnsworth on Contracts,* § 7.2 at 194 (1990). The rule

---

but unanimous agreement that he is bound.... ")

10. The magistrate judge's report correctly notes that MCC has not sought an interpretation of those terms, but rather to exclude them altogether. We agree that such an approach "would render terms of written contracts virtually meaningless and severely diminish the reliability of commercial contracts."

11. Without this crucial acknowledgment, we would interpret the contract and the parties' actions according to article 8(2), which directs courts to rely on objective evidence of the parties' intent. On the facts of this case it seems readily apparent that MCC's affidavits provide *no evidence* that Monzon's actions would have made his alleged subjective intent not to be bound by the terms of the contract known to "the understanding that a reasonable person ... would have had in the same circumstances." CISG, art 8(2).

12. The Uniform Commercial Code includes a version of the parol evidence rule applicable to contracts for the sale of goods in most states:

Terms with respect to which the confirmatory memoranda of the parties agree or which are otherwise set forth in a writing intended by the parties as a final expression of their agreement with respect to such terms as are included therein may not be contradicted by evidence of any prior agreement or of a contemporaneous oral agreement but may be explained or supplemented

(a) by course of dealing or usage of trade ... or by course of performance ...; and

(b) by evidence of consistent additional terms unless the court finds the writing to have been intended also as a complete and exclusive statement of the terms of the agreement.

U.C.C. § 2–202.

does not purport to exclude a particular type of evidence as an "untrustworthy or undesirable" way of proving a fact, but prevents a litigant from attempting to show "the fact itself—the fact that the terms of the agreement are other than those in the writing." *Id.* As such, a federal district court cannot simply apply the parol evidence rule as a procedural matter—as it might if excluding a particular type of evidence under the Federal Rules of Evidence, which apply in federal court regardless of the source of the substantive rule of decision. *Cf. id.* § 7.2 at 196.[13]

The CISG itself contains no express statement on the role of parol evidence. *See* Honnold, Uniform Law § 110 at 170. It is clear, however, that the drafters of the CISG were comfortable with the concept of permitting parties to rely on oral contracts because they eschewed any statutes of fraud provision and expressly provided for the enforcement of oral contracts. *Compare* CISG, art. 11 (a contract of sale need not be concluded or evidenced in writing) *with* U.C.C. § 2–201 (precluding the enforcement of oral contracts for the sale of goods involving more than $500). Moreover, article 8(3) of the CISG expressly directs courts to give "due consideration . . . to all relevant circumstances of the case including the negotiations . . . " to determine the intent of the parties. Given article 8(1)'s directive to use the intent of the parties to interpret their statements and conduct, article 8(3) is a clear instruction to admit and consider parol evidence regarding the negotiations to the extent they reveal the parties' subjective intent.

Despite the CISG's broad scope, surprisingly few cases have applied the Convention in the United States, *see Delchi Carrier SpA v. Rotorex Corp.,* 71 F.3d 1024, 1027–28 (2d Cir.1995) (observing that "there is virtually no case law under the Convention"), and only two reported decisions touch upon the parol evidence rule, both in *dicta.* One court has concluded, much as we have above, that the parol evidence rule is not viable in CISG cases in light of article 8 of the Convention. In *Filanto,* a district court addressed the differences between the UCC and the CISG on the issues of offer and acceptance and the battle of the forms. *See* 789 F.Supp. at 1238. After engaging in a thorough analysis of how the CISG applied to the dispute before it, the district court tangentially observed that article 8(3) "essentially rejects . . . the parol evidence

13. An example demonstrates this point. The CISG provides that a contract for the sale of goods need not be in writing and that the parties may prove the contract "by any means, including witnesses." CISG, art. 11. Nevertheless, a party seeking to prove a contract in such a manner in federal court could not do so in a way that violated in the rule against hearsay. *See* Fed.R.Evid. 802 (barring hearsay evidence). A federal district court applies the Federal Rules of Evidence because these rules are considered procedural, regardless of the source of the law that governs the substantive decision. *Cf. Farnsworth on Contracts* § 7.2 at 196 & n. 16 (citing cases).

rule." *Id.* at 1238 n.7. Another court, however, appears to have arrived at a contrary conclusion. In *Beijing Metals & Minerals Import/Export Corp. v. American Bus. Ctr., Inc.*, 993 F.2d 1178 (5th Cir.1993), a defendant sought to avoid summary judgment on a contract claim by relying on evidence of contemporaneously negotiated oral terms that the parties had not included in their written agreement. The plaintiff, a Chinese corporation, relied on Texas law in its complaint while the defendant, apparently a Texas corporation,[15] asserted that the CISG governed the dispute. *Id.* at 1183 n. 9. Without resolving the choice of law[16] the Fifth Circuit cited *Filanto* for the proposition that there have been very few reported cases applying the CISG in the United States, and stated that the parol evidence rule would apply regardless of whether Texas law or the CISG governed the dispute. *Beijing Metals*, 993 F.2d at 1183 n. 9. The opinion does not acknowledge *Filanto's* more applicable *dictum* that the parol evidence rule does not apply to CISG cases nor does it conduct any analysis of the Convention to support its conclusion. In fact, the Fifth Circuit did not undertake to interpret the CISG in a manner that would arrive at a result consistent with the parol evidence rule but instead explained that it would apply the rule as developed at Texas common law. *See id.* at 1183 n. 10. As persuasive authority for this court, the *Beijing Metals* opinion is not particularly persuasive on this point.

Our reading of article 8(3) as a rejection of the parol evidence rule, however, is in accordance with the great weight of academic commentary on the issue. As one scholar has explained:

> [T]he language of Article 8(3) that "due consideration is to be given to *all relevant* circumstances of the case" seems adequate to override any domestic rule that would bar a tribunal from considering the relevance of other agreements.... Article 8(3) relieves tribunals from domestic rules that might bar them from "considering" any evidence between the parties that is relevant. This added flexibility for interpretation is consistent with a growing body of opinion that the "parol evidence rule"

---

15. The *Beijing Metals* opinion does not state the place of the defendant's incorporation, but the defendant must have been a United States corporation because the court noted that the case was a "diversity action." *Beijing Metals*, 993 F.2d at 1183 n. 9. *Cf.* 28 U.S.C. § 1332 (providing no statutory grant for suits between aliens unless a citizen of a State is present); 15 James W. Moore, *Moore's Federal Practice* § 102.77 (3d ed.1998) (observing that diversity jurisdiction is not present in suits between two foreign citizens).

16. The Fifth Circuit unwittingly may have solved the problem in the very next footnote, where it observed that the agreement between the parties, which attempted to settle a dispute regarding an earlier sales contract, was not itself a contract for the sale of goods and therefore fell outside the Uniform Commercial Code. *Beijing Metals*, 993 F.2d at 1183 n. 10. *See* CISG, art. 1(1) ("This Convention applies to contracts of sale of *goods* ....")(emphasis added).

has been an embarrassment for the administration of modern transactions.

Honnold, Uniform Law § 110 at 170–71.[17] Indeed, only one commentator has made any serious attempt to reconcile the parol evidence rule with the CISG. *See* David H. Moore, Note, *The Parol Evidence Rule and the United Nations Convention on Contracts for the International Sale of Goods: Justifying Beijing Metals & Minerals Import/Export Corp. v. American Business Center, Inc.,* 1995 BYU L.REV. 1347. Moore argues that the parol evidence rule often permits the admission of evidence discussed in article 8(3), and that the rule could be an appropriate way to discern what consideration is "due" under article 8(3) to evidence of a parol nature. *Id.* at 1361–63. He also argues that the parol evidence rule, by limiting the incentive for perjury and pleading prior understandings in bad faith, promotes good faith and uniformity in the interpretation of contracts and therefore is in harmony with the principles of the CISG, as expressed in article 7.[18] *Id.* at 1366–70. The answer to both these arguments, however, is the same: although jurisdictions in the United States have found the parol evidence rule helpful to promote good faith and uniformity in contract, as well as an appropriate answer to the question of how much consideration to give parol evidence, a wide number of other States Party to the CISG have rejected the rule in their domestic jurisdictions. One of the primary factors motivating the negotiation and adoption of the CISG was to provide parties to international contracts for the sale

---

17. *See also* Louis F. Del Duca, et al., *Sales Under the Uniform Commercial Code and the Convention on International Sale of Goods,* 173–74 (1993); Henry D. Gabriel, *A Primer on the United Nations Convention on the International Sale of Goods: From the Perspective of the Uniform Commercial Code,* 7 IND. INT'L & COMP. L.REV. 279, 281 (1997) ("Subjective intent is given primary consideration.... [Article 8] allows open-ended reliance on parol evidence....."); Herbert Berstein & Joseph Lookofsky, *Understanding the CISG in Europe* 29 (1997) ("[T]he CISG has dispensed with the parol evidence rule which might otherwise operate to exclude extrinsic evidence under the law of certain Common Law countries."); Harry M. Fletchner, *Recent Developments: CISG,* 14 J.L. & COM. 153, 157 (1995) (criticizing the *Beijing Metals* opinion and noting that "[c]ommentators generally agree that article 8(3) rejects the approach to the parol evidence questions taken by U.S. domestic law.") (collecting authority); John E. Murray,

Jr., *An Essay on the Formation of Contracts and Related Matters Under the United Nations Convention on Contracts for the International Sale of Goods,* 8 J.L. & COM. 11, 12 (1988) ("We are struck by a new world where there is . . . no parol evidence rule, among other differences."); Peter Winship, *Domesticating International Commercial Law:* Revising U.C.C. Article 2 in Light of the United Nations Sales Convention, 37 LOY. L.REV. 43, 57 (1991).

18. Article 7 of the CISG provides in pertinent part:

(1) In the interpretation of this Convention, regard is to be had to its international character and to the need to promote uniformity in its application and the observance of good faith in international trade.

(2) Questions concerning matters governed by this Convention which are not expressly settled in it are to be settled in conformity with the general principles on which it is based....

CISG, art. 7.

of goods with some degree of certainty as to the principles of law that would govern potential disputes and remove the previous doubt regarding which party's legal system might otherwise apply. *See* Letter of Transmittal from Ronald Reagan, President of the United States, to the United States Senate, *reprinted at* 15 U.S.C. app. 70, 71 (1997). Courts applying the CISG cannot, therefore, upset the parties' reliance on the Convention by substituting familiar principles of domestic law when the Convention requires a different result. We may only achieve the directives of good faith and uniformity in contracts under the CISG by interpreting and applying the plain language of article 8(3) as written and obeying its directive to consider this type of parol evidence.

This is not to say that parties to an international contract for the sale of goods cannot depend on written contracts or that parol evidence regarding subjective contractual intent need always prevent a party relying on a written agreement from securing summary judgment. To the contrary, most cases will not present a situation (as exists in this case) in which both parties to the contract acknowledge a subjective intent not to be bound by the terms of a pre-printed writing. In most cases, therefore, article 8(2) of the CISG will apply, and objective evidence will provide the basis for the court's decision. *See* Honnold, *Uniform Law* § 107 at 164–65. Consequently, a party to a contract governed by the CISG will not be able to avoid the terms of a contract and force a jury trial simply by submitting an affidavit which states that he or she did not have the subjective intent to be bound by the contract's terms. *Cf. Klopfenstein v. Pargeter,* 597 F.2d 150, 152 (9th Cir.1979) (affirming summary judgment despite the appellant's submission of his own affidavit regarding his subjective intent: "Undisclosed, subjective intentions are immaterial in [a] commercial transaction, especially when contradicted by objective conduct. Thus, the affidavit has no legal effect even if its averments are accepted as wholly truthful."). Moreover, to the extent parties wish to avoid parol evidence problems they can do so by including a merger clause in their agreement that extinguishes any and all prior agreements and understandings not expressed in the writing.[19]

Considering MCC's affidavits in this case, however, we conclude that the magistrate judge and the district court improperly

---

19. *See* Ronald A. Brand & Harry M. Fletchner, *Arbitration and Contract Formation in International Trade: First Interpretations of the U.N. Sales Convention,* 12 J.L. & COM. 239, 252 (1993) (arguing that article 8(3) of the CISG will not permit the consideration of parol evidence when the parties have expressly excluded oral modifications of the contract pursuant to article 29); *see also* I Albert Kritzer, *Guide to Practical Applications of the United Nations Convention on Contracts for the International Sale of Goods* 125 (1989) (counseling the use of a merger clause to compensate for the absence of a parol evidence rule in the CISG).

granted summary judgment in favor of D'Agostino. Although the affidavits are, as D'Agostino observes, relatively conclusory and unsupported by facts that would *objectively* establish MCC's intent not to be bound by the conditions on the reverse of the form, article 8(1) requires a court to consider evidence of a party's subjective intent when the other party was aware of it, and the Silingardi and Copelli affidavits provide that evidence. This is not to say that the affidavits are conclusive proof of what the parties intended. A reasonable finder of fact, for example, could disregard testimony that purportedly sophisticated international merchants signed a contract without intending to be bound as simply too incredible to believe and hold MCC to the conditions printed on the reverse of the contract.[20] Nevertheless, the affidavits raise an issue of material fact regarding the parties' intent to incorporate the provisions on the reverse of the form contract. If the finder of fact determines that the parties did not intend to rely on those provisions, then the more general provisions of the CISG will govern the outcome of the dispute.[21]

CONCLUSION

MCC asks us to reverse the district court's grant of summary judgment in favor of D'Agostino. The district court's decision rests on pre-printed contractual terms and conditions incorporated on the reverse of a standard order form that MCC's president signed on the company's behalf. Nevertheless, we conclude that the CISG, which governs international contracts for the sale of goods, precludes summary judgment in this case because MCC has raised an issue of material fact concerning the parties' subjective intent to be bound by the terms on the reverse of the pre-printed contract. The CISG also precludes the application of the parol evidence rule, which would otherwise bar the consideration of evidence concern-

20. D'Agostino attempts to explain and undermine the affidavit of its representatives during the transaction, by calling Silingardi a "disgruntled" former employee.... Silingardi's alleged feelings towards his former employer may indeed be relevant to undermine the credibility of his assertions, but that is a matter for the finder of fact, not for this court on summary judgment.

21. Article 50, which permits a buyer to reduce payment to a seller who delivers nonconforming goods, and article 39, which deprives the buyer of that right if the buyer fails to give the seller notice specifying the defect in the goods delivered within a reasonable time, will be of primary importance. Although we may affirm a district court's grant of summary judgment if it is correct for any reason, even if not relied upon below, *see United States v. $121,100.00 in United States Currency,* 999 F.2d 1503, 1507 (11th Cir.1993), and the parties have touched upon these articles in their briefs, they have not provided us with sufficient information to resolve their dispute under the CISG. MCC's affidavits indicate that MCC may have complained about the quality of the tile D'Agostino delivered, but they have provided no authority regarding what constitutes a reasonable time for such a complaint in this context. Accordingly, we decline to affirm the district court's grant of summary judgment on this basis.

ing a prior or contemporaneously negotiated oral agreement. Accordingly, we REVERSE the district court's grant of summary judgment and REMAND this case for further proceedings consistent with this opinion.

Notes

2–22.　As the court notes, "surprisingly few cases have applied the Convention in the United States." Why is that the case? How did the court happen to apply it in this case? One very useful research tool for finding cases interpreting and applying the CISG—from all jurisdictions that are parties to the convention—is http://www.cisg.law.pace.edu.

2–23.　Review CISG art. 8. Which paragraph governs the situation of the parties in *MCC Marble*? Is it correct to characterize the situation, as the Eleventh Circuit does, as one involving *subjective* intent? How does subjective intent differ from objective intent? If the buyer and seller had both been U.S. firms, would MCC–Marble's "subjective" intent have been relevant? Controlling?

2–24.　What significance does the court attach to the existence of *written* contract terms? (In this regard, review notes 9 and 10 of the court's opinion.) Is it important that the terms signed by Monzon were in a language that he did not understand? Does it matter that Silingardi, with whom he was negotiating, and Copelli, the translator who was an agent of the seller, knew that Monzon did not understand Italian?

2–25.　Does the outcome of this decision itself "render [the] terms of [the] written contract[] virtually meaningless and severely diminish the reliability of commercial contracts," note 10 *supra*. How does the court justify the outcome in this regard?

2–26.　Is application of the parol evidence rule barred by CISG arts. 7 and 8? Would this result, as Moore seems to suggest, really depend upon how formidable and unyielding one thinks the parol evidence rule is? Consider the following experiment: Put aside the CISG for the moment (*e.g.*, assume that both parties are U.S. firms, or that Italy is not a CISG signatory), and ask whether on the facts of the case, the rule would not allow evidence of the parties' mutual intentions as to the formation of their contract and the significance of the written terms.

2–27.　If you represented D'Agostino, and it asked you what it should do when negotiating sales with U.S. firms in the future, what would you recommend?

2–28.　Suppose the contract in MCC–Marble contained the following clause:

> There are no promises, verbal understandings or agreements of any kind, pertaining to this contract other than specified herein.

Does the inclusion of such a so-called "merger clause" in the agreement extinguish prior agreements not referenced in the written contract?

2–29. Is there an Anglo–American legal obsession with contract formality? For domestic sales transactions, the UCC Statute of Frauds provision, § 2–201, makes oral contracts for the sale of goods of $500 or more unenforceable in the absence of a writing or one of several enumerated substitutes evidencing the contract. The UCC parol evidence provision, § 2–202, restricts the admissibility of evidence to clarify the meaning of terms contained in a written contract in domestic sales transactions. In contrast, CISG Article 11 abolishes the writing and other formal requirements for transnational sale of goods transactions. In addition, CISG Article 8 eliminates the use of the parol evidence rule to prohibit introduction of prior oral or written or contemporaneous oral evidence to clarify the intent of the parties as to the meaning of terms used in written contracts in transnational transactions. In a classic comparative law book, two distinguished comparative law experts have commented on the consequences of the Anglo–American tradition of dividing fact-finding and law-application functions between the jury and the judge respectively. They contrast this tradition with the civil law tradition of using judges for *both* fact finding and application of the law. Do you find their evaluation of the impact of the use of juries convincing?

K. ZWEIGERT & H. KÖTZ, AN INTRODUCTION TO COMPARATIVE LAW 258

(Oxford University Press 1998).
By permission of Oxford University Press.

One decisive fact explains many of the peculiarities of Anglo–American procedure: it is that the procedure results from the *jury trial*. Jury trials admittedly occur only in criminal cases in England today, and then only when the crime is serious and the accused has pleaded "not guilty," but even so, civil litigation in England is still instinct with the traditions of the jury trial. For example, all trials, civil as well as criminal, take the form of a single continuous oral hearing, lasting many hours or even days, if necessary. Since one cannot keep recalling the members of a jury, the oral hearing once started must continue without interruption. This compression of the Anglo–American trial into a single oral hearing gives rise to a whole series of further consequences, from the totality of which the Common Law trial has gained its unmistakable characteristics. . . .

There is a complex set of rules, called the "law of evidence," which determines what evidence may be given by witnesses and what questions they may be asked in examination and cross-examination. There is no counterpart for this in the Civil Law, where evidence is heard by professional judges who, in a civil suit, should get to hear *everything*; after all, they are experienced, even hardened, enough to make a "free evaluation of the evidence" and separate the grain from the chaff. In a jury trial, by contrast, a "law of evidence" is necessary to prevent laymen being led up the garden path by "hearsay evidence," suggestive "leading question," and other tricks.

Note

2–30.   Understanding differences in the roles of judges and juries in civil and common law countries and the methods of selecting judges is helpful in understanding the different approaches of the two systems in their treatment of Statute of Frauds and parol evidence issues. The CISG was drafted over a period of fifty years beginning in the early 1930's by representatives of all of the major legal traditions in the world.[11] Initially, it was primarily representatives of countries with civil law traditions who were involved in the drafting process. The United States with its common law tradition became involved only in the 1960's. The influence of the legal systems and legal traditions of the civil law countries on the content and style of the CISG has therefore been profound.

D. THE "BATTLE OF THE FORMS": UCC § 2–207 AND CISG ARTICLE 19[12]

The CISG makes an initial assumption that an "acceptance" with different or additional terms is a counter-offer rather than an acceptance.[13] It does not explicitly contain the U.C.C. concept of "expression of acceptance," which has the same effect as an acceptance.[14] However, the CISG in substance has the practical effect of compromising between the old common-law "mirror image" approach and the U.C.C. approach to contract formation, which merely looks to agreement on essential terms.

11. Louis F. Del Duca and Patrick Del Duca, *Practice Under the Convention On International Sale of Goods (CISG): A Primer for Attorneys and International Traders (Part I)*, 27 UCC L.J. 331, 338 (1995).

12. The discussion that follows is based upon Louis Del Duca, *Implementation of Contract Formation Statute of Frauds, Parol Evidence, and Battle of Forms CISG Provisions in Civil and Common Law Countries*, 38 U.C.C. L.J. 55, 68–70 (2005).

13. CISG Article 19(1) provides:

(1) A reply to an offer which purports to be an acceptance but contains additions, limitations or other modifications is a rejection of the offer and constitutes a counter-offer.

14. U.C.C. § 2–207(1) (2001) provides:

A definite and seasonable expression of acceptance or a written confirmation which is sent within a reasonable time operates as an acceptance even though it states terms additional to or different from those offered or agreed upon, unless acceptance is expressly made conditional on asset to the additional or different terms.

Under CISG Article 19(1), a reply to an offer that purports to be an acceptance but which contains additions, limitations, or other modifications is initially classified as a rejection of the offer and constitutes a counteroffer. By itself this would appear to negate the "expression of acceptance" rule of U.C.C. Section 2–207(1).[15] However, the CISG's apparent absolute negation of this counteroffer approach in Article 19(1) is softened by the immediately following language in Article 19(2) of the CISG, which by implication adopts an "expression of acceptance" approach.[16] This language states that a reply to an offer that purports to be an acceptance but contains additional or different terms that do not "materially" alter the terms of the offer constitutes an acceptance, unless the offeror, without undue delay, objects orally to the discrepancy or dispatches a notice to that effect. If the offeror does not so object, the terms of the contract are the terms of the offer, with the modifications contained in the acceptance. This movement in the direction of permitting a contract to be created on the basis of agreement on essential terms is in turn altered by the immediately following provision, which states that

> [a]dditional or different terms relating among other things to the price, payment, quality and quantity of the goods, place and time of delivery, extent of one party's liability to the other or the settlement of disputes are considered to alter the terms of the offer materially.[17]

Notes

2–31. *High Tech, Inc.* is a manufacturer of medical equipment with its place of business in Illinois. High Tech receives an order for a $300,000 scanner from *Himmel, Inc.* (a German health care provider) with its place of business of business in Hamburg, Germany. Using its standard Order Acknowledgement form, High Tech replies, agreeing with all of the terms in the Himmel offer, but also adding a term, providing that any disputes which might arise between the parties must be resolved by arbitration before the Chicago International Dispute Resolution Association (CIDRA).

(a) Has a contract been formed under CISG Article 19(1)? Does the addition of the arbitration clause in High Tech's response "materially alter" the terms of the offer? *See* CISG Article 19(2)

15. *Id.*

16. CISG Article 19(2) provides:

(2) However, a reply to an offer which purports to be an acceptance but contains additional or different terms which do not materially alter the terms of the offer constitutes an acceptance, unless the offeror, without undue delay, objects orally to the discrepancy or dispatches a notice to that effect. If he does not so object, the terms of the contract are the terms of the offer with the modifications contained in the acceptance.

17. CISG Article 19(3).

and (3); *Filanto, S.p.A. v. Chilewich International Corp.*, 789 F.Supp. 1229 (S.D.N.Y.1992). Among other things, the *Filanto* court concluded that the arbitration clause would constitute a material alteration of the offer under Article 19(3), but goes on to rule that because of the prior practices established between the contracting parties in earlier agreements (*see* CISG Article 9(1)) involving arbitration clauses, the failure of the Seller to object to the arbitration clause included in the Buyer's response to its offer constituted an acceptance of the additional term.

(b) Has a contract been formed under UCC § 2–207(1)? *See* UCC Official Comments 4 and 5; *Marlene Industries Corp. v. Cornac Textiles, Inc.*, 45 N.Y.2d 327, 408 N.Y.S.2d 410, 380 N.E.2d 239, 242 (1978).

2–32.   Assume the same facts as note 2–31, except that instead of containing an arbitration clause, High Tech's reply contained a clause requiring buyer to report defects in the scanner to the seller within 30 days. Has a contract been formed under the CISG? Is the 30–day provision a material or non-material provision? Is the 30–day provision a part of the contract? *See* Case no. 4 O 113/90 (Landgericht Baden–Baden, Germany, 14 Aug. 1991), *available at* http://www.cisg.law.pace.edu/cases/910814g1.html, ruling that the additional clause was a "nonmaterial" modification.

E. IRREVOCABLE OFFERS: UCC § 2–205 AND CISG ARTICLE 16(2)

Although no case law has yet been reported interpreting Article 16(2) of the CISG,[18] one must be wary of the differences between the "firm offer" (irrevocable offer) provisions of UCC § 2–205 and CISG Article 16(2). Section 2–205 of the UCC provides that

[a]n offer by a merchant to buy or sell goods *in a signed writing* which by its terms give assurance that it will be held open is not revocable, for lack of consideration, during the time stated or if no time is stated for a reasonable time, but in no event may such period of irrevocability exceed three months; but any such term of assurance on a form supplied by the offeree must be separately signed by the offeror.

(Emphasis added.) The CISG also gives an additional basis for making the offer irrevocable where "it was reasonable for the offeree to rely on the offer as being irrevocable and the offeree has

---

18. CISG Article 16(2) provides: [a]n offer cannot be revoked:

(a) if it indicates, whether by stating a fixed time for acceptance or otherwise, that it is irrevocable; or

(b) if it was reasonable for the offeree to rely on the offer as being irrevocable and the offeree has acted in reliance on the offer.

acted in reliance on the offer.''[19] Thus. under the CISG an offerer may unintentionally be deemed to make an irrevocable offer without explicitly stating that its offer was irrevocable. To avoid accidentally making an irrevocable offer under the CISG—as a result of stating a fixed time of acceptance—such offers should state something like, "[t]his offer expires after thirty days, but can be revoked at any time." In comparing UCC § 2–205 and CISG Article 16(2), consider also the following problem.

Note

2–33. *General Contractor* was required to submit its competitive bid to *Bigg City* on July 1 for construction of a new office building in which Bigg offices were to be consolidated. Having been delayed in preparing details of its bid, on June 5 General telephoned *Acme Carpets* and requested an estimate and offer to provide all of the carpeting required for the new building. During the lengthy telephone conversation, Acme offered to provide the required carpeting for a total price of $100,000 and assured General that its offer would remain open until July 10, the date on which Bigg, after consideration of all competitive bids it had received, was scheduled to award the general contract for construction of the new office building. On June 20, Acme informed General that because of price increases it was revoking its offer to sell the carpeting for $100,000 but could deliver the required carpeting for $130,000. On July 10, Bigg awarded the contract for construction of the new office building to General. When Acme refused to deliver the carpets at the $100,000 price, General informed Acme that it deemed Acme had breached its contract for delivery of the rugs for $100,000 and proceeded to obtain substitute comparable carpeting from a third party vendor for $115,000.

(a) Under the CISG, does General have a viable cause of action against Acme for $15,000? *See* CISG Article 16(2)(a).

(b) Under the UCC, does General have a viable cause of action against Acme for $15,000? *See* UCC § 2–205.

---

19. *Id*. art. 16(2)(b).

Chapter 3

PERFORMANCE AND BREACH

A. THE MORAL BASIS OF CONTRACT OBLIGATION AND EFFICIENT BREACH

Students of public international law are familiar with the maxim *pacta sunt servanda,* which means that obligations should be observed. The principle, a foundation of public international law that is enshrined in Article 26 of the Vienna Convention on the Law of Treaties, is virtually never questioned, although scholars might differ as to the extent to which and the means by which a state can be forced to abide by those obligations.

The same principle underlies the law of contracts between private parties in the United States and elsewhere. Indeed, a non-lawyer invited to give a definition of a contractual obligation involving private parties would likely say that a contract is an obligation or a promise, and that a person undertaking an obligation or making a promise ought to abide by it. This definition would be meant to have both moral and legal underpinnings. Persons *ought to* abide by their contracts because in the act of promising they have undertaken a moral obligation. If moral suasion is insufficient to persuade them to abide by their promises, then the law should intervene.

In the Anglo–American system of common law, however, a lawyer's definition of contract is usually more qualified and does not include a moral component. The most famous formulation is that given by Justice Oliver Wendell Holmes: "The duty to keep a contract at common law means a prediction that you must pay damages if you do not keep it,—and nothing else."[1] Justice Holmes

---

1. Oliver Wendell Holmes, Jr., *The Path of the Law,* 10 Harv. L. Rev. 457, 462 (1897).

reached this conclusion by adopting the position of the "bad man" who would not abide by his legal duty out of a sense of moral obligation, but only because he would face adverse consequences in the event he failed to do so. Holmes emphasized that damages should remain the same whether the breach was innocent or willful: "If a contract is broken the measure of damages generally is the same, whatever the cause of the breach."[2]

Justice Holmes's formulation was based in part on his observation that common-law courts ordinarily award only substitutional relief in the form of money damages for breach of contract. Specific performance, an order actually to perform one's obligations under a contract, is, for the most part, an exceptional remedy.[3] The focus of the damages remedy is its effect on the breached-against party—damages should be sufficient to make the promisee indifferent as to whether the promisor performed or not—rather than on compelling the promisor to abide by his promise.[4]

Justice Holmes did not phrase his dictum in terms of modern economic theory, but it is easy to see in his writings the precursor to the theory of efficient breach. Efficient breach theory suggests that in some instances breaching a contract leads to greater economic efficiency than would performing it. An efficient breach of contract must be, as economists would say, *Pareto optimal*:[5] no party must be worse off, and at least one party must be better off, as a result of the breach.[6]

For example, imagine that *A* has a contract to deliver 1,000 widgets to *B* at a price of $500 per widget. *C* then approaches *A*, and offers to pay her $750 per widget. Assuming that *B* can obtain

2. *Globe Refining Co. v. Landa Cotton Oil Co.*, 190 U.S. 540, 544, 23 S.Ct. 754, 47 L.Ed. 1171 (1903).

3. It can be viewed as the usual remedy when the action is one for the price owed—payment of the price is then doctrinally a form of specific relief. However, an order to pay damages in the amount of the price is not equivalent to an order for specific performance since, among other things, it is not usually punishable by contempt of court. E. Allan Farnsworth, *Damages and Specific Relief*, 27 Am. J. Comp. L. 247, 249 (1979).

4. E. Allan Farnsworth, *Legal Remedies for Breach of Contract*, 70 Colum. L. Rev. 1145, 1147 (1970).

5. *See Daniel Farber, What (if Anything) Can Economics Say about Equity?* (2003) 101 Mich. L. Rev. 1791, 1795 (2003) ("Pareto superiority is an intuitively appealing standard, since at least one person is better off because of the change and no one else is hurt. Essen-

tially, the Pareto standard avoids the need for interpersonal comparisons by giving each person a veto over changes"). For a general discussion of the economic concept as applied to law and policy, see Louis Kaplow and Steven Shavell, *Fairness versus Welfare: Notes on the Pareto Principle, Preferences, and Distributive Justice*, 32 J. Legal Stud. 331, 342–51 (2003) (analyzing social policies for Pareto optimality).

6. The lawyer-economist Robert Birmingham, currently Professor of Law at the University of Connecticut, is often credited with writing the first article specifically addressed to economic theory and breach of contract. *See* Robert L. Birmingham, *Breach of Contract, Damage Measures, and Economic Efficiency*, 24 Rutgers L. Rev. 273 (1970). *See generally* Richard A Posner, Economic Analysis and the Law § 4.9 (6th ed. 2003).

the widgets from someone else for less than $750 per widget, and assuming that transaction costs are minimal, it is efficient for A to breach her contract with B and to enter into the contract with C. B will be awarded *expectation damages*—the difference between the amount he expected to spend on the widgets ($500) and the amount he actually spent to acquire them from an alternate vendor—and will theoretically be no worse off as a result of the breach. The breaching party is also better off by virtue of her more lucrative contract, and society in the aggregate is also benefited by the more efficient allocation of resources.

Other legal systems take a different view of the moral basis of contractual obligation. While one should be wary of conflating all legal systems just because they are based on a "civil law model," nonetheless some common principles recur. Generally speaking, in the civil law, the assumption is that a contracting party has a moral obligation to perform his contract. For example,

> [j]ust as in matters of mistake and of *réticence dolosive* [misleading silence] French law takes a moral stance while English law emphasizes the security of transactions and economic efficiency, so also French law treats breach of contract as a form of moral wrongdoing, while the Common law looks more to commercial considerations.[7]

The preference that contracts be performed—*id est, pacta sunt servanda*—has two consequences with respect to remedies. One is that the matter of fault on the part of the breaching party has an effect on the available remedy. Under French law, an injured party seeking money damages can get only foreseeable damages if the breaching party breached inadvertently, but can recover all damages proximately caused in the event of an intentional breach.[8] Fault also plays a role in German law, as there it is also a prerequisite to bringing a cause of action in damages.[9] Second, in civil law systems, the remedy of specific performance is generally preferred, subject to certain exceptions.[10] Thus, "German law starts with the principle that the creditor is entitled to judgment for performance."[11] German Civil Code § 241 provides: "By virtue of an obligation the obligee is entitled to demand performance from

7. Barry Nicholas, The French Law of Contract 212 (2d ed. 1992).

8. Richard Hyland, *Pacta Sunt Servanda: A Meditation*, 34 Va. J. Int'l L. 405, 428 (1994).

9. Andreas Heldrich & Beghard M. Rehm, *Modernisation of the German Law of Obligations: Harmonisation of Civil Law and Common Law in the Recent Reform of the German Civil Code, in* Comparative Remedies for Breach of

Contract 123, 131 (Nili Cohen & Ewan McKendrick eds. 2005).

10. *But see* Henrik Lando & Caspar Rose, *On the Enforcement of Specific Performance in Civil Law Countries*, 24 Int'l Rev. L. & Econ. 473 (2004) (arguing that specific performance is in fact rare remedy in Denmark, Germany and France, and under CISG).

11. Sir Guenter H. Treitel, Remedies for Breach of Contract 51 (1988).

the obligor. The performance may also consist of an abstention."[12] The French approach is slightly different, but also leads away from efficient breach:

> [I]n holding a debtor to his obligation to perform the original contract that is less productive than the second, [French law] favors neither the search for efficiency that would come through the breach of a contract to profit from a later, more interesting offer, nor the optimal allocation of resources resulting from such a quest for efficiency by virtue of the postulate according to which the allocation of resources is optimal when those resources return to those who are ready to pay the greatest price to obtain them.[13]

Both approaches are set forth in more detail below. Fuller treatment of contract remedies is provided in Chapter 4, *infra*. For now, consider the following case, written by Judge Richard Posner, which is a classic example of the U.S approach to performance issues and efficient breach.

NORTHERN INDIANA PUBLIC SERVICE CO. v. CARBON COUNTY COAL CO.

799 F.2d 265 (7th Cir. 1986).

POSNER, J.

These appeals bring before us various facets of a dispute between Northern Indiana Public Service Company (NIPSCO), an electric utility in Indiana, and Carbon County Coal Company, a partnership that until recently owned and operated a coal mine in Wyoming. In 1978 NIPSCO and Carbon County signed a contract whereby Carbon County agreed to sell and NIPSCO to buy approximately 1.5 million tons of coal every year for 20 years, at a price of $24 a ton subject to various provisions for escalation which by 1985 had driven the price up to $44 a ton.

NIPSCO's rates are regulated by the Indiana Public Service Commission. In 1983 NIPSCO requested permission to raise its rates to reflect increased fuel charges. Some customers of NIPSCO opposed the increase on the ground that NIPSCO could reduce its

---

12. The translation is taken from John Dawson, *Specific Performance in France and Germany*, 57 MICH. L. REV. 495, 529 (1959). The German Civil Code was updated in 2002, but Civil Code section 241 did not change. The new code does, however, contain a new § 275(1), which provides for damages as the remedy when performance is unavailable due to impossibility. This change may indicate some shift in approach from the primacy of the performance remedy, or it may illustrate only a recognition that in some circumstances performance is not a feasible remedy.

13. Bernard Rudden & Philippe Juilhard, La Théorie de la violation efficace, 8 Revue Internationale de droit comparé 1016, 1036 (1986) (trans. by Andrea K. Bjorklund).

overall costs by buying more electrical power from neighboring utilities for resale to its customers and producing less of its own power. Although the Commission granted the requested increase, it directed NIPSCO, in orders issued in December 1983 and February 1984 (the "economy purchase orders"), to make a good faith effort to find, and wherever possible buy from, utilities that would sell electricity to it at prices lower than its costs of internal generation. The Commission added ominously that "the adverse effects of entering into long-term coal supply contracts which do not allow for renegotiation and are not requirement contracts, is a burden which must rest squarely on the shoulders of NIPSCO management." Actually the contract with Carbon County did provide for renegotiation of the contract price—but one-way renegotiation in favor of Carbon County; the price fixed in the contract (as adjusted from time to time in accordance with the escalator provisions) was a floor. And the contract was indeed not a requirements contract: it specified the exact amount of coal that NIPSCO must take over the 20 years during which the contract was to remain in effect. NIP-SCO was eager to have an assured supply of low-sulphur coal and was therefore willing to guarantee both price and quantity.

Unfortunately for NIPSCO, however, as things turned out it was indeed able to buy electricity at prices below the costs of generating electricity from coal bought under the contract with Carbon County; and because of the "economy purchase orders," of which it had not sought judicial review, NIPSCO could not expect to be allowed by the Public Service Commission to recover in its electrical rates the costs of buying coal from Carbon County. NIPSCO therefore decided to stop accepting coal deliveries from Carbon County, at least for the time being; and on April 24, 1985, it brought this diversity suit against Carbon County in a federal district court in Indiana, seeking a declaration that it was excused from its obligations under the contract either permanently or at least until the economy purchase orders ceased preventing it from passing on the costs of the contract to its ratepayers. In support of this position it argued that the contract violated section 2(c) of the Mineral Lands Leasing Act of 1920, 30 U.S.C. § 202, because of Carbon County's affiliation with a railroad (Union Pacific), and that in any event NIPSCO's performance was excused or suspended—either under the contract's *force majeure* clause or under the doctrines of frustration or impossibility—by reason of the economy purchase orders.

On May 17, 1985, Carbon County counterclaimed for breach of contract and moved for a preliminary injunction requiring NIPSCO to continue taking delivery under the contract. On June 19, 1985, the district judge granted the preliminary injunction, from which NIPSCO has appealed.... Trial did begin then, lasted for six weeks, and resulted in a jury verdict for Carbon County of $181 million. The judge entered judgment in accordance with the verdict, rejecting Carbon County's argument that in lieu of damages it should get an order of specific performance requiring NIPSCO to comply with the contract. Upon entering the final judgment the district judge dissolved the preliminary injunction, and shortly afterward the mine—whose only customer was NIPSCO—shut down. NIPSCO has appealed from the damage judgment, and Carbon County from the denial of specific performance and from the district judge's order staying execution of the damage judgment without requiring NIPSCO to post a bond guaranteeing payment of the judgment should NIPSCO lose on appeal.

[The court rejected each of NIPSCO's appeals.]

This completes our consideration of NIPSCO's attack on the damages judgment and we turn to Carbon County's cross-appeal, which seeks specific performance in lieu of the damages it got. Carbon County's counsel virtually abandoned the cross-appeal at oral argument, noting that the mine was closed and could not be reopened immediately—so that if specific performance (*i.e.*, NIPSCO's resuming taking the coal) was ordered, Carbon County would not be able to resume its obligations under the contract without some grace period. In any event the request for specific performance has no merit. Like other equitable remedies, specific performance is available only if damages are not an adequate remedy, Farnsworth, *supra*, § 12.6, and there is no reason to suppose them inadequate here. The loss to Carbon County from the breach of contract is simply the difference between (1) the contract price (as escalated over the life of the contract in accordance with the contract's escalator provisions) times quantity, and (2) the cost of mining the coal over the life of the contract. Carbon County does not even argue that $181 million is not a reasonable estimate of the present value of the difference. Its complaint is that although the money will make the owners of Carbon County whole it will do nothing for the miners who have lost their jobs because the mine is closed and the satellite businesses that have closed for the same reason. Only specific performance will help them.

But since they are not parties to the contract their losses are irrelevant. Indeed, specific performance would be improper as well as unnecessary here, because it would force the continuation of production that has become uneconomical. Cf. Farnsworth, *supra*, at 817–18. No one wants coal from Carbon County's mine. With the collapse of oil prices, which has depressed the price of substitute fuels as well, this coal costs far more to get out of the ground than it is worth in the market. Continuing to produce it, under compulsion of an order for specific performance, would impose costs on society greater than the benefits. NIPSCO's breach, though it gave

Carbon County a right to damages, was an efficient breach in the sense that it brought to a halt a production process that was no longer cost-justified ..... The reason why NIPSCO must pay Carbon County's loss is not that it should have continued buying coal it didn't need but that the contract assigned to NIPSCO the risk of market changes that made continued deliveries uneconomical. The judgment for damages is the method by which that risk is being fixed on NIPSCO in accordance with its undertakings.

With continued production uneconomical, it is unlikely that an order of specific performance, if made, would ever actually be implemented. If, as a finding that the breach was efficient implies, the cost of substitute supply (whether of coal, or of electricity) to NIPSCO is less than the cost of producing coal from Carbon County's mine, NIPSCO and Carbon County can both be made better off by negotiating a cancellation of the contract and with it a dissolution of the order of specific performance. Suppose, by way of example, that Carbon County's coal costs $20 a ton to produce, that the contract price is $40, and that NIPSCO can buy coal elsewhere for $10. Then Carbon County would be making a profit of only $20 on each ton it sold to NIPSCO ($40–$20), while NIPSCO would be losing $30 on each ton it bought from Carbon County ($40–$10). Hence by offering Carbon County more than contract damages (i.e., more than Carbon County's lost profits), NIPSCO could induce Carbon County to discharge the contract and release NIPSCO to buy cheaper coal. For example, at $25, both parties would be better off than under specific performance, where Carbon County gains only $20 but NIPSCO loses $30. Probably, therefore, Carbon County is seeking specific performance in order to have bargaining leverage with NIPSCO, and we can think of no reason why the law should give it such leverage. We add that if Carbon County obtained and enforced an order for specific performance this would mean that society was spending $20 (in our hypothetical example) to produce coal that could be gotten elsewhere for $10—a waste of scarce resources.

As for possible hardships to workers and merchants in Hanna, Wyoming, where Carbon County's coal mine is located, we point out that none of these people were parties to the contract with NIPSCO or third-party beneficiaries. They have no legal interest in the contract.... Of course the consequences to third parties of granting an injunctive remedy, such as specific performance, must be considered, and in some cases may require that the remedy be withheld..... The frequent references to "public interest" as a factor in the grant or denial of preliminary injunction invariably are references to third-party effects.... But even though the formal statement of the judicial obligation to consider such effects extends to orders denying as well as granting injunctive relief, see, e.g., *Kershner v. Mazurkiewicz*, 670 F.2d 440, 443 (3d Cir. 1982) (en banc), the actuality is somewhat different: when the question is whether third parties would be injured by an order denying an injunction, always they are persons having a legally recognized interest in the lawsuit, so that the issue really is the adequacy of relief if the injunction is denied. In *Mississippi Power & Light Co. v. United Gas Pipe Line Co.*, 760 F.2d 618 (5th Cir. 1985), for example, a public utility sought a preliminary injunction against alleged overcharges by a supplier. If the injunction was denied and later the utility got damages, its customers would be entitled to refunds; but for a variety of reasons explained in the opinion, refunds would not fully protect the customers' interests. The customers were the real parties in interest on the plaintiff side of the case, and their interests had therefore to be taken into account in deciding whether there would be irreparable harm (and how much) if the preliminary injunction was denied. See *id. at 623–26*. Carbon County does not stand in a representative relation to the workers and businesses of Hanna, Wyoming. Treating them as real parties in interest would evade the limitations on the concept of a third-party beneficiary and would place the promisor under obligations potentially far heavier than it had thought it was accepting when it signed the contract. Indeed, if we are right that an order of specific performance would probably not be carried out—that instead NIPSCO would pay an additional sum of money to Carbon County for an agreement not to enforce the order—it becomes transparent that granting specific performance would make NIPSCO liable in money damages for harms to nonparties to the contract, and it did not assume such liability by signing the contract. . . .

Moreover, the workers and merchants in Hanna assumed the risk that the coal mine would have to close down if it turned out to be uneconomical. The contract with NIPSCO did not guarantee that the mine would operate throughout the life of the contract but only protected the owners of Carbon County against the financial consequences to them of a breach. As Carbon County itself emphasizes in its brief, the contract was a product of the international oil cartel, which by forcing up the price of substitute fuels such as coal made costly coal-mining operations economically attractive. The OPEC cartel is not a source of vested rights to produce substitute fuels at inflated prices.

. . . To summarize, the appeal from the grant of the preliminary injunction is dismissed as moot; the other orders appealed from are affirmed. No costs will be awarded in this court, since we have turned down Carbon County's appeals as well as NIPSCO's.

Notes

3–1. Judge Posner describes NIPSCO's actions as an efficient breach. Many commentators doubt whether there is any such thing as an efficient breach given the societal harms and costs that stem from a breach of contract but which do not "count" for the purpose of calculating damages stemming from the breach. What examples of such costs are evident in *NIPSCO*? In *NIPSCO*, who would have benefited the most from specific performance? Should U.S. Courts take a broader view of what constitutes the public interest in considering matters such as orders of specific performance?

3–2. Nowhere does Judge Posner indicate a concern about the morality of entering into a contract and then breaking it when performing it becomes economically unattractive. Should he have?

3–3. It is usually said that an efficient breach is facilitated by the preference for an award of money damages in lieu of specific performance.[14] It is important to note that efficient breach is not a defense that a breaching party may raise to defeat a claim that she is in breach of a contract: the efficient breacher *still* owes money damages. Yet the efficient breacher can enter into the substitute contract knowing that she can fulfill the terms of the new contract, and pay to extricate herself from the obligations of the prior one. How might the actions of both parties in *NIPSCO* have been affected if specific performance were a readily available remedy? How and why might specific performance actually lead to a more effective remedy?

3–4. What assumptions about the quantification of damages underlie the theory of efficient breach? What other assumptions does Judge Posner make about the market's functioning?

B. CIVIL LAW APPROACHES TO PERFORMANCE

While specific performance is the preferred remedy in the civil law, the preference for specific performance is not without limits, and it is arguable that the differences between the civil and common law systems are greater in theory than in practice. Many injured parties prefer a damages remedy to a specific performance remedy, and tailor their court action appropriately when they have the option to demand damages. Yet it is important both symbolically and in practice that the baseline presumption is in favor of performance.

---

14. *See, e.g.,* E. Allan Farnsworth, *Damages and Specific Relief,* 27 Am. J. Comp. L. 247 (1979); Anthony T. Kronman, *Specific Performance,* 45 U. Chi. L. Rev. 351 (1978). Some recent scholarship has suggested that the availability of specific performance might in some instances lead to greater efficiencies in the allocation of resources. *See* Alan Schwartz, *The Case for Specific Performance,* 89 Yale L.J. 271, 291–92 (1979); Ian R. Macneil, *Efficient Breach of Contract: Circles in the Sky,* 68 Va. L. Rev. 947 (1982).

1. Is There a "Right to Performance"?

One fundamental difference between common law and civil law approaches to contract law involves the implications of a "right to performance."[15] As we have seen, the common law tradition favors damages as the typical remedy for contract breach.[16] The concept of the "efficient breach" is favored in contemporary common law of contracts, as well as in the UCC.

In the civil law tradition, the obligation to perform the contract as agreed—*pacta sunt servanda*—is the generally accepted formal expectation and legal norm. This principle is expressed in the following general terms in the UNIDROIT PRINCIPLES:

Article 1.3

A contract validly entered into is binding upon the parties. It can only be modified or terminated in accordance with its terms or by agreement or as otherwise provided in these Principles.

That this principle leads to a right to performance is emphasized later in the UNIDROIT PRINCIPLES, as follows:

Article 7.2.2

Where a party who owes an obligation other than one to pay money does not perform, the other party may require performance, unless

(a) performance is impossible in law or in fact;

(b) performance or, where relevant, enforcement is unreasonably burdensome or expensive;

(c) the party entitled to performance may reasonably obtain performance from another source;

(d) performance is of an exclusively personal character; or

(e) the party entitled to performance does not require performance within a reasonable time after it has, or ought to have, become aware of the non-performance.

Differences in the implications of the binding nature of a valid contract may represent a cultural divide between the common law

---

15. *See generally* Robert Bejesky, *The Evolution in and International Convergence of the Doctrine of Specific Performance in Three Types of States*, 13 IND. INT'L & COMP. L. REV. 353 (2003) (analyzing differing approaches to contract enforcement in United States and UK (characterized as "reactive states"), France and Germany ("semi-active states"), and Russia and China ("activist states")).

16. *See* REST. (2d), § 359 (injunctive relief unavailable where "damages would be adequate to protect the expectation interest of the injured party"); UCC § 2–716(1) (specific performance available "where the goods are unique or in other proper circumstances").

and civil law traditions.[17] In that regard, one noted European commentator—the father of the PRINCIPLES OF EUROPEAN CONTRACT LAW—has noted that *pacta sunt servanda*

> is a basic principle in the laws of all countries. Many laws and courts stick to it with rigor. It is stated in the famous article 1134(1) of the French Civil Code. "The agreements validly concluded are regarded as law for the parties," the [UNIDROIT PRINCIPLES] states in art. 1.3. "A contract validly entered into is binding upon the parties. It can only be modified or terminated in accordance with its terms or by agreement or as otherwise provided in these Principles." A contracting party must be able to rely on the contract and exercise the rights granted to him or her under the contract. As the draftsmen of the CISG, the [Commission on European Contract Law] considered the principle to be so obvious that it was not stated in a special rule. It is, however, implied in several articles, including CISG art. 79.... It is also implied in art. 6.111 (*l*) of the [PRINCIPLES OF EUROPEAN CONTRACT LAW] on change of circumstances, which provides that a party is bound to fulfil its obligations even if performance becomes more onerous.[18]

Notes

3–5. At common law, and under the UCC as well, specific performance and other injunctive relief are discretionary—and generally disfavored. What about article 7.2.2 of the UNIDROIT PRINCIPLES? Comment 2 to this article states that "under the Principles specific performance is not a discretionary remedy, *i.e.* a court must order performance, unless one of the exceptions laid down in [article 7.2.2] applies." In light of the exceptions, how far apart are the common law and article 7.2.2 in practice?

3–6. Assume that *A Corp.*, a national of a developing country where foreign exchange is relatively scarce, buys a machine from *B*, a U.S. manufacturer. *A* has paid the price of the machine in U.S. dollars, but *B* does not deliver. Could *A* obtain specific performance under the UCC? What if the UNIDROIT PRINCIPLES applied to this transaction?

3–7. Assume that *C Architects* have entered into an agreement with *D* to design a seaside resort complex. *C* later obtains a contract to

---

17. *Cf.* Ana M. López-Rodríguez, *Towards a European Civil Code Without a Common European Legal Culture? The Link Between Law, Language and Culture*, 29 BROOK J. INT'L L. 1195 (2004) (arguing that EU legislative measure to create European contract law should be preceded by or should run parallel with promotion of European legal discourse, ultimately crystallizing into European legal culture).

18. Ole Lando, *CISG and its Followers: A Proposal to Adopt Some International Principles of Contract Law*, 53 AM. J. COMP. L. 379, 388 (2005) (footnotes omitted). *See also* KLAUS PETER BERGER, THE CREEPING CODIFICATION OF THE LEX MERCATORIA Annex 1, Principle No. 3 (1999) (concerning binding nature of contract obligation).

design the World Trade Center Memorial in New York City and decides to repudiate its contract with *D*. Could *D* obtain specific performance under the common law? Under the UNIDROIT PRINCIPLES?

3–8. Assume that *Mr. E*, a world-famous architect agreed to design the new Parliament Building for the Government of *G*, expressing the "spirit of the citizens of *G* in the face of the Twenty–First Century." *E* has discovered that the citizens of *G* "don't inspire [him]," and he has therefore repudiated the agreement with *G*. Could *G* obtain specific performance under the common law? Under the UNIDROIT PRINCIPLES?

3–9. Assume that *H Company* has contracted with *I International Marine* to carry *H*'s shipment of oil, worth $2 million, from Saudi Arabia to the Port of Baltimore on board *I*'s tanker, the Pearl. The Pearl sinks in coastal waters off South Carolina in a heavy storm. Assume that, at a cost of $3 million, *I* could raise the Pearl from the bottom of the sea. Could *H* obtain specific performance under the common law? Under the UNIDROIT PRINCIPLES?

2. French Law

French law distinguishes between obligations "to give" and obligations "to do or not do" with respect to the availability of remedies. As to a breach of an obligation to give, *exécution en nature*, which reasonably translates to specific performance, is the preferred remedy. Indeed, title passes when a contract of sale is signed, and a party may obtain a court order directing seizure of the asset as promised. As observed by Professor Dawson,

> It would seem at first glance that French law had solved most of the problems of specific performance of contract in the simplest possible way, allowing direct execution in sales of both land or goods, in contracts of exchange, promises of gift (when duly notarized), and promises to lease—and all this without the harassing nuisance of an adequacy-of-alternative-remedies test.[19]

The situation is more complicated with respect to obligations to do or not do. The French Civil Code is concerned with safeguarding the personal liberty of the debtor. Thus, Civil Code Article 1142 provides that "Every obligation to do or not to do resolves itself into damages in the case of non-performance by the debtor." In practice, however, the seemingly broad reach of Article 1142 is subject to several limitations. As explained by Professor Nicholas:

> The Code itself provides (article 1144) that the creditor may be authorized to obtain performance by a third party at the expense of the debtor. Thus, where a seller fails to deliver, the buyer may buy replacement goods, or a tenant may cause

---

19. Dawson, *supra* note 12, at 511–12.

repairs to be carried out. It must be emphasized that this is not a form of self-help. The creditor must first get a court order, except in cases governed by commercial law, where a notice . . . to the debtor is sufficient, and generally in cases of extreme urgency. Similarly, the Code provides (article 1143) that in the case of an obligation [not to do] the creditor is entitled to have what has been done in breach of the obligation destroyed at the expense of the debtor. Such 'destruction' may include the reversal of a juridical act, such as an alienation. These two instances of performance in kind at the expense of the debtor constitute *exécution en nature*, in the sense that the creditor gets what he was promised, but for practical purposes they differ little from the award of damages: the creditor still has to obtain payment from the debtor and the risk of the debtor's insolvency is on the creditor. On the other hand, the creditor does not have to show damage (*préjudice*). So where one party to a building scheme had put up a building which exceeded the limits laid down in the scheme and the court below had refused to authorize the demolition sought by another party to the scheme, the ground for the refusal being that the plaintiff had shown no *préjudice*, the *Cour de cassation* quashed the decision. This ruling is one of a series in the last twenty years which seem largely to deny any element of discretion in cases such as this. Earlier decisions had conceded that it lay within the [court's inherent power] to award damages rather than to authorize destruction, and courts had therefore taken account of such matters as the disproportion between the benefit to the creditor and the loss to the debtor, the relation of the excess to the whole building, the shortage of housing, or the interests of the tenants of the part to be demolished. The *Court de cassation* now, however, insists on a strict interpretation of article 1143, which says that the creditor has a 'right' to the destruction of what has been done.[20]

In addition, French courts have also developed the doctrine of *astreinte*, which is a judgment for performance accompanied by a stipulated fine that the debtor must pay (usually daily) during the time he is in default. The coercive nature of the *astreinte* would seem to be utterly inconsistent with the language of Article 1142, but, with some exceptions, it has become an accepted tool that judges can use to compel performance. It developed in the mid-nineteenth century, and courts initially justified themselves by suggesting that they were merely assessing damages as permitted under Article 1142. This pretense soon wore thin, especially after

20. NICHOLAS, *supra* note 7, at 217–18 (internal citations omitted).

... the Court of Cassation suggested that such judgments did not need to have any relation to the plaintiff's injury, since the defendant's "unlawful resistance becomes a more serious wrong and it is proper, in order to overcome it, to decree a judgment in accordance with the interests involved, a proportion which it is the function of the lower court to measure in its unlimited discretion." The famous *affaire de Beauffremont* involved a dispute in the 1870's between two well-known members of café society over custody of their children. The judgment against the disobedient wife, Princess Bibesco, was at first 500 francs a day, was then raised to 1,000 francs a day, and totaled at one stage 1,000,000 francs (about $200,000 at the then existing rate of exchange). In their opinions in this case the French courts used language of surprising bellicosity. With this and other examples of money awards by French courts that were plainly punitive, it became a hollow pretense to assert that these obligations were being resolved in the "damages" that were authorized by article 1142. Although confusion persisted in many court opinions, it became increasingly clear in the opinions of the Court of Cassation that the *astreintes*, as they were beginning to be called, were purely threats, coercive in purpose, provisional and revisable, and therefore exempt from review or control.[21]

There are two kinds of *astreinte*: one provisional and one definitive. Professor Treitel illustrates the two approaches:

> *Provisional astreinte.* The provisional *astreinte* simply fixes a sum which is to be paid for each specified period of non-performance. The sum so fixed is not based on the actual or prospective loss to the creditor; its object is not to compensate the creditor but to coerce the debtor into complying with the judgment to perform the principal obligation. It may therefore be assessed with reference to such factors as the means of the debtor, the degree of his fault, and the extent of the obstinacy which the order seeks to overcome. This form of *astreinte* is called provisional because (whether or not the debtor eventually performs) the creditor has no automatic right to recover the amount specified. He must make a fresh application to the court for this purpose; and at this stage the *astreinte* is subject to revision or 'liquidation'. When this process takes place, the court may have regard to the creditor's actual loss, so that the *astreinte* may become compensatory by being reduced to the amount of the actual loss suffered. Conversely, if the debtor continues to be recalcitrant, the *astreinte* may be increased in amount with a view to overcoming his obstinacy.

---

21. Dawson, *supra* note 12, at 514 (internal citations omitted).

In theory, the process of reduction of the *astreinte* to the actual loss suffered would appear to deprive it of its coercive effect; but in practice the assessment of damages on the liquidation of a provision *astreinte* tends to be somewhat severe on the debtor. It may also take account of his fault, not only in relation to the non-performance of the original contractual obligation, but also in relation to his disobedience to the court's decree. Certainly, an *astreinte* may be upheld even though it exceeds the creditor's actual loss; it has been held in a leading case that the court is not bound to 'liquidate' the *astreinte* at the loss actually suffered. In the case in question an electric company was condemned in the sum of Frs. 900,000 (in 1956 about £900) for refusing, after repeated and increasing *astreintes* to modify works done in violation of a landowner's rights. It was held on appeal that the lower court had acted correctly in awarding this sum, even though it bore no direct relation to the loss suffered by the landowner.

The original judgment will normally fix a period during which the *astreinte* operates; if at the end of the period the debtor has still not performed, the creditor may apply for a liquidation of the *astreinte* and for the issue of a further *astreinte*.

Definitive *astreinte*. The definitive *astreinte*, as its name suggests, is not subject to revision unless the defendant's failure to perform is due to certain events outside his control. Except in such a case the creditor is entitled simply to the fixed sum multiplied (where appropriate) by the number of periods of delay specified in the judgment. This form of *astreinte* may, like the provisional *astreinte*, be fixed at an amount greater than the prejudice actually suffered (or likely to be suffered) by the creditor, and in view of its definite nature it would appear to have a considerably greater coercive force than the provisional *astreinte*.[22]

In practice, then, "a judgment for [specific performance] will be given in respect of all obligations except those positive obligations which require personal performance and those negative obligations the enforcement of which would result in such an interference with personal liberty as would be offensive to current morality."[23] Finally, Article 1184 of the French Civil Code governs the termination of contracts based on consideration in which one party has not fulfilled his undertaking. In such a case the aggrieved party can seek a judicial order demanding performance or seek a judicial order terminating the contract and the award of any damages incurred.

---

22. TREITEL, *supra* note 11, at 60–61 (internal citations omitted).

23. NICHOLAS, *supra* note 7, at 218–19.

The notion of moral obligation buttressing French law helps to explain why French courts have not embraced the theory of efficient breach, although there is at least theoretically room for them to do so with respect to obligations to do or not do. A thorough study of the position efficient breach could occupy within French law was undertaken by Bernard Rudden and Philipe Juilhard in 1986. They concluded that:

> [French] jurisprudence has not, however, ratified the theory of efficient breach. The possibility has been open to it, but it has preferred to place the emphasis on the obligatory force of contracts. In affirming that "all creditors can demand performance of an obligation when such performance is possible" within the framework of Article 1142 of the [French] Civil Code, but especially that "a debtor commits an actionable breach when with deliberation he refuses to abide by his contractual obligations, even if this refusal is not dictated by an intention to cause harm" ... , the Court of Cassation strongly discourages parties to a contract to breach their initial obligations to realize an efficient breach.[24]

3. German Law

The German Civil Code, first established in a newly confederated Germany in the late nineteenth century, firmly entrenched the principle that contracts should be performed, subject to certain exceptions. Professor John Dawson's classic work on specific performance describes in exquisite detail the moral concerns underpinning the German approach, and the broad powers given to judges to ensure their orders were carried out.[25] The German legislature debated adopting an approach that would distinguish between an obligation to do and an obligation to give, much in the way that the French Code does in Article 1142, but rejected that approach. Thus, the German courts could levy a fine against, or even arrest, a defendant who refused to carry out an act he was bound to perform. "It is intolerable and inconsistent with the basic principles of the modern law of obligations that an obligor without property should be able to defeat the execution of a judgment merely through his own disobedience."[26] In addition, there is the possibility of getting an order for substitute performance that might consist of the delivery of goods equivalent to those irrevocably disposed of; while not equivalent to the Anglo–American notion of specific performance, such an order is closer to performance than to dam-

---

24. Rudden & Juilhard, *supra* note 13, at 1041 (trans. by Andrea K. Bjorklund).

25. Dawson, *supra* note 12, at 529–30.

26. *Id.* at 526 (internal citation omitted).

ages.[27] Professor Dawson eloquently described the German approach:

> But one main point should be noted. The Code sets limitations on resort to damage remedies in contract cases, requiring at least a formal notice with demand for performance and in some cases a formal court order fixing a time limit for rendition of the promised performance. But despite such formal limitations the damage remedy is in fact resorted to, by the choice of litigants, in a high percentage of cases, especially in sales of goods and other commercial transactions that are standard subjects of damage actions with us. Another main point, however, is that in contract cases where specific enforcement is desired for any reason by the promisee, the courts have not claimed for themselves a discretion to refuse specific relief that is appropriate and possible.... Unlike our own equity courts, German courts in general have not asserted a discretionary power to refuse specific performance, through a morality too delicate and refined to satisfy the more robust tests used in damage actions. The double standard of morality that is so characteristic of our system simply does not exist in German law. This is mainly because, in ways that are too complex and pervasive to be documented here, specific performance, not the damage remedy, is conceived as the normal recourse. In short, the legislative mandate is accepted and applied. When a judgment has been rendered and the case has reached the stage of execution—a stage that is formally distinct from the pre-judgment stage—the court entrusted with execution will normally be ready, without hesitation, to order specific enforcement when requested by the judgment plaintiff. The main reservations are for cases where specific relief is impossible, would involve disproportionate cost, would introduce compulsion into close personal relationships or compel the expression of special forms of artistic or intellectual creativity. Presumably German courts, like French courts and our own, would not affirmatively order painters to paint pictures or singers to sing.[28]

Professor Dawson did not always endorse the German dedication to specific performance. He criticized robustly a decision made by German courts in the aftermath of World War II that ordered Volkswagen to honor contracts it had made in the late 1930s to sell automobiles to thousands of German. These Germans had pre-paid for cars yet to be manufactured; before they could be manufactured, war broke out. At the end of war Russia took the account

27. TREITEL, *supra* note 11, at 51–52.   28. Dawson, *supra* note 12, at 529–30 (internal citations omitted).

that contained the pre-paid funds. Two plaintiffs asked a German court to enforce the contracts (although they conceded that the price charged for the cars should be higher), which the *Bundesgerichtshof* eventually decided were enforceable. It then remanded to the lower courts to enforce the contracts not only as to the two plaintiffs, but also as to all others similarly situations, which meant the court would have to trace thousands of people who had been displaced during the war. Dawson's view was that the court should not have granted enforcement because the basic premises underlying the contract had been destroyed by the war and performance of the contracts was simply not feasible.

Professor Dawson's view was likely colored by his common-law viewpoint. Consider the following passage from eminent comparative law scholar Vivian Curran:

> To Dawson, the Court clearly was in error. As he saw it, under German contract law, the contract's foundations had been destroyed by the catastrophic events of the war, such that performance was no longer feasible, and, therefore, the Court should have rescinded the contracts.... Dawson believed that the non-feasibility was in part a function of the overwhelming burden on the court that would result from a judicial revision of the contracts. He reached this conclusion through a common-law perspective, however. The German standard for enforcing contracts did not look to judicial burden. As Dawson himself reported, the German standard required a contract to be enforced if feasible, and contracts were deemed feasible if at least a rough approximation of the original promise still could be performed. As the German court saw it, since the defendant still manufactured cars, the defendant could still perform at least an approximation of its original promise, albeit with a different kind of car, and at a price to be determined by the court.

> Significantly, Dawson reproduced the sentence from the *Bundesgerichtshof's* decision which in my opinion contains the clue to its holding, but found it neither significant nor illuminating: The Court set forth the principle that "in law it is a basic premise that contracts should be performed." Dawson dismissed this statement as beside the point: "Wholly laudable though this proposition might ... be, there would remain one other question—whether it had anything whatever to do with this case."

> It had everything to do with the case, and everything to do with the difference between the common and civil law perspectives of contract law. The binding nature of a promise is of utmost importance to the civil law, and the courts accordingly

bind individuals to their promises. [Germany's Civil Code] sets forth explicitly in Section 241 that, "the effect of an obligation is that the creditor is entitled to claim performance ..." As Professors Flour and Aubert write in their appropriately titled book on the French law of contracts, *Obligations*, morality dominates civilian contract law. They state unequivocally that "the legal obligation incumbent on the contracting party to perform is none other than the moral duty to honor one's word, once given." The civilian focus on morality contrasts with the common law's concern for efficiency as the primary priority. The contrast between the two systems is not only pervasive but fundamental, influencing the courts' assessments of factual criteria.[29]

The German Code underwent a significant revision in 2002. The revisions made it easier for aggrieved parties to get damages, particularly in commercial contracts for the sale of goods. Yet damages remedies, in most instances, continue to depend on a finding that the debtor was at fault. If a party does not perform, its fault is in general assumed, and that party bears the burden of proof to demonstrate that the non-performance was not due to its fault. Only in very limited instances does German law recognize strict liability in contract. Moreover, a creditor who seeks a damages remedy must allow the debtor additional time actually to perform the contract. "The right of the debtor corresponds with the creditor's right to specific performance and stresses the principle of *pacta sunt servanda.*"[30] Finally, in many cases specific performance remains the preferred remedy.

Notes

3–10. What effect, if any, might a default remedy of specific performance have on the actions of contracting parties in the United States? Should the legal system be concerned with non-monetary damages stemming from contract breach? Think again about the *NIPSCO* case. How do you think it would have been decided by a French court? A German court? Is the law more effective if it contains a moral dimension?

3–11. Should a party have a right to select her preferred remedy without its availability being subject to the discretion of the court?

3–12. What are the ramifications for economic development in a country with a legal system that actively discourages efficient breach?

29. VIVIAN GROSSWALD CURRAN, COMPARATIVE LAW: AN INTRODUCTION 24–25 (2002) (internal citations and quotations omitted).

30. Dagmar Coester–Waltjen, *The New Approach to Breach of Contract in*

German Law, in COMPARATIVE REMEDIES FOR BREACH OF CONTRACT 135, 150 (Nili Cohen & Ewan McKendrick eds. 2005).

4. Hardship as a Contract Defense

At common law, and under the traditional civil law principle of *force majeure*, contract liability is all or nothing—performance is or is not excused. Under the UNIDROIT PRINCIPLES (and some contemporary civil law systems), the approach is that each party gets a "piece of the loss"—and a "piece of the cake." What a contrast! The RESTATEMENT (2d) § 261 takes the position that when performance of a contract is rendered "impracticable," through no fault of a contracting party, by the occurrence of an event the nonoccurrence of which was a basic assumption of the contract, the party's duty to render performance is "discharged, unless the language or circumstances indicate the contrary."[31] The UCC has a comparable provision giving an "excuse" for delay in performance or for non-performance "if performance as agreed has been made impracticable by the occurrence of a contingency the non-occurrence of which was a basic assumption on which the contract was made."[32] The UNIDROIT PRINCIPLES, however, are premised on the notion that "[w]here the performance . . . becomes more onerous for one of the parties, that party is nevertheless bound to perform its obligations" subject to the excuse of "hardship."[33] The concept of hardship is defined for these purposes as follows:

Article 6.2.2

There is hardship where the occurrence of events fundamentally alters the equilibrium of the contract either because the cost of a party's performance has increased or because the value of the performance a party receives has diminished, and

(a) the events occur or become known to the disadvantaged party after the conclusion of the contract;

(b) the events could not reasonably have been taken into account by the disadvantaged party at the time of the conclusion of the contract;

(c) the events are beyond the control of the disadvantaged party; and

(d) the risk of the events was not assumed by the disadvantaged party.

Superficially, impracticability and hardship bear certain family resemblances, as illustrated by Figure 1, *infra*. However, the comments to article 6.2.2 emphasize the *fundamental* "alteration of the equilibrium of the contract," a notion that is not explicitly identi-

31. *Cf.* REST. (2d) § 265 (providing for similar discharge of performance upon substantial frustration of party's principal purpose).

32. UCC § 2–615(a).

33. UNIDROIT PRINCIPLES, art. 6.2.1. Comment 2 to the article notes cognate concepts in various systems, such as "frustration of purpose, *Wegfall der Geschäftsgrundlage, imprévision, eccessiva onerositá sopravenuta*" and the like.

fied in the RESTATEMENT provision.[34] Essentially, substantial increase in cost of performance or substantial decrease in value of performance would exemplify such a fundamental alteration of contract equilibrium.[35]

Figure 1

Impracticability *v.* Hardship

REST. 2D § 261	*UNIDROIT PRINCIPLES, art. 6.2.2*
disadvantaged party's performance made "impracticable" (§ 261) [or principal purpose substantially frustrated (§ 265)]	fundamental alteration of equilibrium of contract: increase in cost or diminishment of value
"after contract is made"	events occur or become known after conclusion of contract
nonoccurrence of event a basic assumption on which contract was made	events could not have been reasonably taken into account by disadvantaged party at conclusion of contract
"without his fault"	events beyond control of disadvantaged party
"unless the language or circumstances indicate the contrary"	risk of events not assumed by disadvantaged party

While one can imagine many factual situations in which either of these concepts could be invoked, there is a significant difference in the legal consequences that follow from each provision. In the case of the RESTATEMENT, impracticability (or, in some jurisdictions, frustration of purpose) would have the effect of discharging the disadvantaged party's remaining contract obligations.[36] Under the UNIDROIT PRINCIPLES, however, the disadvantaged party has the right to request renegotiation of the contract, to be made without undue delay.[37] Significantly, such a request "does not in itself entitle the disadvantaged party to withhold performance."[38] The following decision illustrates the application of the hardship concept.

[CLAIMANT] v. [RESPONDENT]

ICC International Court of Arbitration.
Arbitral Award No. 9994 (December 2001).

On [the matter of whether the respondent was right or wrong to refuse delivery of certain biological products at a new price], the

---

34. *See* UNIDROIT PRINCIPLES, art. 6.2.2, comment 2 (discussing fundamental alteration).

35. *Id.*, comment 2(a)-(b).

36. REST. (2d) §§ 261, 265. *But cf. id.* § 272 (providing for claim for relief in-

cluding restitution for either party, as circumstances dictate).

37. UNIDROIT PRINCIPLES, art. 6.2.3(1).

38. *Id.*, art. 6.2.3(2).

Arbitral Tribunal finds that the issue of the alleged existence of an oral agreement between Messrs [A, of claimant company] and [B, the respondent's CEO and its negotiator of the contract] to renegotiate the Agreement in case of more stringent demands of the [government agency] regarding the approval of the product can be left undecided.... Assuming that on [this] issue[], [Respondent]'s contention should prevail, this would not discharge [Respondent] from its duty to renegotiate the agreement in the event that the conditions set forth by French law for such a renegotiation would be met.... As correctly stated by [Claimant] ..., French law requires from each party to perform the agreement in good faith (see c. civ. 1134, al. 2). Good faith imposes upon the parties the duty to seek out an adaptation of their agreement to the new circumstances which may have occurred after its execution, in order to ensure that its performance does not cause, especially when the contract at stake is a long term agreement, the ruin of one of the parties.... This principle is also prevailing in international commercial law (see UNIDROIT PRINCIPLES, art. 6.2.2 and 6.2.3).

[W]hen negotiating the agreement, the parties were under the impression that the [government agency] would not impose a control ..., although they did not exclude such an eventuality. Now, some time after the signature of the Agreement, the [government agency] required individual donors' screening and that severe demand was certainly one of the cause [*sic*] of the increase of the cost of the [raw material] well above the US$ ... per gram agreed upon in the Agreement.... [T]his was certainly a somehow unexpected event. Furthermore, the fact that the "Force Majeure Clause" ... of the Agreement, did not expressly contemplate the risk of a potential regulatory change, does not "per se" exempt [Respondent] from renegotiating the contract price as, according to the French doctrine ... this duty is already imposed upon the contracting parties by the rule of good faith and that rule cannot be defeated by any divergent contractual provisions. Therefore and on this point, the Arbitral Tribunal finds that due to the new request of the [government agency] relating to the control of the [biological product], [the Claimant] was entitled to a renegotiation of the contract price, but that does not mean at all that [Claimant] was entitled to impose upon [Respondent] its own view on what should be the correct price.

Notes

3–13. How would this dispute have been decided under U.S. law?

3–14. If you were an arbitrator in this dispute, trained in the tradition of U.S. contract law, how would you have decided this case?

3–15. There are also critical procedural differences in the application of the concepts of impracticability and hardship. Presumably, an assertion of impracticability would ordinarily arise as an affirmative defense to an action for breach of contract; if successful, performance would be discharged. In the case of a hardship claim, however, failure to conclude the renegotiation within a reasonable time would allow "either party [to] resort to the court."[39] If the court were to find hardship, it would have the discretion to

if reasonable,

>   (a) terminate the contract at a date and on terms to be fixed,

or

>   (b) adapt the contract with a view to restoring equilibrium.[40]

In effect then, absent a successful renegotiation, the parties might find themselves subjected to the obligation to terminate or to perform on new terms imposed by the court.[41] Furthermore, if the court determined that neither termination nor adaptation was "reasonable" under the circumstances, Article 6.2.3 allows it to "direct the parties to resume negotiations ... or ... confirm the terms of the contract as they stand." Which of these two procedures seems to be more efficient in terms of giving the parties what they thought they were negotiating in forming the contract? In terms of distributing the loss?

3–16. Assume that *A Corp.*, a national of *Country X*, entered into a contract to supply *B Hotels Company*, a national of *Country Y*, with premium beers for three years, payable in *Y* currency. Due to an unexpected devaluation in the currency of *X*, A's actual cost of the beer increases dramatically. What recourse would *A* have if U.S. law applied to the contract? What if the UNIDROIT PRINCIPLES applied?

3–17. Assume that the facts are the same as in 3–16, except that the contract included a price indexation clause relating to the cost of the beer. Would *A* or *B* have an affirmative defense under U.S. law if either terminated the contract? Would either have a right to request renegotiation under the UNIDROIT PRINCIPLES?

3–18. Assume that *A* has entered into the three-year contract with *B*. Two years after the conclusion of the contract, *Y* enacts new legislation prohibiting the retail sale and consumption of alcoholic

---

39. *Id.*, art. 6.2.3(3).

40. *Id.*, art. 6.2.3(4)(a)-(b).

41. In "adapting" the contract to restore its equilibrium, the court would seek to make a fair distribution of the losses between the parties. This may or may not, depending upon the nature of the hardship, involve a price adaptation. However, if it does, the adaptation will not necessarily reflect in full the loss entailed by the change in circumstances, since the court will, for instance, have to consider the extent to which one or the parties has taken a risk and the extent to which the party entitled to receive a performance may still benefit from that performance.

Id., art. 6.2.3, comment 7.

beverages within the territory of *Y*. Would *A* or *B* have an affirmative defense under U.S. law if either terminated the contract? Would either have a right to request renegotiation under the UNIDROIT PRINCIPLES? What circumstances might influence the outcome of litigation under article 6.2.3(4)? In answering these questions, consider the following arbitral decision involving a trademark agreement.

[CLAIMANTS] v. [DEFENDANT]

ICC International Court of Arbitration.
Arbitral Award No. 9479 (February 1999).

[A trademark licensing agreement between the parties covering use of registered trademarks within the territory of the European Union was later affected by changes in EU law with respect to trademarks. To take advantage of the benefits of the newly revised EU trademark law, the licensee wanted the original agreement to be modified. Licensor resisted such modification of the agreement.]

... On the basis of article 6.2 of the UNIDROIT PRINCIPLES, [Defendant argues that it] is entitled to an equitable modification of the [trademark licensing] Agreement so that, on the territory of the European Union, [Defendant] might benefit from the liberal solutions resulting from the application of [a newly applicable EEC] Directive. As a further justification for its requests, [Defendant] also refers to article 1467 of the Italian Civil Code....

The Claimants first stress that the law of the State of New York is applicable to [Defendant]'s request for equitable modifications of the Agreement and that, under the New York law, a Court (or an arbitrator) should not modify a contract because of a change of law, even should this change create additional burdens or advantages for either party. The Claimants, although on a slightly different basis, come to the same conclusion by application of Italian law. In particular, they point out that the entry into force of the EEC Directive cannot be seen as an "extraordinary and unforeseeable event".

... [T]he Arbitral Tribunal has found that the law of the State of New York only applies to the validity of the Agreement and that [Defendant]'s request for equitable modification of the Agreement cannot be characterized as a question of validity of the Agreement. Moreover, the Arbitral Tribunal has found that besides the law of New York, no national law had been made applicable to the Agreement. Thus, since the provisions of the Agreement do not contemplate the possibility of its modifications on equitable grounds, the Arbitral Tribunal will turn to the usages of international trade in order to supplement the provisions of the Agreement. In this respect, [Defendant] has referred to the UNIDROIT PRINCIPLES which the Arbitral Tribunal recognize as an accurate representation, although incomplete, of the usages of international trade. [The tribunal then quoted articles 6.2.2 and 6.2.3(4) of the UNIDROIT PRINCIPLES.]

However, these provisions must be read in conjunction with article 6.2.1. . . .

On the basis of the above-mentioned definitions, the Arbitral Tribunal admits that it would be entitled to make an equitable modification of the Agreement, but it is not convinced that [Defendant] is being faced with a situation which maybe characterized as "hardship". . . . Indeed, the thrust of [Defendant]'s submission is that since the EEC Directive has been made, the Agreement imposes on the use of the name . . . restrictions which have disappeared from the laws of all countries members of the European Union. As a result, the Agreement, into which [Defendant] entered in order to meet the requirements of [Italian law] deprives it of a freedom in the use of the name . . . that it would enjoy in the absence of the Agreement. It is the reason why [Defendant] requests the Arbitral Tribunal to substitute article 7(b) of the Agreement with the terms of article 6 of the EEC Directive as far as its effects on the territory of the European Union is concerned. [Defendant] would obtain more or less the same result with its subordinate counterclaims aiming at obtaining the termination of the Agreement at least as regards its effects in Europe.

The Arbitral Tribunal does not accept the view, expressed by the Claimants, that a change in the law cannot be the source of hardship. It may well be the case, when a new law makes the performance of the contractual obligations of a party more onerous or when the value it receives from the performance of the other party is severely reduced. However, the Arbitral Tribunal has already found that the introduction of the EEC Directive had no effect on the performance of the Agreement by the parties.

In reality, [Defendant]'s position, in a nutshell, is that it would have had no reason to enter into the Agreement should the EEC Directive have been introduced before [the date of the Agreement]. This has nothing to do with hardship, which is a notion which may play a role when the performance of a contract is at stake but has no function in the formation of contracts. Even if it is probable that [Defendant] would have entered into the Agreement, as drafted in 1987, after the adoption of the EEC Directive in 1989, a subsequent evolution of the legislative context of a contract does not constitute a hardship when it does not destroy the balance of the parties' respective obligations. Moreover, without denying that the parties had in mind [Italian law] when they executed the Agreement, it was not made to be enforced in Italy only nor in Europe. The

Agreement is a global arrangement, due to be enforced in the whole world. . . .

. . . [T]he parties wanted to enter into a final settlement of their conflicts relating to the use of the trademark . . . by agreeing on an arrangement applicable whenever in the world. This probably explains [why] they limited the scope of the law of New York to the validity of the Agreement, since its worldwide application was at odds with the intervention of a specific national law to govern its performance.

Irrespective of the fact that the adoption of EEC Directive does not constitute a situation of hardship, [Defendant]'s contention that the Agreement be modified in so far as its effects in the territory of the European Union are concerned is in direct contradiction with the intention of the parties to organize their relations as to the use of the trademark . . . by harmonized solutions applicable in any jurisdiction, whatever be the content of the law in that jurisdiction.

. . . For the above-mentioned reasons, the Arbitral Tribunal decides to dismiss [Defendant]'s first and principal counterclaim.

In a subordinate counterclaim, [Defendant] requests the Arbitral Tribunal to terminate the Agreement, due to hardship, at least as regards its effects in Europe.

. . . In reality, the termination of the Agreement is one of the two solutions available in case of hardship. As indicated in article 6.2.3, para. 4 of the UNIDROIT PRINCIPLES, a Court (or an Arbitral Tribunal) may either terminate a contract or adapt it with a view to restoring its equilibrium.

As the Arbitral Tribunal has found that the existence of a situation of hardship had not been established and as modifying the Agreement, in its scope in the case of partial termination, in view of the evolution of the law in a specific country or in a group of countries is incompatible with the real intention of the parties which wanted a global application of the Agreement, [Defendant]'s subordinate counterclaim must be dismissed as well as its principal counterclaims. . . .

Notes

3–19. The Licensor (claimants) argued that the applicable law of New York would not allow "equitable modification" of the agreement, absent Licensor's consent. What is the basis at common law for Licensor's argument? Is it saying in effect that Licensee did not have a defense of impracticability?

3–20. Does the result urged by Licensor or by Licensee seem to be more efficient in terms of giving the parties what they thought they were negotiating in forming the contract? In terms of distributing the loss or the increased cost of the agreement?

3–21. The Arbitral Tribunal found that New York law applied only to "the validity of the Agreement," but that Licensee's request for equitable modification "cannot be characterized as a question of validity of the Agreement." Why not? If the parties are in effect fighting over impracticability of the agreement, why is that not an issue of validity? After all, if the agreement *is* impracticable, the parties are discharged without performing further, aren't they?

3–22. The Arbitral Tribunal decided to apply "the usages of international trade in order to supplement the provisions of the Agreement," *e.g.*, the UNIDROIT PRINCIPLES, which the tribunal recognized as "an accurate representation, although incomplete, of the usages of international trade." How do "the usages of international trade" become part of the contract between the parties? Could this ever happen under U.S. law? *Cf.* UCC §§ 1–205(2), (4)-(6) (concerning "usage of trade"), 2–208(2) (explaining interrelationship of usage of trade with express terms, course of performance, and course of dealing).

C. PERFORMANCE AND BREACH UNDER THE CISG

1. The Significance of "Fundamental Breach"[42]

At common law, performance of a contract is the norm, and a breach of a party's obligation gives rise to a cause of action in favor of the breached-upon party. However, the latter's obligations under the contract may continue, absent a material breach by the former. Under the UCC, the parties' performance obligations are specified by part 5 of Article 2.[43] If there is any breach by the seller—"if the goods or the tender of delivery fail in any respect to conform to the contract"[44]—the buyer can accept or reject the delivery in whole or in part.[45] The buyer is still required to pay for any goods accepted.[46] If either party "repudiates"[47] the contract before his or her performance is due, the other party may treat the repudiation as a breach of the contract, *i.e.*, an "anticipatory repudiation" of the contract.[48] Notice that this right to consider an anticipatory repudi-

---

42. For discussion of the concept of "fundamental breach" from the perspective of contract remedies, see Chapter 4, *infra*, § D.1.

43. UCC §§ 2–501–2–515.

44. *Id.* § 2–601.

45. *Id.* § 2–601(a)-(c).

46. *Id.* § 2–607(1).

47. The term "repudiate" would include any language by the buyer or sell-

er "that a reasonable person would interpret to mean that the other party will not or cannot make a performance still due under the contract or voluntary, affirmative conduct that would appear to a reasonable person to make a future performance by the other party impossible." *Id.* § 2–610(2).

48. *Id.* § 2–610(1).

ation as a breach is available only if the anticipated loss "will substantially impair the value of the contract" to the non-repudiating party.[49] For a current breach by a seller, however, in theory it does not matter how insubstantial the breach might be—the buyer's rights in breach are triggered.[50]

Under the CISG, Article 25 is the key provision for the law of performance and breach. It defines the concept of "fundamental breach," which is of central importance to the CISG remedial system. The existence of a "fundamental breach" triggers significant legal consequences, for instance:

(a) the breached-upon party's right to avoid the contract under CISG arts. 49(1)(a), 51(2), 64(1)(a), 72(1), 73(1) & (2);

(b) the buyer's right to substitute delivery under CISG art. 46(2); and,

(c) the allocation of risk in case of delivery of defective goods under CISG art. 70.

Thus, the legal consequences of a fundamental breach depend upon more specific provisions of the CISG or of the contract itself. The following article explores the interplay among CISG provisions that essentially define the law of performance and breach under the CISG.

FRANCO FERRARI, FUNDAMENTAL BREACH OF CONTRACT UNDER THE UN SALES CONVENTION—25 YEARS OF ARTICLE 25 CISG

25 J.L. & Com. 489 (2006).

I. Introduction . . .

The reason for limiting particularly drastic legal consequences (such as the avoidance of the contract) to cases in which the breach of contract is fundamental lies, on the one hand, in ensuring the performance of the contract despite a (non-fundamental) breach to avoid considerable unnecessary and unproductive costs,[14] such as

---

49. *Id.*

50. *Id.* § 2–601. There is some conflicting case law and commentary concerning the efficacy of this so-called "perfect tender" rule. For discussion of this controversy, see William H. Lawrence, *Appropriate Standards for a Buyer's Refusal to Keep Goods Tendered by a Seller*, 35 Wm. & Mary L.Rev. 1635 (1994). UCC § 2–612, governing breaches of installment contracts, creates an exception to the perfect tender rule and requires "substantial impair[ment]" or material breach for buyer's rejection of

the whole contract. *See Midwest Mobile Diagnostic Imaging, L.L.C. v. Dynamics Corp. of America*, 965 F.Supp. 1003, 1010–1011 (W.D.Mich.1997), *affirmed* 165 F.3d 27 (6th Cir. 1998) (contrasting UCC §§ 2–601, 2–612).

14. Compare Clemens Pauly, *The Concept of Fundamental Breach as an International Principle to Create Uniformity of Commercial Law*, 19 J.L. & Com. 221, 225 (2000): The remedy of contract avoidance is supposed to be a remedy of last resort, and a court is supposed to try to save the deal as much as possible.

those associated with the return or storage of the goods. On the other hand, this limitation helps to contain the number of cases in which the damaged party may take advantage of the defaulting party's breach in order to revise an agreement based on a specific economic situation or to shift the risk of a change in the market conditions to the other party.

II.   THE CONCEPT OF THE FUNDAMENTAL BREACH OF CONTRACT

1.   The Breach of an Obligation as a Prerequisite for the Fundamental Breach of Contract

Article 25 defines the fundamental breach autonomously, *i.e.*, independently from any domestic preconceptions. In doing so, Article 25 complies with the obligation set forth in Article 7(1) to interpret the CISG in light of its international character[18] and prevents recourse to domestic legal concepts, which would compromise the unification efforts pursued by the CISG. One must not, therefore, assimilate the Convention's concept of the fundamental breach to the identically worded notion in English contract law. Indeed, a "nationalistic" interpretation of the CISG must be avoided even in the (rare) cases where the original versions of the CISG use terms which have a precise meaning in a particular legal system[21] (such as "fundamental breach"),[22] at least as long as the

Under CISG, the stake for the aggrieved buyer to return non-conforming goods to the seller, or to require substitution, is considerably higher than the prerequisites for a claim for damages. The explanation for this high burden of proof lies in the international character of the transactions. In a CISG setting, goods are being shipped around the world, generating immense costs for shipping, insurance, storage, financing, etc. The goal of saving those deals thus not only reduces costs, but also promotes performance and assures that the parties can rely on their agreements. *See also* BERNARD AUDIT, LA VENTE INTERNATIONALE DE MARCHANDISES, CONVENTION DES NATIONS UNIES DU 11 AVRIL 1980 at 118–19 (1990); [ALEJANDRO GARRO & ALBERTO ZUPPI, COMPRAVENTA INTERNACIONAL DE MERCADERIAS] at 135 [(1990)].

18. *See*, for example, Franco Ferrari, *Uniform Interpretation of The 1980 Uniform Sales Law*, 24 GA. J. INT'L & COMP. L. 183 (1994); Franco Ferrari, *La jurisprudence sur la CVIM: un nouveau défi pour les interprètes?*, 4 INT'L BUS. L.J. 495 (1998).

21. For a similar statement, see also James Bailey, Facing the Truth: Seeing

the Convention on Contracts for the International Sale of Goods as an Obstacle to a Uniform Law of International Sales, 32 CORNELL INT'L L.J. 273, 289 (1999); FRANK DIEDRICH, AUTONOME AUSLEGUNG VON INTERNATIONALEM EINHEITSRECHT. COMPUTERSOFTWAREIM WIENER KAUFRECHT 74 (1994); Franco Ferrari, DER BEGRIFF DES "INTERNATIONALEN PRIVATSRECHTS" NACH ART. I ABS. I LIT.(B) DES UN–KAUFRECHTS, ZEITSCHRIFT FÜR EUROPÄISCHES PRIVATRECHT 162, 166 (1998); Franco Ferrari, Internationales Kaufrecht einheitlich ausgelegt—Anmerkungen anläilch eines italienischen Urteils (Trib. Vigevano, 12.07.2000), INTERNATIONALES HANDELSRECHT 56, 57–58 (2001); JAN KROPHOLLER, INTERNATIONALES EINHEITSRECHT. ALLGEMEINE LEHREN 265 (1975); Paul B. Stephan, The Futility of Unification and Harmonization of International Commercial Law, 39 VA. J. INT'L L. 743, 774 (1999); for a similar statement in case law, see MCC–Marble Ceramic Inc. v. Ceramica Nuova d'Agostino S.p.A., 144 F.3d 1384, 1391 (11th Cir. 1998) (U.S. Court of Appeals (11th Circuit), 29 June 1998); for a different opinion, see Rod N. Andreason, MCC–Marble Ceramic Center: The Parol Evidence Rule and Other Domestic Law Under the Convention on Contracts for the In-

drafters have not intentionally borrowed those terms from a particular domestic legal system. Where, however, the drafting history
suggests that a particular concept is based upon a domestic concep-
tion, "the aim it serves in the domestic context may be taken into
account for the purposes of its comprehension and interpretation."

Pursuant to Article 25, a breach of contract—whatever its
nature—is fundamental when it substantially deprives the other
party of what it is entitled to expect under the contract, provided
that the party in breach did not foresee and a reasonable person of
the same kind in the same circumstances could not have foreseen
such a result.

As pointed out by legal scholars and courts alike, the definition
of fundamental breach is very vague. Whether, however, the concept can only be defined through its practical application, as some
suggest, must be doubted. On the contrary, in this author's opinion,
it is possible to define the concept of "fundamental breach" on the
basis of the elements by which it is characterised (such as breach of
an obligation, detriment, legitimate expectations, and foreseeability) in a way that can prove useful for the CISG's practical
application.

The most important precondition of the CISG's concept of
"fundamental breach" is the breach of an obligation deriving from
either the contract, the practice established between the parties, or
the usages referred to in Article 9 of the CISG.[28] Where no such
breach occurred, Article 25 cannot apply. Thus, there can be no
fundamental breach where a party whose behaviour is incompatible
with its obligations is entitled not to comply with those obligations,
as in the case where the debtor exercises the right to refuse
performance or where the creditor fails to collaborate with the
debtor thus making it impossible for the latter to perform.

The CISG does not distinguish between the breach of principal
and ancillary obligations. "[E]ven the violation of an obligation
which is not a principal obligation under the contract, but an
ancillary one can [thus] be fundamental,"[34] as long as the obligation

ternational Sale of Goods, 1999 BYU L.
REV. 351, 355; Larry DiMatteo, An Inter-
national Contract Law Formula: The In-
formality of International Business
Transactions Plus the Internationaliza-
tion of Contract Law Equals Unexpected
Contractual Liability, 23 SYRACUSE J.
INT'L L. & COM. 67, 79 (1997).

22. FABIAN BURKART, INTERPRETATIVES
ZUSAMMENWIRKEN VON CISG UND UNI-
DROIT PRINCIPLES 146 (2000); Franco
Ferrari, *The Relationship Between the
UCC and the CISG and the Construction*

of Uniform Law, 29 LOY. L.A.L. REV.
1021, 1026 (1996); [JOHN O. HONNOLD,
UNIFORM LAW FOR INTERNATIONAL SALES UN-
DER THE 1980 UNITED NATIONS CONVENTION
(3d ed. 1999)] at 89.

28. Andrew Babiak, *Defining "Fundamental Breach" under the United Nations Convention on Contracts for the
International Sale of Goods*, 6 TEMPLE
INT'L & COMP. L.J. 113, 127, 133
(1992). . . .

34. Oberlandesgericht Frankfurt,
Germany, 17 Sept. 1991, available at

is closely connected to the exchange of goods or the parties have subjected it to the rules of the CISG. It is thus not surprising that a French court has applied Article 25 to the breach of a contractually agreed upon re-import prohibition;[37] nor is it surprising that a German court has held that "the buyer may, in accordance with Article 49(1)(a), request the avoidance of the contract if the non-performance constitutes a fundamental breach of the contract, which may also be the case where an ancillary obligation arising for instance from an exclusivity agreement is breached."[38]

Article 25 does not distinguish between the various types of breaches, such as non-delivery, non-payment, impossibility, delay etc., but rather creates a unitary concept of the breach of contract.

2. The Detriment as a Precondition for Fundamental Breach

"Fundamental breach" further requires the damaged party to suffer a detriment such that it is substantially deprived of what it could have expected under the contract. The term "detriment," which is not being used in any other provision of the CISG and which is nowhere defined in the Convention, must be construed extensively and is not to be analogized to the concept of "damages" referred to in Article 74. The concept of "detriment" comprises all (actual and future) negative consequences of any possible breach of contract, not only actual and future monetary loss, but also any other kind of negative consequences.[48]

A breach of contract is fundamental when the detriment suffered by the damaged party is such that it is "substantially deprived of what [it] is entitled to expect under the contract."[49] The wording of Article 25 clearly indicates that the fundamental character of the breach—to be assessed by the judge[50]—does not, contrary

---

http://cisgw3.law.pace.edu/cases/910917g1.html. . . .

37. *See* Cour d'appel Grenoble, France, 22 Feb. 1995, available at http://cisgw3.law.pace.edu/cases/950222f1.html.

38. Oberlandesgericht Koblenz, Germany, 31 Jan. 1997, available at http://www.cisg-online.ch/cisg/urteile/256.htm.

48. Compare . . . Angela Maria Romito & Charles Sant'Elia, *Italian Court and Homeward Trend*, 14 PACE INT'L L. REV. 179, 198 (2002). *See*, however, Babiak, *supra* note 28, at 120 ("the drafters simply and naturally intended the word 'detriment' to be synonymous with monetary injury or harm, or of a consequential harm").

49. In case law see, for instance, Landgericht Landshut, Germany, 5 Apr.

1995, available at http://cisgw3.law.pace.edu/cases/950405g1.html (stating that the delivery of garments that shrink up to two sizes after washing amounts to a fundamental breach); Roder Zelt-und Hallenkonstruktionen GmbH v. Rosedown Park Pty Ltd and Reginald R Eustace, Federal Court of Australia, South Australian District, Adelaide, 28 Apr. 1995, available at http://cisgw3.law.pace.edu/cases/951130a2.html ("the appointment of an administrator . . . and the placement of the company under administration, in the circumstances of this case, resulted in such detriment to [the seller] as substantially to deprive it of what it was entitled to expect under the contract.").

50. For this statement in case law, see, e.g., Bundesgerichtshof, Germany, 3 Apr. 1996, available at http://

to what had been provided for by the 1978 draft, depend on the extent of the detriment. Rather, it depends upon the impairment of the justified contractual expectations of the damaged party. This impairment must be so serious that it suppresses the damaged party's interest in the performance of the contract or that said party can no longer be expected to be satisfied with less drastic remedies such as damages, price reduction or repair.[55] This is in line with the basic principle inspiring the CISG, according to which the avoidance of the contract in cases of fundamental breach should constitute an *ultima ratio* remedy.[56] Whether the impairment is, in fact, of such seriousness must be decided on a case-by-case basis.[57] It is, however, possible to identify certain lines of cases which strongly suggest the existence of a fundamental breach of contract. . . .

From the language of Article 25, it can be derived that the extent of the detrimental consequences of a breach of contract must be assessed by reference to what the damaged party "could have expected under the contract."[59] This does not mean, however, that one must take into consideration the non-defaulting party's will or the interests it wanted to reach. As the express reference in Article 25 to the contract indicates,[61] one must rather take into account the more objective[62] contractual expectations as they result from the specific contract. This is a matter of contract interpretation. In this context, one must have regard not only to the contractual language, but also to the practice established between the parties, and other

cisgw3.law.pace.edu/cases/960403g1. html. . . .

55. [F]or a similar statement in case law, see Oberlandesgericht Hamburg, Germany, 14 Dec. 1994, available at http://www.cisg-online.ch/cisg/urteile/ 216.htm; Oberlandesgericht Frankfurt, Germany, 18 Jan. 1994, available at http://www.cisg-online.ch/cisg/urteile/ 123.htm; Landgericht Kassel, Germany, 21 Sept. 1995, available at http://www. cisg-online.ch/cisg/urteile/192.htm; Bundesgericht, Switzerland, 28 Oct. 1998, available at http://www.cisg-online.ch/ cisg/urteile/413.htm.

56. [F]or similar statements in case law, see, for instance, Oberlandesgericht Köln, Germany, 14 Oct. 2002, available at http:// cisgw3.law.pace.edu/cases/ 021014g1.html ("The buyer shall be authorised to request avoidance only as a last resort."); Landgericht Munich, Germany, 27 Feb. 2002, available at http://cisgw3.law.pace.edu/cases/ 020227g1.html ("since restitution as a

result of the avoidance of a contract is— as is clearly illustrated by the case at hand—particularly burdensome in the international context, avoidance should only be a remedy of last resort."); Oberster Gerichtshof, Austria, 7 Sept. 2000, available at http://www.cisg.at/8_ 2200v.htm (mentioning that the avoidance of the contract constitutes an "ultima ratio" remedy).

57. For a similar conclusion, see Bundesgericht, Switzerland, 28 Oct. 1998, available at http://www.cisg-online.ch/cisg/urteile/413.htm. . . .

59. Bundesgericht, Switzerland, 28 Oct. 1998, available at http:// www.cisg-online.ch/cisg/urteile/413.htm.

61. *See also* Oberlandesgericht Hamburg Germany, 14 Dec. 1994, available at http://www.cisg-online.ch/cisg/urteile/ 216.htm.

62. *[S]ee* Bundesgericht, Switzerland, 28 Oct. 1998, available at http:// www.cisg-online.ch/cisg/urteile/413.htm.

circumstances preceding the conclusion of the contract[67] (such as the contractual negotiations)....

IV. CONCLUDING REMARKS

The preceding remarks clearly show the central importance of the concept of the "fundamental breach." It is, therefore, not surprising that there are a growing number of decisions involving the application of Article 25.[150] The first decision applying the CISG in the year of its twenty-fifth anniversary[151] also dealt with that provision. It held that the breach of a contractually agreed upon obligation to clean and disinfect, prior to the delivery of the purchased animals, the stables in which sick animals had earlier been kept, amounts to a fundamental breach.

Notes

3–23.   Applying CISG Article 25 is unlikely to be a problem where the parties expressly or implicitly agree that a specific aspect of performance or a specific kind of detriment is to be regarded as fundamental.[51] The issue becomes more problematic where the parties use standard terms, the validity of which is *not* subject to the CISG.[52] How should courts approach the problem of determining the existence of a fundamental breach? In the cases cited or excerpted below, we shall see some examples of how courts make this determination. In counseling a client negotiating a contract that might be subject to the CISG, would you advise the inclusion of a provision in which the parties agree on what breaches or detriments would constitute fundamental breaches? If so, which breaches or detriments would you want included if you represented the buyer? The seller?

3–24.   In the absence of guidance in the contract language, determining what would constitute a fundamental breach would presumably involve a question of contract interpretation governed by the CISG itself.[53] The importance that a particular performance would have for a

---

67. *See* CISG art. 8(3).

150. For recent case law, see Cour d'Appel Paris, France, 4 June 2004, available at http://cisgw3.law.pace.edu/cases/040604f1.html (the delivery of non-conforming goods the use of which does not warrant the same degree of safety as the contractually agreed goods constitutes a fundamental breach of contract).

151. Tribunale di Padova, Italy, 11 Jan. 2005, available at http://www.unilex.info/case.cfm?pid=1&do=case&id=1005&step=Abstract.

51. How likely is it that parties (or their counsel) would have that much

foresight? Considering how many cases we have seen where the parties—and even the court—seemed unsure of whether the CISG applied, it probably strains credibility to expect that degree of foresight.

52. CISG, art. 4.

53. *See id.* art. 8, which provides:

(1) For the purposes of this Convention statements made by and other conduct of a party are to be interpreted according to his intent where the other party knew or could not have been unaware what that intent was.

(2) If the preceding paragraph is not applicable, statements made by

specific non-defaulting party would obviously be determined on a case-by-case basis.[54] Nevertheless, the following problems offer some likely assumptions from which we might start in determining whether a specific breach is fundamental or not.[55]

(a) What if the defaulting party did not foresee the detrimental consequences? Would it make a difference whether or not a "reasonable person," of the same kind and in the same circumstances as the defaulting party, would have foreseen these consequences? The CISG suggests that foreseeability should be measured against an objective standard.[56]

(b) What if one of the parties simply fails to perform at all? Complete non-performance would undoubtedly be considered a fundamental breach of contract,[57] so long as the non-performance was not justified or excused.[58]

(c) What if there is a delay in delivery of the goods? There is a significant body of case law arguing that delivery delay cannot *per se* amount to a fundamental breach.[59] Under what circumstances would a delay in delivery constitute a fundamental breach? In answering the question, consider *Valero Marketing & Supply Co. v. Greeni Oy*, excerpted in Chapter 4, *infra* at § D.1.

and other conduct of a party are to be interpreted according to the understanding that a reasonable person of the same kind as the other party would have had in the same circumstances.

(3) In determining the intent of a party or the understanding a reasonable person would have had, due consideration is to be given to all relevant circumstances of the case including the negotiations, any practices which the parties have established between themselves, usages and any subsequent conduct of the parties.

54. *See, e.g.,* Andrew Babiak, *Defining "Fundamental Breach" under the United Nations Convention on Contracts for the International Sale of Goods*, 6 TEMPLE INT'L & COMP. L.J. 113, 120 (1992) (so arguing).

55. The problems are based on discussion in Franco Ferrari, *Fundamental Breach of Contract under the UN Sales Convention—25 Years of Article 25 CISG*, 25 J. L. & COM. 489 (2006), not included in the selection from the article excerpted *supra*.

56. CISG, art. 8(2).

57. For cases so holding, see Pretura di Parma–Fidenza, Italy, 24 Nov. 1989, available at http://cisgw3.law.pace.edu/cases/891124i3.html; Landgericht Ellwangen, Germany, 21 Aug. 1995, avail-

able at http://cisgw3.law.pace.edu/cases/950821g2.html.

58. Cf. Oberlandesgericht Celle, Germany, 24 May 1995, available at http://cisgw3.law.pace.edu/cases/950524g1.html; Schiedsgericht Hamburger Freundschaftliche Arbitrage, Germany, 29 Dec. 1998, available at http://cisgw3.law.pace.edu/cases/981229g1.html.

59. *See, e.g.,* Oberlandesgericht München, Germany, 1 July 2002, available at http://cisgw3.law.pace.edu/cases/020701g1.html ("a delay in the delivery does not amount to a fundamental breach of contract in the sense of Article 25 CISG."); Landgericht München, Germany, 20 Feb. 2002, available at http://cisgw3.law.pace.edu/cases/020220g1.html ("Non-delivery at the contractually agreed delivery date does not constitute a fundamental breach of contract in the sense of a Article 49(1)(a)."); Oberlandesgericht Hamburg, Germany, 28 Feb. 1997, available at http://www.cisg-online.ch/cisg/urteile/261.htm ("late delivery should not generally be viewed as a fundamental breach of contract."); Oberlandesgericht Düsseldorf, Germany, 18 Nov. 1993, available at http://www.cisg-online.ch/cisg/urteile/92.htm ("late delivery does not constitute a fundamental breach under Article 25 as long as performance is possible and the debtor has not finally refused to perform."); Court of Arbitra-

(d) What about delivery of defective goods? Some case law suggests that delivery of such goods is a fundamental breach only if the defect is such that the non-defaulting party cannot be expected to be made whole through damages or price reduction.[60] What if the defect can only be cured within an unreasonable period of time or with excessive effort? There is case law suggesting that, in such a situation, the defect should be considered a fundamental breach of contract.[61] Do you agree? Consider the following excerpt from a case considering this issue:

> [S]ince, as long and insofar as (even) a serious defect may be cured through repair or substitute delivery, performance by the seller remains possible and the buyer's interest in performance is intact. According to legal writers and case law under the CISG, a serious defect does therefore not constitute a fundamental breach of contract if the defect can be cured and the seller is willing to do so, as long as the buyer does not suffer undue delay or any other burden.

Handelsgericht Kanton Aargau, Switzerland, 5 Nov. 2002, available at http://cisgw3.law.pace.edu/cases/021105s1.html.

(e) What if buyer miscalculates in considering a delivery of defective goods to be a fundamental breach? What actions might you expect such a mistaken buyer to take? What happens when, well after the fact, a court determines that the delivery of the defective goods was *not* a fundamental breach? In answering these questions, consider the following case.

SHUTTLE PACKAGING SYSTEMS, L.L.C. v. TSONAKIS

2001 WL 34046276 (W.D.Mich. 2001).

ENSLEN, J.

[A Greek seller agreed to supply thermoforming lining equipment for the manufacture of plastic gardening pots to a U.S. buyer,

tion of the International Chamber of Commerce, Award No. 8128, 1995, available at http://www.unilex.info/case.cfm?pid=1&do=case&id=207&step=Full Text (*"Le simple retard ne constitue cependant pas une contravention essentielle d'après l'article 25 de la Convention."*).

60. *See, e.g.,* Oberlandesgericht Hamm, Germany, 22 Sept. 1992, available at http://www.cisg-online.ch/cisg/urteile/57.htm (non-conformity of only 0.005% of delivered goods does not warrant avoidance of contract as to remaining goods to be delivered); Landgericht Landshut, Germany, 5 Apr. 1995, available at http://cisgw3.law.pace.edu/cases/950405g1.html (shrinking of all pieces of

clothing purchased); Bundesgerichtshof, Germany, 3 Apr. 1996, available at http://cisgw3.law.pace.edu/cases/960403g 1.html (discussing CISG preference for damages or price reduction, rather than avoidance of contract; Oberlandesgericht Köln, Germany, 14 Oct. 2002, available at http://cisgw3.law.pace.edu/cases/021014g1.html).

61. *See, e.g.,* Oberlandesgericht Köln, Germany, 14 Oct. 2002, available at http://cisgw3.law.pace.edu/cases/021014g1.html ("Even a serious defect does not constitute a fundamental breach of contract when the seller is willing to deliver conforming goods and when such delivery is not excessively burdensome for the buyer").

Shuttle Packaging Systems. The contract included terms relating to, *inter alia*, the supply of the technology and assistance in the use of the equipment, and a non-competition agreement, the full terms of which were to be contained in a separate document. The parties then concluded the non-competition agreement applying to an undefined "restricted area," and agreeing not to disclose or use trade information or customer lists of the buyer. The contract did not specify the law applicable to the purchase of goods but did state that the non-competition agreement was to be enforced in accordance with Michigan law.

[The buyer had problems with the equipment and believed that it did not conform to the seller's specifications or to industry standards. The seller thought that the buyer had negligently operated the machinery. The buyer unilaterally suspended payment for the goods, and the seller began to compete in the market for distribution of plastic gardening pots, an apparent violation of the non-competition agreement. The buyer brought suit, seeking damages for breach of contract and violation of the non-competition agreement. In a motion before the Court, the buyer sought to restrain the seller from selling pots in the North American market pending the outcome of the case.]

I. Procedural Background

Plaintiff Shuttle Packaging Systems, L.L.C. ("Plaintiff") filed this action against Defendants Jacob Tsonakis, INA S.A. ("INA") and INA Plastics Corp. ("INA Plastics") on October 24, 2001. Plaintiff's sole member is Calvin Diller, who is a citizen of Michigan. This decision refers in many parts to East Jordan Plastics, Inc. ("EJP"), which company is related to Plaintiff by its ownership and operation.

On October 24, 2001, Plaintiff filed motions for a temporary restraining order and preliminary injunction. By Order of October 25, 2001, this Court denied the Motion for Temporary Restraining Order on the ground that Plaintiff had not shown that it was likely to sustain irreparable harm before the Motion for Preliminary Injunction could be heard....

II. Factual Background

A. *Allegations of Complaint and Answer*

Plaintiff's Verified Complaint alleges that on November 1, 2000, it agreed to a purchase agreement with Defendants. Plaintiff alleges that under the purchase agreement Defendants were required to supply thermoforming line equipment for the manufacture of plastic gardening pots together with the technology and assistance to use the equipment.... The Contract also included other terms relating to payment schedules, non-competition, warranties, notices, expenses, interest, and an integration clause.... The non-competition term did not include the specific terms for non-competition, but required the further execution of a non-competition agreement....

According to the Complaint, on November 2, 2000, the parties entered into a non-competition agreement which contained various covenants of the seller not to engage in selling its equipment and processes within the "Restricted Area," not to disclose its technical manufacturing processes to others, and not to disclose or use trade information and customer lists of the buyer.... The non-competition agreement contained no covenants for the buyer, but listed the payment of the purchase price under the purchase agreement as the consideration.... The "Restricted Area" was defined as "any jurisdiction throughout the world where the Company is, or in which Seller has reason to know the Company expects to engage in, the Business. The jurisdictions included in the Restricted Area as of the date of this Agreement are listed on Schedule I hereto." ... No Schedule I was attached to the document. Plaintiff interprets the "Restricted Area" as North America. The non-competition agreement also stated that it was to be interpreted and enforced in accordance with the laws of the State of Michigan....

Plaintiff's Complaint is stated in three state law counts, each premised on diversity jurisdiction. Count One alleges breach of the non-competition agreement and specifically that Defendants are soliciting customers of Plaintiff in North America for the purpose of selling equipment subject to the agreement. Count Two alleges breach of the purchase agreement and more specifically both that Defendants have not provided all of the services required under the agreement and that the equipment has not performed as promised. Count Three alleges a breach of warranty as to the equipment in that the equipment was not in good working order, did not manufacture to the contract specifications and failed to meet industry standards for manufacturing. Count One is pertinent to the request for Preliminary Injunction since it includes the request that the Court temporarily and permanently enjoin violation of the non-competition agreement.

Defendants have also answered the Complaint. The Answer contests most of the factual allegations, but admits jurisdiction and venue. The Answer also contends that Defendant INA Plastics has dissolved and is no longer in business....

B. Plaintiff's Affidavits and Exhibits ...

Gary Gurizzian is the CFO [chief financial officer] for Plaintiff and the Financial Projects Manager at EJP.... EJP is located in East Jordan, Michigan, which is also Plaintiff's principal place of business.... Gurizzian states in his affidavit that Jacob Tsonakis, the President of INA, made representations to him, Calvin Diller and Al Druskin concerning the plastic technology manufacturing equipment sold by his company in July 2000.... Gurizzian further states that EJP then provided a loan or advance of funds of $600,000 with the idea that the parties, EJP and INA, would form a joint venture.... The joint venture did not occur, but Shuttle was formed in place of EJP as a possible participant in the joint venture.... The parties eventually settled on a purchase agreement for the equipment instead of a joint venture.... At the time of the purchase agreement, a contract term requiring non-competition was critical to Plaintiff.... Plaintiff has made payments on the equipment consistent with the payment schedule in the contract.... [One machine] was delivered on January 25, 2001, which was after its scheduled date of December 18, 2000.... Upon delivery, Plaintiff discovered that the equipment had been damaged in shipping.... These circumstances required Plaintiff to order pots from INA for sale to its customers instead of manufacturing the pots itself.... Due to constant failure of the equipment, Plaintiff suspended payment to INA.... Gurizzian believes (for unspecified reasons) that INA is competing in the North American market and underselling Plaintiff, so as to cause Plaintiff an undeterminable financial loss and so as to threaten Plaintiff's business viability....

Alan Druskin is the Vice President of Marketing of EJP and by an administrative agreement also manages the marketing of Plaintiff.... Druskin worked with Jacob Tsonakis to solicit sales for Plaintiff.... Druskin claims "on information and belief" that Tsonakis solicited customers of Plaintiff for his own business beginning in February 2001 and made his products available to these customers at prices which undercut Plaintiff's prices.... According to Druskin, he has been told by his customers that they will buy from INA instead of Plaintiff because of the cost difference....

C. Defendants' Affidavit and Exhibits

Defendants have filed the very lengthy Affidavit of Jacob Tsonakis, which includes some 185 numbered paragraphs and some 67 attachments.... Paragraphs 27 through 33 describe the events giving rise to the approval of the purchase agreement. Those paragraphs describe those events in a similar manner to Plaintiff's representatives' descriptions. However, one important difference is that Defendant indicates that he engaged in tele-facsimile correspondence with Calvin Diller on September 28, 2000 in which he indicated that the lines might not be completed until January 15, 2001.... The January date was used because much of the described equipment, which was quite large, needed to be shipped by container ship from Greece to the port of Charleston and then shipped by truck to the Plaintiff's plant in Forest City, North Carolina....

Paragraphs 45 through 54 of the Affidavit describe the approval of the non-competition agreement. According to Tsonakis, he inquired of Gurizzian why the balance of the down payment of $450,000 had not been sent. When he asked this question, Gurizzian told him that the balance would not be paid until he agreed to the terms of a non-competition agreement. When he reviewed the proposed agreement, he told Gurizzian that the term relating to the "Restricted Area" was unreasonable because it referred to any jurisdiction in the whole world. Gurizzian responded that he should not be concerned since the document was "simply something 'for the file.' " Tsonakis then faxed a signed and initialed copy to Gurizzian. The copy referenced did not include a Schedule I, the schedule describing more particularly the jurisdictions referenced in the agreement. After receiving the balance of the down payment from Plaintiff, Tsonakis turned over his customers in the United States to Plaintiff (though he did not deem himself required to do so)....

According to [paragraphs 55 through 66], certain accessory equipment was not part of the contract and Tsonakis advised Plaintiff of this, without objection, upon his arrival to install the equipment. According to Tsonakis, the only defect in the machinery, a bent cabinet from damage in shipping, was quickly repaired....

Paragraphs 75 to 91 of the Affidavit relate to the negligent operation of the [equipment], which Tsonakis claims to have witnessed during his assistance at the plant. According to Tsonakis, the machinery was unsafe and inefficient due to Plaintiff's refusal to purchase necessary accessories for the machinery.... Also, according to Tsonakis, Plaintiff attempted to use the machinery without a mixer by having employees attempt to manually mix 700 pounds per hour of molten plastic with a shovel over the hot extruder of the line.... These compromises caused problems with the homogeneity of the plastic, lack of quality control, and other production problems.... Plaintiff's production also suffered from high turnover of the work force and the drug addiction of one key employee who operated the lines.... According to Tsonakis, there was a shortage of employees to operate the second line when it arrived in March 2001.... Tsonakis also explained in paragraphs 92 through 99 that Plaintiff had some production problems because its workers ignored his production engineer's advice to use some virgin material in mixtures and to avoid contaminants. . . .

D. Defendants' Supplementary Evidence . . .

An examination of Plaintiff's affiants' testimonies show them to be generally consistent with the affidavits, but also contain many admissions helpful to the Defendants. Wayne DeCamp admitted that the high degree of manual labor associated with Plaintiff's operation of the lines made training difficult. . . . He also admitted that the line operated inefficiently due to employee breaks . . . and that the four inch line had not been set up and run by Plaintiff (which was required because of Defendants' expectation of the additional performance payment) and that the necessary part to set up the line (the extruder) had been warehoused. . . . DeCamp also confirmed his authoring the email attributed to him by Tsonakis, relating to the adequacy of the line training.

Gary Gurizzian's deposition is also somewhat helpful to Defendants' position. He admitted that he had not complained about late delivery or about the failure to include accessory equipment with the lines. . . . Gurizzian's credibility on other points is also undermined by his deposition testimony. For instance, his explanation of his spreadsheet analysis concerning the operation of the lines shows it to be mistaken in significant parts. This spreadsheet analysis appears to bill Defendants for the ordinary operation of the machinery, including repair costs, and accessories which were not included within the Purchase Agreement. . . .

III. LEGAL ANALYSIS

A. Likelihood of Success . . .

The first factor, likelihood of success, in this case relates to the likelihood of success of the merits of its claim for injunctive relief to enjoin the violation of the non-competition agreement and, more specifically, to enjoin competition in places in North America wherein Plaintiff is active in selling greenhouse pots. Jacob Tsonakis has not denied that his companies are competing in North America and his email of August 2001 indicated his intent to compete in North America because of Plaintiff's non-payment. Thus, the Court regards that the substance of this dispute is not over whether Defendants are competing, but whether they are bound by the terms of non-competition agreement to not compete in North America.

To begin this discussion, the Court must make an initial and preliminary assessment of the likely source of law to be applied to this controversy. The Court's preliminary assessment is that this controversy is governed by the United Nations Convention on Contracts for the International Sale of Goods ("CISG"), 19 I.L.M.

671 (May 1980), with one exception. The exception is the legal question of the enforcement of the non-competition agreement, which is governed by Michigan law under the parties' forum selection clause. This assessment is based on the several pertinent facts. The United States and Greece are signatories to the Convention.... The goods sold in this case are commercial goods of the type subject to the Convention. While the purchase agreement does not specify the application of any body of law as to the purchase, the non-competition agreement specifies the application of Michigan law, but only as to the enforcement of the non-competition agreement. Also, given the law cited by the parties, they are in apparent agreement as to this choice of law.

With this backdrop, the Court must assess whether Defendants now have a legal right to compete for this business in North America. Defendants make several arguments in opposition to the Motion. One argument made by Defendants is that the non-competition agreement is ineffective because of lack of consideration for the agreement. This argument fails. First of all, the non-competition agreement was made part and parcel with the purchase agreement and assumed that the consideration for the non-competition agreement was the consideration for the purchase agreement. Second, under the Convention, a contract for the sale of goods may be modified without consideration for the modification. *See* CISG, Art. 29; Michael Van Alstine, 37 Va. J. Int. Law 1 & n. 47 (Fall 1996) (reaching this conclusion based on the U.N. Secretariat's Commentary on the Draft Convention, U.N. Doc. A/Conf. 97/5 (1979))....

Defendants' final argument relating to likelihood of success is that the Plaintiff committed the first material breach of the contract and, as such, Defendants are no longer bound by the terms of the non-competition agreement. Defendants also make a related argument that because Plaintiff delayed in complaining about the performance of the equipment, it is not entitled to suspend payment of money owed under the purchase agreement.

This related argument concerns Articles 38 and 39 of the Convention, which require the buyer to "examine the goods ... within as short a period as is practicable in the circumstances" and which further state the buyer "loses the right to rely on a lack of conformity of the goods if he does not give notice to the seller specifying the nature of the lack of conformity within a reasonable time...." Article 39 also provides a two-year time period as the outer limit of time for a buyer to notify the seller of a lack of conformity (unless the goods are subject to a longer contractual period of guarantee).

This related argument fails. The wording of the Convention reveals an intent that buyers examine goods promptly and give notice of defects to sellers promptly. However, it is also clear from the statute that on occasion it will not be practicable to require notification in a matter of a few weeks. For this reason, the outer limit of two years is set for the purpose of barring late notices. In this case, there was ample reason for a delayed notification. The machinery was complicated, unique, delivered in installments and subject to training and on-going repairs. The Plaintiff's employees lacked the expertise to inspect the goods and needed to rely on Defendants' engineers even to use the equipment. It is also wrong to say, in light of this record, that notification did not occur until July 6, 2001. Long before the July 6 correspondence, there was a steady stream of correspondence between the parties relating to the functioning of the equipment which may have constituted sufficient notice of the complaints. The international cases cited by Defendants are not apposite to this discussion because they concern the inspection of simple goods and not complicated machinery like that involved in this case.

Nevertheless, the Court does accept Defendants' contention that the Plaintiff's non-payment of progress payments on the machinery did constitute a "fundamental breach of contract." Article 25 of the Convention defines a "fundamental breach of contract" as one "which results in such detriment to the other party as substantially to deprive him of what he is entitled to expect under the contract. . . ." *See Delchi Carrier v. Rotorex Corp.,* 71 F.3d 1024, 1028 (2nd Cir.1995) (discussing definition). This is a significant definition in that Article 64 provides the seller a right to declare the contract avoided due to a "fundamental breach of contract." The Convention affords the buyer a right to avoid the contract under Article 49 for a fundamental breach. It likewise affords both buyer and seller the right to suspend or avoid an installment contract due to fundamental breach under Articles 71–73. Article 64 is also specifically worded to give the implication that non-payment of the purchase price is the most significant form of a fundamental breach by a buyer, since, as to a serious non-payment, no additional notifications are required for avoidance of the contract.

In this case, the buyer has had some legitimate complaints concerning the machinery throughout the delivery and training process. However, on the whole, the Court concludes that the evidence submitted best supports the proposition that these complaints did not constitute either a fundamental or even a substantial breach of the contract by the seller. This is particularly true since the context for this dispute—namely, the machinery has been successfully operated with Defendants' assistance and Plaintiff is a cash-strapped business raising performance questions only after formal inquiries have been made as to non-payment—tends to show that complaints about performance were opportunistic and not genuine in character. On the other hand, the Court determines that it is likely that non-payment of the large sums due for the performance payments was a fundamental breach of contract and that it excused Defendants' performance of non-competition obligations under the purchase agreement and non-competition agreement. As such, the Court concludes that Plaintiff is unlikely to succeed on the merits.

B.   Irreparable Harm to Plaintiff

Plaintiff has cited cases for the proposition that loss of goodwill and loss of business opportunities are the kinds of losses which are irreparable because they cannot later be sufficiently quantified for damage purposes. *See, e.g., Basicomputer v. Scott,* 973 F.2d 507, 511–12 (6th Cir.1992). While the Court agrees with that legal proposition, it finds it inapplicable here. Because the Plaintiff had, most likely, committed a fundamental breach of the contract by nonpayment, it has also most likely surrendered its right to seek enforcement of the non-competition agreement. As such, on the present record, the Court does not find that Plaintiff is likely to suffer irreparable harm because of Plaintiff's own fundamental non-performance of its duties under the contract.

C.   Harm to Others

This factor focuses on the harm to Defendants caused by a possible wrongful injunction. The Court believes that this factor sorts out like the other factors above. Namely, since the Plaintiff has, most likely, wrongfully failed to pay amounts due under the contract, the Defendants should not be expected to honor obligations for which they have not been paid. As such, the Court determines that this factor disfavors granting relief.

D.   Public Interest

Of course, the public, in the abstract, cares very little concerning which group of manufacturers should manufacture pots in the United States during the course of this lawsuit. However, the public does have an interest in seeing that these pots, which are produced at a more cost-efficient basis than other agricultural pots, are readily available in the market. Thus, the public's interest is best supported by a resolution which would cause both the parties to manufacture pots in the market pending the resolution of this suit. This is particularly true since the Plaintiff's manufacturing abilities have proven suspect such that the market might be jeopardized by licensing the market solely to Plaintiff-a producer who operates its manufacturing on a shoestring budget. Although, as Plaintiff points out, this resolution might threaten its long-term viability, it seems apparent that there are ample threats to Plaintiff's long-term viability even absent denial of this preliminary injunction motion.

Notes

3–25. Why did the parties not realize from the first that their contract was subject to the CISG? And why did plaintiff allege diversity jurisdiction, rather than federal question jurisdiction under the CISG? (*Cf. Asante*), *supra* at 4. (discussing federal question jurisdiction under CISG); note 1–14, *supra* (discussing jurisdictional function of CISG).

3–26. The *Shuttle Packaging* court does make a "preliminary assessment" that the case is governed by the CISG, except for the non-competition agreement, which was governed by Michigan law as the parties had agreed. What if the parties had not given any indication of choice of law governing the non-competition agreement? Would the CISG apply? Even though non-competition is not a good, but a service?

3–27. The court believed that the non-competition agreement was supported by consideration—as part of the sales agreement—and that the agreement could be modified to include the non-competition agreement because, under the CISG, a contract for the sale of goods may be modified without consideration for the modification. The relevant provision—not cited by the court—is Article 29, which provides:

(1) A contract may be modified or terminated by the mere agreement of the parties.

(2) A contract in writing which contains a provision requiring any modification or termination by agreement to be in writing may not be otherwise modified or terminated by agreement. However, a party may be precluded by his conduct from asserting such a provision to the extent that the other party has relied on that conduct.

3–28. As the court notes, CISG Articles 38 and 39 require a buyer to "examine the goods . . . within as short a period as is practicable in the circumstances" and specify that a buyer "loses the right to rely on a lack of conformity of the goods if he does not give notice to the seller specifying the nature of the lack of conformity within a reasonable time," with two years as the outer limit of time for notification unless the contract provides a longer period. CISG, art. 39. How does this compare with the UCC, which provides:

(1) Acceptance of goods occurs when the buyer

(a) after a reasonable opportunity to inspect the goods signifies to the seller that the goods are conforming or that he will take or retain them in spite of their non-conformity. . . .

UCC § 2–606(1)(a).[62]

---

62. *See, e.g., Miron v. Yonkers Raceway, Inc.,* 400 F.2d 112 (2d Cir. 1968) (where there are defects discoverable by customer inspection at time of sale, buy-

3–29. The court found that Shuttle's non-payment of progress payments on the machinery constituted a "fundamental breach of contract" under CISG Article 25. How does the court define a "fundamental breach"? What are the legal consequences of this finding for the plaintiff's case?

3–30. The date of delivery may be a fundamental issue depending upon the nature of the goods, *e.g.*, seasonal goods.[63] However, some cases resist the notion that a short delay could ever be fundamental absent an agreement of the parties to that effect.[64] A substantial delay in delivery would generally be considered a fundamental breach.[65]

3–31. Could the buyer's failure to take delivery of the goods constitute a fundamental breach of contract? Case law suggests that it does not.[66] What if the seller has a particular interest in timely taking of delivery by the buyer, perhaps because of burdensome storage or maintenance costs?

3–32. What about the obligation of the buyer to pay for the goods? Could delay in payment be considered a fundamental breach in the sense of Article 25? In answering these questions, consider the following case.

DOWNS INVESTMENTS P/L v. PERWAJA STEEL SDN BHD

[2001] QCA 433.
Supreme Court of Queensland, Australia—Court of Appeal.

WILLIAMS, JA

[The claim arose out of a contract between Downs, an Australian seller, and Perwaja, a Malaysian buyer, where the former agreed to sell 30,000 metric tons of scrap metal to the latter. The seller asked for termination of the contract and damages on the grounds that the buyer had failed to establish a requested letter of credit. The trial court applied the CISG and concluded that the

---

er will not be excused from making inspection and rejecting goods within a reasonable time on ground that there are possible critical defects which only more thorough inspection would disclose).

63. Oberlandesgericht Düsseldorf, Germany, 24 Apr. 1997, available at http://cisgw3.law.pace.edu/cases/970424g 1.html; Corte d'Appello Milano, Italy, 20 Mar. 1998, available at http://cisgw3.law. pace.edu/cases/980320i3.html; Court of Arbitration of the International Chamber of Commerce, Award No. 8786, Jan. 1997, available at http://cisgw3.law.pace. edu/cases/978786i1.html.

64. Landgericht Oldenburg, Germany, 27 Mar. 1996, available at http:// www.cisg-online.ch/cisg/urteile/188.htm; Amstgericht Ludwigsburg, Germany, 21 Dec. 1990, available at http://www.cisg-online.ch/cisg/urteile/17.htm   (two-day delay in delivery).

65. Bundesgericht, Switzerland, 15 Sept. 2000, available at http:// cisgw3. law.pace.edu/cases/000915s1.html;   Pretura Parma–Fidenza, Italy, 24 Nov. 1989, available at http://cisgw3.law.pace. edu/cases/891124i3.html.

66. *But see* Kantonsgericht Zug, Switzerland, 12 Dec. 2002, available at http://cisgw3.law.pace.edu/cases/021212s 1.html (taking contrary position).

buyer was in fundamental breach of its obligations under the contract by failing to establish the appropriate letter of credit as promised. The buyer appealed.]

This is an appeal from Ambrose J who concluded that the respondent was entitled to recover from the appellant a total of US$1,280,347.80 for damages including interest. The claim arose out of a contract between the parties in terms of which the respondent agreed to sell scrap metal to the appellant. As the respondent was in Australia and the appellant in Malaysia it was held that the United Nations Convention on Contracts for the International Sale of Goods, made relevant by the Sale of Goods (Vienna Convention) Act 1986, applied to the transaction. The learned trial judge held on the evidence that the appellant had fundamentally breached the contract and assessed damages pursuant to Articles 74 and 75 of the Convention. From that decision the appellant has appealed on a variety of grounds.

The first matter that must be considered is the appellant's contention that "in fairness" the respondent was not entitled to a judgment based on the Convention. . . .

In the respondent's pleadings, as they stood at the first day of trial, there was no reference either to the Sale of Goods Act 1986 ("the Act") or the Convention. Arguably the material facts pleaded by the respondent could have supported a claim either under the Act or the Convention. . . .

At the start of day 3 of the trial, before the respondent had closed its case, its counsel asked for and was granted leave to amend the statement of claim. That application was not opposed by counsel for the appellant. . . .

Counsels' addresses began on day 6 of the trial. In the course of the address by counsel for the respondent reference was made to the Convention and in particular to Articles 74 and 75 thereof relating to the calculation of damages. In submissions in reply counsel for the appellant contended that the respondent was estopped by its conduct of the trial from relying on the Convention. The learned trial judge reserved his decision.

Some 44 days later the learned trial judge had the matter relisted and indicated that the applicability of the Convention had emerged as an important consideration. The learned trial judge on that occasion invited counsel for the appellant to call any additional evidence that would overcome any prejudice that might otherwise be occasioned to the appellant because it arguably only became obvious at a late stage in the trial that the Convention was an important consideration. There was at that stage no need for the respondent to formally amend its statement of claim. . . . It is sufficient to record that the appellant stated it might reopen its case if the respondent amended its pleading but ultimately decided that no additional evidence would be called. However supplementary written submissions dealing with the Convention were given to the trial judge. . . .

. . . Given the statements . . . made by counsel for the respondent in the course of opening and at the time of seeking leave to make the amendments, it must have been obvious that the respondent's case included a contention that damages should be assessed on some basis other than that set out in s 51(3) of the Act. That should have put the appellant on notice that the respondent's case was based, at least in the alternative, on propositions not included in s 51(3). It is not as if the appellant and its legal advisers were not aware of the Convention. Counsel for the appellant conceded that the Convention had been considered some two years prior to the hearing and been put "back on the shelf because it wasn't relevant to the case".

The basis of liability pleaded by the respondent was that it had elected to terminate the contract because of fundamental breach by the appellant. That case was in no way affected by the issue whether the Convention applied or not; the evidence and findings would have been precisely the same. Any difference between Article 25 and the common law was not material given the facts of this case. The only possible difference between the Act and Convention for present purposes is with respect to the calculation of damages. . . . Ultimately the learned trial judge held on the evidence that there was a substitute transaction entered into [by the seller] in a reasonable manner and within a reasonable time after avoidance and it is difficult to see how those findings could be upset by the calling of further evidence.

The trial was vigorously contested on a number of issues and a lot of documentary evidence was placed before the court. I cannot see that there was anything unfair about the trial because of the alleged belated concentration on the Convention.

In all the circumstances I am not satisfied that the appellant has made out a case that the decision should be set aside on the ground of unfairness. The appellant did not suffer any irremediable prejudice. Further, I cannot see that anything was said or done by the respondent, or its counsel, in the course of the trial which would preclude it from relying on the Convention.

Grounds 3 to 9 inclusive in the notice of appeal raise in various ways the issue whether the respondent proved the appellant's liability pursuant to the Convention. Article 64(1) relevantly provides that the seller may declare the contract avoided if the failure by the buyer to perform any of its obligations under the contract or the Convention amounts to a "fundamental breach of contract";

that expression is defined in Article 25. Essentially a breach will be fundamental if it deprives a party of what he is entitled to expect under the contract. Much of the appellant's case in this regard depended on whether or not time remained of the essence. Before the issue so raised can be determined it is necessary to set out the terms of the contract and record certain events which occurred that are relevant to the question whether or not the appellant was in fundamental breach. . . .

The relevant contract was made on 7 May 1996. It was negotiated between Anderson[, manager of the seller,] and Rohani Basir, the purchasing officer of the appellant at the material time. . . . In broad terms [the duly executed contract] provided for the sale by the respondent to the appellant of approximately 30,000 tonnes (plus/minus 10% at seller's option) of heavy melting scrap at a price of USD 164.00 per tonne to be delivered at Kemaman, Malaysia. Also at the seller's option 5,000 tonnes of shredded scrap could be included in the goods supplied. The contract provided that the buyer had the right to inspect material at any time prior to loading and during loading. Shipment was to be from "any Australian ports" during July 1996.

The contract provided that vessel details and descriptions were to be submitted by the respondent to the appellant for its approval prior to charter party acceptance. However, the learned trial judge accepted evidence that it was agreed between the parties that the respondent need not formally comply with that requirement. As they had done business on a number of occasions previously, it was agreed that the respondent knew the appellant's requirements with respect to the standard of ship which was to be used to carry the scrap metal to Kemaman.

The contract expressly provided that payment was to be by "Irrevocable Letter of Credit" to be established by 1 July. Any disputes were to "be settled by the laws prevailing in Brisbane". The other terms of the agreement need not be quoted.

The copy of the agreement executed by Wan Ghani[, the managing director of the buyer,] and bearing Anderson's signature was returned by fax under the hand of Basir on 21 May 1996. The learned trial judge found that on the same day the appellant stated in a letter to the respondent that it was prepared to agree to the respondent's request that the Letter of Credit be valid for two months provided that the respondent bore the charges for the additional month. On that basis the letter said that the Letter of Credit would be established from 8 June 1996 and be valid for two months.

At the request of the respondent the establishment of the Letter of Credit was delayed until July or upon nomination of the vessel to carry the goods. Then by letter of 2 July 1996 the respondent requested a further delay in the timing of the shipment from July to August 1996. The learned trial judge found that those variations were agreed to by Wan Ghani on behalf of the appellant during a visit to Australia. That appears to have been in July 1996. On 18 July the respondent sent a fax to the appellant setting out a proposed loading schedule from 19 August to 10 September and requesting that the Letter of Credit issue on 1 August expiring on 30 September. The appellant replied by letter of 22 July stating that it would "establish L/C as per your request once you have confirmed the vessel of the contract".

I now turn to how those matters were dealt with in the pleadings. After setting out the terms of the agreement the respondent alleged in para 5 of its Statement of Claim that there was implied from the express terms of the contract a provision that time was of the essence of the appellant's obligation to issue the Letter of Credit. That allegation was admitted in para 1 of the defence of the appellant. In para 7 of the Statement of Claim the respondent alleged the variation of the original terms of the contract by postponing the last date for the issue of the letter of credit from 1 July to 1 August 1996 and agreeing that the appellant would establish the Letter of Credit when the respondent confirmed the vessel to ship the scrap metal. It was then alleged in para 8 that time remained of the essence of the appellant's obligation to establish the Letter of Credit. Those allegations were dealt with in para 7 of the defence which included in subpara (c) an allegation that time was of the essence of the contract as relevantly varied. There was also a general allegation in para 3(b)(ii) of the defence that time was of the essence with respect to the obligations of each party to the contract.

In July the respondent entered into a charter agreement with respect to the vessel "Dooyang Winner". On 31 July 1996 the respondent advised the appellant of all relevant details with respect to the vessel and giving a loading program commencing 8 August, concluding 29 August, with an estimated time of arrival in Kemaman of 10 September. The defence admitted receipt of that detail.

The sending of those details on 31 July 1996 meant that the respondent had complied with all preliminary matters and in accordance with the appellant's letter of 22 July the Letter of Credit was to be established immediately, that is, by 1 August. That was not done and on 5 August the solicitor for the respondent wrote to the appellant setting out those matters and then stating:

> "We are now instructed to request you to establish the Letter of Credit for the full price of US $4,920,000 by the close of business on Wednesday 7th August, 1996 as the vessel will

commence loading on 8th August, 1996. Should you fail to establish the Letter of Credit by then, our clients will deem it that you do not wish to honour your obligations under the Agreement and have repudiated the Agreement and in such an event they will take action to dispose of the said steel scrap, cancel the charter of the vessel, if possible, and revert to you for any damages which they may sustain herein".

The reply from the appellant's solicitors, dated 7 August 1996, was materially in these terms:

"As your client is probably aware our client is now under different (interim) management and transactions are still under review. The new management team is still studying this matter. In the meantime our client makes no admission of liability".

The solicitors for the respondent replied as follows:

"As you may know, our clients have enjoyed a good business relationship with your clients for over a period of several years. It has been unfortunate that the shipment of scrap metal in question has been delayed, however, our clients cannot wait indefinitely for the shipment of the cargo as that would attract substantial expense.

In view of the foregoing kindly revert by 12 noon of Friday the 9th of August 1996 as to whether your clients are prepared to honour the contract in question".

The reply from the appellant's solicitors to that was dated 9 August 1996, and was in these terms:

"Unfortunately, we are unable to obtain any positive instructions from Perwaja Steel Sdn Bhd within this short time. We understand that the board is meeting some time later this month".

That then resulted in the respondent's letter of 9 August 1996, materially in these terms:

"2. Our clients regret that as at the date hereof your clients have failed, refused and/or otherwise neglected to establish the requisite Irrevocable Letter of Credit in respect of the above contract in question between our respective clients and are therefore in breach of the same.

3. Our clients are unable to wait indefinitely for your clients to establish the said Letter of Credit as our clients will incur substantial loss and damage and will be put to enormous expense if they were to do so.

4. Furthermore, despite our client's repeated requests, your clients have still not indicated in any way whatsoever that

your clients intend to honour their obligations under the said contract.

5. By reason of the foregoing, your clients have demonstrated an intention no longer to be bound by their obligations under the said contract and have thereby repudiated the same, which repudiation our clients hereby accept".

There was no reply to that letter until the fax of 15 August. It merely said: "Though our clients note, the contents of your letter, our clients do not admit any liability. Nor do they agree with your views and conclusions". Against that background it is necessary to consider the findings as to the change in management personnel of the appellant and the new management's attitude to the contract.

The learned trial judge found that prior to 10 July 1996 the respondent had become aware through newspaper articles that the management structure of the appellant was to be changed. On or about 24 July Teo[,the seller's agent in Malaysia,] called on Yunus[, a member of the buyer's new management team after about July 1996,] to congratulate him on his appointment to the new management and mentioned the contract in question in the course of discussion. Yunus replied that he had no idea of the existence of such a contract and was surprised to hear of one. When Teo next spoke to Yunus on 26 July he handed him copies of the contract, purchase order and other relevant correspondence. Again Yunus affected surprise at that information. On 29 or 30 July Anderson and Teo together visited Datuk Abu[, who had replaced Wan Ghani as the buyer's managing director,] and Yunus. There was discussion of the signed contract, purchase order and other correspondence but Yunus kept reiterating that he had no knowledge of the particular contract. Datuk Abu said he was very sorry that this was not part of the hand-over notes between the previous management and that which he headed and said that had he known that there was this outstanding contract he would have asked the officials from the Ministry of Finance to issue the Letter of Credit. He also said he would have to ask the "executive committee" that was running the company for permission to issue the Letter of Credit. Anderson informed Datuk Abu that the respondent had already arranged for a ship and that it was not possible to cancel that charter. He stated that if the Letter of Credit did not issue the respondent would suffer significant loss. The learned trial judge found that Datuk Abu responded by saying: "Since you have already committed to a vessel perhaps you could ship the cargo first and we will pay you later or alternatively sell the shipment to another company.... if you do it this way in future Perwaja will buy scrap metal from you under the new management". Anderson said he could not accede to that request, mentioning the drop in prices since the contract was made. Datuk Abu suggested Anderson and Teo come back later because the decision was not his to make, the decision had to be made by the committee.

There was a further meeting between Anderson and Teo on behalf of the respondent and Yunus and Datuk Abu on behalf of the appellant on 31 July. The latter said that he had not been able to get the committee to approve the Letter of Credit but he might still be able to help and suggested he be telephoned on 2 August. Anderson and Teo again pointed out that the vessel had been chartered and that the respondent stood to suffer significant losses if the Letter of Credit did not issue.

There was a meeting of the executive committee on 2 August 1996 and the Minutes form part of the evidence. Those Minutes record in relation to the transaction in question that the "Management is authorised to re-negotiate and recommend appropriate action in relation to the supply of scrap initiated on 22 July 1996". The learned trial judge found that on the evening of 2 August Teo had a conversation with Datuk Abu in the course of which the latter said that he had brought the matter to the attention of the executive committee and one of the committee members objected that the committee could not proceed with the issuing of a Letter of Credit because the contract had not been made during the tenure of office of the present management. Datuk Abu informed Teo that he would "try again" on 22 August when the board next met. Significantly at no stage up to 15 August did the appellant allege that the respondent was in any way in breach of its obligations under the contract.

Based on those findings of fact the learned trial judge reached the following conclusions in the course of his judgment:

> "The refusal to establish a timely Letter of Credit was clearly a fundamental breach within the meaning of Article 25 and Article 64(1)(a) of the Convention. . . .
>
> In my view the refusal by Perwaja to establish the Letter of Credit at a time when the 'Dooyang Winner' was standing by at Bells Bay in Tasmania to commence loading the scrap steel so that it might complete its loading program either as advised on 18 July 1996 or as subsequently advised on 31 July 1996 was a clear breach by Perwaja of an essential term of the contract as varied. . . .
>
> Whatever may be the explanation for the avowal of Mr Yunus that he had no knowledge of the contract between Perwaja and Wanless there is no doubt that on 24 July 1996 Mr Teo advised him of its existence. On 26 July 1996 Mr Teo handed to Mr Yunus copies of all documents, purchase orders, etc. relating to that contract. He was then also advised that the

shipment of the scrap steel the subject of the contract 'was so to speak actually on the way'.

Thereafter in my view the evidence indicates a simple procrastination on the part of Perwaja to meet its contractual obligation. There is nothing in the evidence to suggest that the appropriate arrangements for the issue of the letter of credit could not have been made within a day or so. Indeed, Rohani Basir had undertaken to do that 'once you have confirmed the vessel of this contract'. . . .

In my view Perwaja by the officers who succeeded Rohani Basir and Wan Ghani in its management clearly evinced an intention not to meet Perwaja's contractual obligation. It is clear when one reads the 'Payment' clause and the letter from Wanless to Perwaja of 18 July 1996 that the provision of the letter of credit prior to the commencement of loading of the shipment to Perwaja of scrap metal was an essential term of the contract. It is clear in my view that Perwaja indicated that it did not intend to comply with that requirement. It is equally clear from the resolution of the committee meeting of 2 August 1996 that Perwaja proposed instead of meeting its contractual obligations with Wanless to embark upon a 'renegotiation' of that contract—presumably in the light of the fall in the current market value of scrap steel. . . .

In my judgment Wanless was entitled to avoid the contract and to recover the loss it suffered as a consequence of Perwaja's repudiation and/or non-compliance with an essential term of its contract with Wanless."

In my view all of those conclusions were clearly open on the findings of basic fact made by the learned trial judge. The establishment of a Letter of Credit prior to shipment was essential from the respondent's perspective. Failure to meet that obligation deprived the respondent of what it was entitled to expect under the contract, and entitled the respondent to rescind the contract. (cf. Trans Trust S.P.R.L. v. Danubian Trading Company Ltd [1952] 2 QB 297 at 301–302 and 305–306 and Ian Stach Ltd v. Baker Bosley Ltd [1958] 2 QB 130 at 139–144). But the findings went even further. On the findings the appellant had no intention of meeting its obligations under the contract; that also entitled the respondent to rescind the contract.

Much of the attack mounted by counsel for the appellant on those findings is dependent upon the proposition that as at 1 August 1996 time had ceased to be of the essence of the contract. That to my mind is at odds with the assertion in the defence that with respect to the obligations of each party time was of the essence; and the further admission that time remained of the essence after the initial time-frame was varied. In any event commercial commonsense would require the Letter of Credit to be established before shipment commenced and at least to that limited extent (disregarding the admissions in the pleadings) there would be imputed to the parties an intention that time was of the essence.

The next attack on the reasoning in the judgment was based on Article 63 of the Convention; it was submitted that the time-frame fixed by the letters of 5 August and 8 August was too short. Paragraph (1) of that Article provides: "The seller may fix an additional period of time of reasonable length for performance by the buyer of his obligations". Article 64(1)(b) then provides that if the buyer does not, within the additional period of time so fixed, perform its obligation the seller may declare the contract avoided.

It is difficult to see the relevance of Article 63 if time was of the essence. If that were so, when the letters of 5 and 8 August were written the appellant was already in fundamental breach of its obligations by not establishing the Letter of Credit. But in any event the appellant had been under notice throughout July, and in particular from and after 27 July, that it would have to establish the Letter of Credit on 1 August provided that by then details of the ship had been given by the respondent. In those circumstances the times set by the letters of 5 and 8 August for extended compliance with the obligation were not unreasonable.

There is also nothing in the argument that the respondent could not terminate the contract because it had not afforded the appellant the opportunity of examining the goods before payment: Article 58(3). That matter is sufficiently addressed in the reasons for judgment of the learned trial judge. . . .

Clearly in the passages quoted above the learned trial judge concluded that the failure to establish the Letter of Credit amounted to a fundamental breach of contract and the respondent in consequence declared the contract avoided by its letter of 9 August.

Ground 13 in the notice of appeal challenges the finding of fact made by the learned trial judge that at all material times the respondent had the capacity to meet its contractual obligations— that is, it had on hand sufficient scrap of required quality to meet its contractual obligations. In so finding the learned trial judge said he had "no hesitation in accepting the evidence of Mr Anderson" to that effect. Anderson had been cross-examined at some length on the issue and the finding was dependent to a not insignificant degree upon the acceptance of him as a credible witness. In consequence the appellant faces significant hurdles in seeking to establish this ground of appeal.

Counsel for the respondent relies on (and inferentially so did the learned trial judge) the fact that the chartered vessel was en route to commence loading at the first port on 8 August 1996. That strongly supports the oral evidence of Anderson that sufficient scrap was readily available to satisfy the respondent's contractual obligations. Apparently some of the respondent's records relating to available stock had been destroyed in a flash flood at its premises, but there was other documentary material tending to confirm the existence of stock in question. That is also supported by the fact that the respondent entered into substitute transactions involving the sale of 30,000 tonnes of scrap of a description which would have satisfied its obligations under this contract.

I am not satisfied that the appellant has made out a case for setting aside the finding by the learned trial judge that the respondent had the ability to complete this contract.

2. CISG and Comparative Aspects of Performance and Breach

Given the general preference for specific performance in the civil law realm, and the general preference for money damages in the common-law realm, it is not surprising that the issue is a difficult one whenever nations attempt to adopt a unified approach to an area of law. For example, the European Union has directed that the governments of its member States adapt their laws to protect consumers in accordance with an EC directive on the subject. Accordingly, in Britain in 2002, Parliament amended the Sale of Goods Act to implement the EC Directive with respect to consumer protection (Directive 1999/44/EC). Part 5A of the Sale of Goods Act 1979 gives certain "additional rights" to a consumer who receives defective goods from a seller. One of these rights, found in § 48B, is the ability to require the seller to repair or replace the goods (subject to certain limitations).[67] The Act further provides that "On the application of the buyer the court may make an order requiring specific performance or, in Scotland, specific implement by the seller of any obligation imposed on him by virtue of section 48B above."[68] Thus, by virtue of its membership in the EU, the English preference for damages over specific performance has been limited somewhat in the area of consumer protection.

Reconciling the different approaches to performance, and hence to damages, was a difficult one for those drafting the Convention on Contracts for the International Sale of Goods (CISG). At first blush, the CISG appears to favor specific performance at the election of the injured party. Article 46(1) provides that "The buyer may require performance by the seller of his obligations unless the

---

67. Part 5A of the Sale of Goods Act 1979 was added by the Sale and Supply of Goods to Consumers Regulations 2002, SI 2202/3045.

68. *Id.* § 48E(2).

buyer has resorted to a remedy which is inconsistent with this requirement." Sellers have similar recourse under Article 62: "The seller may require the buyer to pay the price, take delivery, or perform his other obligations, unless the seller has resorted to a remedy which is inconsistent with this requirement." Article 28, however, also applies:

> If, in accordance with the provisions of this Convention, one party is entitled to require performance of any obligation by the other party, a court is not bound to enter a judgment for specific performance unless the court would do so under its own law in respect of similar contracts of sale not governed by this Convention.

These three articles illustrate the compromise reached by the CISG drafters: a court is not bound to enter a judgment for specific performance if such would not be the usual remedy under the local law that the court would apply. A quick reading of this provision might suggest that a court must apply its local law on specific performance, thereby making that remedy likely to be available if it is a civil-law court and unlikely to be available if it is a common-law court. Yet the language is less prescriptive than that; it says only that a court is not *bound* to award specific performance under Articles 46(1) or 62 of the Convention unless it would do so under its own law in an analogous non-CISG context. The implication is that the court may award such performance if it chooses, and that it need not necessarily treat the case as it would one involving only domestic parties. The court might want to consider, for example, whether or not cover is reasonably available to an aggrieved buyer, or whether the parties had different expectations about possible remedies given the international nature of the transaction.

Even under this interpretation, the potential for differential implementation exists. A litigant with a case that falls under the CISG might choose to file his suit in the State with a more favorable approach to specific performance in lieu of filing, for example, in the United States, if that option is open to him. One of the goals of the CISG is to enhance the predictability of transactions by ensuring that the parties know which law—the CISG—governs their transaction notwithstanding the cross-border nature of the transactions that fall under the CISG. The reference back to local law in Article 28 tends to undermine that certainty by inviting different laws to govern the availability of specific performance depending on the forum.

Remarkably few cases have addressed specific performance under Articles 46, 62, or 28. In a case between an Italian seller of wine and a German buyer, a German court, at the behest of the

Italian wine merchant, ordered the contract price to be paid in Italian lira rather than in German marks:

APPELLATE COURT (KAMMERGERICHT) BERLIN

24 January 1994 [2 U 7418/92].

REASONS FOR THE DECISION

The admissible appeal is partially successful.

The [seller]'s assignee, Appellant, is not entitled to demand from the [buyer] payment of Deutsche Mark [*DM*] 37,143.60. Instead, he may claim payment of Italian Lira [*It£*] 26,601,522.

1.   [Applicable law]

The legal relationship between the parties is governed by Italian law, that is, by the United Nations Convention on Contracts for the International Sale of Goods (CISG) and the *Codice civile*. The sales contracts between the parties regarding the delivery of wine were concluded in the year 1990. At that point in time, the CISG was not effective in the Federal Republic of Germany. The Convention did not enter into force for Germany until 1 January 1991. Up until then, the Uniform Law on the International Sale of Goods (ULIS) was in effect. However, Italy ceased being a Contracting State to ULIS on 31 December 1987 and was already a Contracting State to the CISG at the time of the formation of contract between the parties. The law governing international contracts is primarily determined by the parties' choice of law. The parties to the present case did not make an explicit choice of law. In the absence of a choice of law clause, the law at the seller's place of business is decisive according to Art. 28(2) sent. 1. Therefore, Italian law principally applies to the dispute, because both the [seller] and the [seller]'s assignee have their places of business in Italy. The CISG is part of the Italian legal regime. Consequently, the Convention also applies if it is in effect in one Contracting State. In order to exclude the applicability of the Convention, it is necessary that such an exclusion correspond to the actual intentions and not solely to the hypothetical intentions of the parties. This is not the case in the present dispute, as the [seller]'s assignee also discussed the application of the CISG.

2.   [...]

a.   [Currency of payment of purchase price]

[Seller]'s assignee changed its claim ... and now requests payment of the purchase price in Italian currency. The [seller]'s assignee was not entitled to demand payment of the purchase price in Deutsche Mark. The invoices state the amount in Italian Lira.

The question in which currency the purchase price needs to be paid is primarily determined by the agreement between the parties. In the absence of such an agreement, payment is to be rendered in the currency of the place of payment. The content of the [seller]'s invoices indicates that, under the parties' agreement, payment was to be effected in the Italian currency. In case such an agreement was not reached, the [seller's] place of business in Florence is decisive, following Art. 57(1)(a) CISG.

Notes

3–33. Why would the parties argue about the appropriate currency for payment of a debt, and why would the court endorse the view that payment had to be in a specific currency? Isn't money fungible? Could the Italian wine seller have received specific performance in a common-law court in the United States? What circumstances, if any, might cause a common-law court to order payment in a certain currency?

3–34. The language of Article 28 is carefully crafted. An earlier draft stated "a court is not bound to award specific performance unless it could do so under its local law." The word "could" was replaced by "would" at the request of representatives from one of the countries negotiating the agreement. What effect does this change have, and why might it have been considered desirable?

3–35. How does the availability of specific performance affect a plaintiff's duty to mitigate? The CISG provides that mitigation is a limitation on the availability of damages, but not on other remedies. CISG art. 77. Yet other obligations such as good faith might nonetheless require mitigation, even in the context of specific performance.

3–36. The CISG is an international law of sales, and can be ratified by any country. In developing countries, in particular, the availability of specific performance is often considered to be especially desirable. Why is that?

3–37. In one CISG case, a Russian producer of raw aluminum had an installment contract extending over several years to supply a group of companies operating aluminum casting works in Hungary and Argentina with raw aluminum. The Russian seller was privatized in 1994, and the seller's new owners stopped delivery of aluminum to the buyers in early 1995, pending an internal investigation. The deliveries were never resumed. The buyer brought a case before an arbitral tribunal, claiming that the seller had breached, and asking for specific performance, or, alternatively, money damages. The arbitral tribunal determined that the seller had breached the contracts, and that the breach was not excused by any conduct on the part of the buyer. It also concluded that the CISG applied to the contracts, but did not grant specific performance to the buyer. "[T]he Arbitral Tribunal fails to see how specific performance could be an appropriate remedy for [buyers] in this case. They can hardly expect to be able, under the New York Convention [for the Recognition and Enforcement of Arbitral Awards] or otherwise, to have an award enforced in Russia providing that [seller] must specifically perform its obligations under the various contracts for the next eight or ten years, producing the aluminum and delivering it to buyers."[69]

3–38.   The New York Convention is the mechanism whereby parties to an international arbitration can be assured that local courts will recognize and enforce an arbitral award in their favor. The Convention permits a successful party in an arbitration to seek enforcement of the award against the losing party wherever the losing party has assets, so long as the award was rendered in a nation that has ratified the convention, and so long as the assets are in a nation that has ratified the convention. With over 135 signatory countries, including Russia, the reach of the New York Convention is broad. Why was the arbitral tribunal so reluctant to grant specific performance to the buyers in this case? Do issues of supervision of the performance affect the availability of the performance remedy? Should they, given the CISG's apparent preference for performance?

69. Zurich Arbitration Proceeding, 31 May 1996, *available at* http://cisgw3. law.pace.edu/cases/960531s1.html.

Chapter 4

REMEDIES

A. INTRODUCTION TO CISG REMEDIES

Unlike Article 2 of the Uniform Commercial Code, which—perhaps artificially—distinguishes between damages a seller or buyer may recover, the CISG provides sellers and buyers with the same array of damages.[1] But damages are only the beginning of the story as far as CISG remedies are concerned. Articles 46 through 52 provide additional buyers' remedies, including a buyer's rights to demand specific performance (Article 46), to extend the time for the seller's performance (Article 47), to avoid a contract due to the seller's fundamental breach (Article 49), and to reduce the price it owes the seller to reflect the diminished value of nonconforming goods (Article 50). Likewise, Articles 62 through 65 provide additional sellers' remedies, including a seller's rights to demand specific performance (Article 62), to extend the time for the buyer's performance (Article 63), and to avoid a contract due to the buyer's fundamental breach (Article 64).

As is true with Article 2 remedies, the general principle underlying the CISG's remedial structure is to afford the nonbreaching party the benefit of its bargain by, for example, requiring the breaching party to perform as promised (Articles 46 and 62) or to compensate the nonbreaching party for the difference in price the nonbreaching party paid or received for goods conforming to the contract and the price it expected to pay or receive if the breaching party had honored its contractual obligations (Article 75).

---

1. *Compare* CISG arts. 74–78 *with* U.C.C. §§ 2–706 to 2–710 (sellers' damages) *and id.* §§ 2–712 to 2–715 (buyers' damages).

B. AGREED REMEDIES

The various remedies the CISG affords buyers and sellers are cumulative,[2] subject to the parties' contrary agreement.

... Defendant asserts that the alleged contract contains a provision that limits liability to the purchase price of the software, $10,995, and precludes recovery for incidental or consequential damages. In contrast, Plaintiffs argue that they have suffered damages in the amount of $981,758 as a result of Defendant's breach of contract, and they contend that the liquidated damages provision contained in the alleged contract is invalid because the CISG does not permit a limitation on damages....

Article 74 of the CISG states that damages for breach of contract may consist of "a sum equal to the loss, including loss of profit, suffered by the other party as a consequence of the breach." CISG art. 74. However, such damages are limited to that "which the party in breach foresaw or ought to have foreseen at the time of conclusion of the contract, in the light of the facts and matter of which he then knew or ought to have known, as possible consequence of the breach of contract." *Id*. Plaintiffs allege that the damages and loss of anticipated profits suffered by Plaintiffs ... were a direct consequence of Defendant's breach. Plaintiffs claim that such damages were foreseeable, or ou[gh]t to have been foreseeable to Defendant at the time of the conclusion of the contract terms and were a direct consequence of Defendant's breach....

The terms and conditions and all limitations contained in the alleged contract are not completely superceded by the provisions of the CISG. Article 6 states that parties may, by contract, "derogate from or vary the effect of any of [the CISG's] provisions." CISG art. 6; *see Ajax Tool Works, Inc. v. Can–Eng Mfg. Ltd.*, No. 01 C 5938, 2003 WL 223187, at *3 (N.D. Ill. Jan. 30, 2003) ("[t]he CISG does not preempt a private contract between parties; instead, it provides a statutory authority from which contract provisions are interpreted, fills gaps in contract language, and governs issues not addressed by the contract"). Thus, under the CISG, Plaintiffs and Defendant were free to agree to liquidate damages in the event of a breach of contract.

American Mint LLC v. GOSoftware, Inc., No. Civ. A. 1:05–CV–650, 2006 WL 42090, at **5–6 (M.D. Pa. Jan. 6, 2006). More generally,

the parties may agree to set a minimum or a maximum sum for the damages payable. They may also agree upon a liquidated damages clause, under which the party liable to pay damages for breach of contract must pay a specified sum regardless of

---

2. CISG arts. 45(2) & 61(2).

the size of the actual loss. Nor does the Convention preclude the parties from agreeing upon a contractual penalty, the function of which is to both provide compensation and act as a threat. The admissibility and effect of such clauses are matters for the applicable domestic law.

COMMENTARY ON THE UN CONVENTION ON THE INTERNATIONAL SALE OF GOODS (CISG) art. 74, ¶ 46 (Peter Schlechtriem ed. 2d ed. 1998, Geoffrey Thomas trans.).

JOSEPH LOOKOFSKY, UNDERSTANDING THE CISG IN THE USA
143–44 (2d ed. 2003).

Since the CISG is a default set of rules, the provisions of the Convention apply only to the extent that the parties have not agreed to put something else in their place. And the remedial rules of the CISG are among the provisions which contracting merchants most often seek to amend or displace. . . .

The actual content of the contract will, among other things, depend on the relative positions of the parties. . . . Buyers who enjoy superior bargaining power might, for example, seek advance agreement on a high liquidated damages figure which a defaulting seller would be liable to pay irrespective of [the] buyer's actual loss. Another kind of pro-buyer clause might expressly provide for a right to reject goods which fail to conform to the contract "in any respect."

Well-positioned sellers, on the other hand, often seek protection in standard terms which contain a combination of so-called "disclaimer clauses" which limit both the seller's obligations and the buyer's remedies for breach. Depending on the circumstances, such terms might purport to . . . disclaim the seller's liability for "indirect or consequential loss." . . . [I]n the case of a serious (fundamental and incurable) defect which would entitle the buyer to avoid, the seller's liability would be limited to the selling price (perhaps a bit more).

The starting point seems clear enough: the CISG parties are free to make their own deal, not only with respect to substantive duties, but also as regards their remedial rights. . . . On the other hand, the parties' power to displace certain rights and duties under the CISG . . . may be limited by various factors (within and without the Convention). . . . To be sure, the law still seeks to hold merchants to their promises and to protect their expectations, but a court or arbitrator is not likely to hold a promise binding if to do so would lead to an unfair result. In other words, the traditional laissez faire (freedom-of-contract) view is today sometimes, at least in some places and contexts, tempered by a paternalistic (protection-of-the-weak) view of fairness, so that—even in a commercial environment—an unreasonable or unconscionable "expectation" does not always equate with an "expectation interest" worthy of (full) protection.

Notes

4–1. *American Mint* is not the ideal decision to rely upon for the enforceability of liquidated damages provisions under the CISG because, before opining on the issue, the court had already held that the CISG did not govern the parties' contract due to the plaintiffs' inability to satisfy the court that the foreign parent, rather than the domestic subsidiary, had bought the defendant's goods. However, such is the current state of domestic CISG case law: lacking a case on point, dicta is more persuasive than silence.

4–2. If you were going to start a law library, could only afford two books about the CISG, and solicited the advice of seasoned international commercial lawyers, many—including your authors—would likely counsel you to purchase the most current (translated) edition of PETER SCHLECHTRIEM, COMMENTARY ON THE UN CONVENTION ON THE INTERNATIONAL SALE OF GOODS, quoted above, and the most current edition of JOHN O. HONNOLD, UNIFORM LAW FOR INTERNATIONAL SALES, cited in several of the opinions and book and article excerpts that follow. (Indeed, Professor Lookofsky cites both books repeatedly in his chapter on agreed remedies under the CISG, a portion of which is excerpted above.)

4–3. The excerpts from *American Mint* and the Schlechtriem book focus on—and the excerpt from Lookofsky also mentions—liquidated damages: an agreed sum that a breaching party will pay a nonbreaching party regardless of the actual damages the nonbreaching party suffers. Liquidated damages are only one form of agreed remedy.[3] The parties might also agree to limit the seller's liability to repairing or replacing the nonconforming good or refunding the purchase price. With any form of agreed remedy, it is important to ascertain whether the agreed remedy is exclusive. *Cf.* UCC § 2–719(1)(b) ("[R]esort to [an agreed remedy] is optional unless the remedy is expressly agreed to be exclusive, in which case it is the sole remedy").

4–4. In the excerpt above, Professor Lookofsky suggests another "pro-buyer" agreed remedy: allowing the buyer "to reject goods which fail to conform to the contract 'in any respect.'" Anyone familiar with UCC Article 2's "perfect tender rule" might not think such an agreed remedy would be particularly pro-buyer; after all, under the perfect tender rule, a buyer has the statutory right to reject goods "if the goods or the tender of delivery fail in any respect to conform to the contract." UCC § 2–601. However, there is no counterpart to UCC § 2–601 in the text of the CISG. A CISG buyer can "reject" goods only

---

3. For example, the next section includes an excerpt from an article by Professor Amy Kastely discussing the parties' ability to contract for the remedy of specific performance.

if the buyer has the right to avoid the contract. Avoidance is discussed more fully in Chapter 3 and below. Suffice it to say, for now, that avoidance requires more than nonconformity "in any respect."

4–5. Mastiff Trailer Sales, Inc. manufactures and sells a wide variety of over-the-road trailers. Bunyan Timber, Inc. harvests timber and transports the felled trees to third-party commercial saw mills for processing. Mastiff is incorporated in Ontario, Canada. Its factory and corporate headquarters are located in Mississauga, Ontario. Bunyan is incorporated in Minnesota and its principal place of business is in Brainerd, Minnesota. On or about March 1, 2006, Bunyan agreed to purchase two 65,000–pound capacity pulpwood trailers from Mastiff for US$35,000 each. The sales agreement limited Mastiff's liability, in the event one or both trailers failed to perform in accordance with any express or implied warranty, to repairing or replacing any defective parts and any other parts damaged as a result of any defective part, up to and including repairing or replacing an entire trailer, for one year from the date of purchase. The sales agreement also excluded consequential damages.

(a) In September 2006, Bunyan began experiencing serious problems with one of the trailers it purchased from Mastiff. What remedy or remedies should Bunyan have against Mastiff?

(b) If Bunyan lost a valuable contract while Mastiff was repairing its trailer, should Bunyan be able to recover from Mastiff the profit Bunyan lost on that contract?

(c) Suppose that Mastiff was unable to repair the trailer to Bunyan's good faith satisfaction and the replacement trailer that Mastiff supplied Bunyan failed to perform to Bunyan's good faith satisfaction. How might that affect your answer to subparagraph (a) or (b)? *Cf. Great Dane Trailer Sales, Inc. v. Malvern Pulpwood, Inc.*, 301 Ark. 436, 785 S.W.2d 13 (1990).

4–6. In the absence of an enforceable liquidated damages clause or other exclusive remedy, disappointed buyers and sellers may resort to one or more of remedies discussed in the following sections.

C. SPECIFIC PERFORMANCE

The most instinctively appealing remedy for breach of contract is specific performance: compelling the breaching party to do what it promised to do.[4] What could be more straightforward? While simple in theory, doing *what* you promised to do, *when* you promised to do it, *where* you promised to do it—and for the price you promised to do it—often is not so simple in practice. Moreover, American common law and the Uniform Commercial Code general-

---

4. Indeed, under certain circumstances, traditional civil law principles favor specific performance as the preferred contract remedy. *See* Chapter 3, *supra*, § B.1 (discussing right to contract performance).

ly prefer to award a disappointed party monetary damages than to compel a breaching party to perform. What of the CISG? Articles 46(1) and 62 purport to give a disappointed buyer or seller, respectively, the right to require its seller or buyer to perform as promised, as long as the disappointed party has not already resorted to an inconsistent remedy (*e.g.*, buying substitute goods from, or selling the subject goods to, a third party.[5] However, Article 28 rations the availability of specific performance to situations in which the forum court would award specific performance under its domestic law.

Convention Art. 46(1) provides that a buyer may require the seller to perform its obligations unless the buyer has resorted to a remedy inconsistent with that requirement. As such, that provision would appear to make specific performance routinely available under the Convention. But Convention Art. 28 conditions the availability of specific performance.... Simply put, [Article 28] looks to the availability of such relief under the UCC....

Under UCC § 2–716(1) a court may decree specific performance "where the goods are unique or in other proper circumstances." That provision's Official Commentary instructs that inability to cover should be considered "strong evidence" of "other proper circumstances." UCC § 2–716 was designed to liberalize the common law, which rarely allow[s] specific performance. *See, e.g.*, 4A Ronald A. Anderson, Uniform Commercial Code § 2–716:11 (3d ed. 1997). Basically courts now determine whether goods are replaceable as a practical matter—for example, whether it would be difficult to obtain similar goods on the open market.

Magellan Int'l Corp. v. Salzgitter Handel GmbH, 76 F. Supp. 2d 919, 926 (N.D. Ill. 1999) (footnotes and citation omitted).

Notes

4–7. The *Magellan International* court held that the plaintiff had adequately pleaded the difficulty of cover to state a claim for specific performance and, thus, avoid dismissal. Because of the procedural posture of the case, the court did not find that the plaintiff was, in fact, entitled to specific performance. No further proceedings in the case resulted in a published opinion. Presumably, the parties settled before the plaintiff was required to prove its entitlement to specific performance.

5. By contrast, UCC Article 2 affords only buyers the right to demand specific performance. *See* U.C.C. § 2–716. That said, a seller's right to recover the contract price, *see id.* § 2–709, includes arguably the most significant element of specific performance.

4–8.   Notice that CISG Article 28 *requires* a court to order specific performance if the court would grant specific performance applying non-CISG domestic law. Article 28 *does not prohibit* a court from awarding specific performance in a situation in which the court would not grant specific performance applying non-CISG domestic law.

AMY KASTELY, THE RIGHT TO REQUIRE PERFORMANCE IN INTERNATIONAL SALES: TOWARD AN INTERNATIONAL INTERPRETATION OF THE VIENNA CONVENTION

63 Wash. L. Rev. 607, 638–40 (1988).

Article 28 provides that a court "is not bound" to order specific performance in a dispute governed by the Convention unless it would do so "under its own law in respect of similar contracts of sale not governed by the Convention." If the domestic law of the forum court would require an order of specific performance in a similar contract of sale, the court must order specific performance if the party otherwise has a right to performance under the Convention. If, on the other hand, the domestic law of the forum court does not require an order of specific performance, does the court nevertheless have discretion under the Convention to enforce the right to performance? The best interpretation of article 28 would hold that it does.

The negative phrasing in article 28 is consistent with its purpose. This provision was adopted in order to avoid forcing national courts to issue orders that either were not authorized or were considered unwise under domestic law.... In short, article 28 does not require a court to apply its law to a contract governed by the Convention; it simply allows the court to follow domestic law if it so chooses.

Article 7 further supports the interpretation of article 28 as discretionary. Article 7 requires that the Convention be interpreted consistently with its international character and with the need to promote uniformity in its application. An interpretation of article 28 allowing a court to give effect to the right to performance recognized in articles 46 and 62 without regard to domestic law furthers these principles. Most civil law courts will readily enforce the right to performance under the Convention's remedial provisions; certainly courts in common law nations should be encouraged to do the same.

Interpreting article 28 as discretionary is also consistent with the broad discretion given to courts under Anglo–American ... law to determine when specific performance of a contract should be ordered. Section 2–716 of the Uniform Commercial Code, for example, allows the court to order specific performance where the goods are unique or "in other proper circumstances." In exercising that discretion, a court appropriately considers all of the circumstances of the case, including its international character. Three factors suggest that ... American ... courts should order specific performance more readily in disputes governed by the Sales Convention than they would in other contexts.

First, the difficulties of cover and resale are often aggravated in international transactions. Even though alternative suppliers exist, for example, it may be difficult for a buyer in one country to locate a new seller in another country and to negotiate a contract with him. Similarly, a seller of goods with an international market often will have added difficulty locating and contracting with a new buyer. This suggests that even under American law, the ability to cover or resell in international contracts should be carefully evaluated. While fungible goods may be readily covered or resold in a domestic market, this may not be true in international trade.

Second, the expectations of the parties to an international contract may be quite different than those to a domestic contract. The civil law system, which generally recognizes and enforces a right to performance, has influenced much of the world. Although the expectations of the parties are not determinative in American law governing specific performance, still a court may consider them in exercising its discretion to order specific relief. If one of the parties is from a jurisdiction influenced by the civil law, and the other deals regularly within a civil law system or under the Sales Convention, an American court should more readily enforce the Convention's right to performance as consistent with the parties' general, albeit unspoken, expectation.

Finally, an American court may recognize, in the exercise of its discretion to order specific performance, the need to promote uniformity in the application of the Sales Convention. The Convention's general remedial provisions give the aggrieved party the choice whether to enforce a right to performance or to seek damages.... Courts in most civil law nations and in many other states likely will give effect to this approach and will allow the aggrieved party to choose specific performance so long as this is not unduly burdensome to the other side. If so, American courts will significantly further the goal of uniformity by granting specific performance when the aggrieved party requests it....

Notes

4–9. Other commentators have also argued that specific performance should be freely available under the CISG. *See, e.g.,* Steven Walt, *For Specific Performance Under the United Nations Sales Convention,*

26 Tex. Int'l. L.J. 211, 249–51 (1991) (arguing that, given the CISG's documentary history and existing domestic caselaw, U.S. courts should routinely grant specific performance in CISG cases).

4–10. Despite her apparent conviction (shared by Professor Walt and others) that courts *should* read Article 28 as empowering them to grant specific performance if domestic non-CISG law would require it, rather than constraining them to grant specific performance only if domestic non-CISG law would permit it, Professor Kastely seemed less certain that courts *would* so read Article 28. Consequently, she also explored the possibility of the parties contractually agreeing to specific performance.

AMY KASTELY, THE RIGHT TO REQUIRE PERFORMANCE IN INTERNATIONAL SALES: TOWARD AN INTERNATIONAL INTERPRETATION OF THE VIENNA CONVENTION

63 Wash. L. Rev. 607, 641–47 (1988).

Contracting parties may avoid the post-breach uncertainty created by article 28 by specifying in the contract that specific performance will or will not be available in the event of a breach. Although such terms have been relatively rare in the past, still under the Convention such a term may be advisable. The difficult question is whether such a term will be effective to assure or preclude an order of specific performance in the event of a breach.

In general, the Convention embraces the principle of freedom of contract, and article 6 expressly recognizes contractual choice.... [Q]uestions arise, however, regarding the effectiveness of a contractual term governing specific performance. First, if the contract provides that specific performance should be granted in the event of a breach, can this term overcome article 28? Second, if the Convention does give effect to such a contract term, will the term nevertheless be subject to domestic rules denying enforcement to contract clauses regarding specific performance? In particular, does article 4 preserve such a domestic rule as a rule of validity? ...

A. Contractual Waiver of Article 28

.... Enforcement of a contract term providing for specific performance would require that the court order specific performance even if the court would not normally do so in similar contracts. The contract term, then, attempts to waive, or change, the application of article 28.

Article 6, the "freedom of contract" provision, specifies that contracting parties may "derogate from or vary the effect of any of [the Convention's] provisions." The Secretariat's Commentary to this section describes the Convention as "non-mandatory" and makes clear the goal of giving autonomy to contracting parties to determine their own governing rules....

On balance ... article 6 should be interpreted to permit waiver of article 28....

B.   CONTRACTUAL PROVISION AS AN ISSUE OF VALIDITY

... [A] court may refuse to give effect to a clause requiring specific performance, not under article 28, but rather under its own domestic law, preserved by article 4....

... [T]he drafting history of article 4 suggests that the UNCITRAL representatives considered issues of validity to include only issues such as fraud, duress, unconscionability, and incapacity. The UNCITRAL delegates may have chosen to defer to domestic law on these matters because they involve very significant issues of public policy and the protection of parties. Regard for the principles of internationalism and uniformity can be achieved by a definition of validity that gives deference to very important public policies in the various contracting states, but at the same time limits the category of validity issues to those matters that involve very significant public policies and does not include the vast array of detailed regulatory provisions that exist throughout the world. Domestic rules against contract terms regarding specific performance do not involve considerations of the same magnitude as those underlying issues such as fraud, duress, and incapacity.... A national rule denying enforcement to such terms should not be treated as a rule of validity within the meaning of article 4.

An express contract term concerning specific performance should be enforceable ... under the general provisions of articles 30 and 53. These provisions require the parties to comply with their obligations under the contract. If the contract provides that specific performance ... should be granted, then the court should do so, in order to carry out the agreement of the parties.

Notes

4–11. Recall the essential facts of the problem in note 4–5, *supra.* On or about March 1, 2006, Mastiff, a Canadian corporation, contracted to sell two 65,000–pound capacity pulpwood trailers for US$35,000 each to Bunyan, a Minnesota corporation. Suppose that the contract requires the trailers to be a specific length (based on the standard length to which felled trees are cut before transport). Suppose, further, that the contract is silent about what remedy or remedies Bunyan can seek if Mastiff breaches.

 (a) Should Bunyan be able to obtain specific performance from Mastiff if Bunyan experiences serious performance problems with one of the trailers it purchased from Mastiff?

(b) Should Bunyan be able to obtain specific performance from Mastiff if the trailers Mastiff delivered to Bunyan are ten feet shorter than the contractually-specified length? (In answering, suppose that the substantially shorter length poses transport safety problems that will either require Bunyan to change the way it cuts felled trees or change the way it transports the cut timber.)

(c) Now, suppose that the sales agreement between Mastiff and Bunyan includes the following: "In the event of a nonconformity in one or more trailers due to Mastiff's fault or negligence, Bunyan may insist that Mastiff deliver conforming trailers and withhold payment until Mastiff complies." How might that affect your answer to subparagraph (a) or (b)?

4–12. The art world is all aflutter over a recently discovered oil painting, titled "Snapdragons," attributed to French master Claude Monet. Las Vegas hotelier and art collector Stefan Lüzz, wishing to purchase "Snapdragons" after learning of its discovery, entered into a written contract to purchase the painting from its owner, Sophie Chanceaux, who resides in rural France, for US$12.5 million. The contract requires Lüzz to pay US$1.25 million within 48 hours after the written contract is fully executed; Chanceaux, or her Paris-based agent, Richárd Bonhomme, to deliver the painting to Lüzz within 10 days after receiving the initial US$1.25 million from Lüzz; and Lüzz to pay the balance of US$11.25 million within 7 days of receipt, subject to a mutually-acceptable expert confirming that the painting Lüzz received was the original "Snapdragons" attributed to Claude Monet. Suppose that, after executing the contract and receiving Lüzz's wire transfer of US$1.25 million, Mme. Chanceaux changed her mind and decided not to sell the painting. She promptly notified Lüzz of her decision and saw that his US$1.25 million was promptly refunded. Should Lüzz be able to sue Chanceaux for specific performance and compel her to sell him "Snapdragons" for the agreed price?

D. AVOIDANCE AND FUNDAMENTAL BREACH

A key to many of the CISG's remedies is the disappointed party's ability to *avoid* the contract. Avoidance is not the same thing as rescission—although an avoiding party may elect simply to cancel the contract. Article 49(1) empowers a buyer to avoid a contract if (a) the seller fails to perform one or more of its contractual obligations amounting to a fundamental breach or (b) the seller fails to deliver the goods on time, or within any extension of time the buyer has granted the seller under Article 47(1), or the seller declares that it will fail to deliver the goods within the time permitted by the contract or extended by the buyer. Article 64(1) parallels Article 49(1), empowering a seller to avoid a contract if (a) the buyer fails to perform one or more of its contractual obligations amounting to a fundamental breach or (b) the buyer fails to pay for or take delivery of the goods on time, or within any extension of time the seller has granted the buyer under Article 63(1), or the buyer declares that it will fail to pay for or take delivery of the goods within the time permitted by the contract or extended by the seller. Articles 49(2) and 64(2) constrain a nonbreaching buyer's or seller's respective right to avoid in cases where the breaching seller has delivered the goods or the breaching buyer has paid the contract price.

1. Fundamental Breach[6]

Article 25 defines a fundamental breach as one that "results in such detriment to the other party as substantially to deprive him of what he is entitled to expect under the contract, unless the party in breach did not foresee and a reasonable person of the same kind in the same circumstances would not have foreseen such a result." Article 2 of the Uniform Commercial Code lacks a counterpart. Typically, a buyer need only prove that the good, its tender or delivery, or both failed to conform to the contract. This so-called "perfect tender rule" is the Article 2 norm. The exception is provided by U.C.C. § 2–608, which requires a buyer seeking to revoke its prior acceptance of a good to prove that the later-discovered nonconformity *substantially impaired* the value of the good. CISG Articles 49 and 64 require a party seeking to avoid a contract for reasons other than untimely performance to prove substantial deprivation—a more onerous burden than the perfect tender rule imposes.

In some cases, fundamental breach is easy to prove; in others, it is not. In *Shuttle Packaging Systems, L.L.C. v. Tsonakis*, excerpted in Chapter 3, *supra*, § C.1., for example, the plaintiff agreed to purchase from the defendants certain equipment for manufacturing plastic gardening pots and services necessary to enable the plaintiff to use the equipment. Ancillary to the purchase agreement, the parties allegedly entered into a non-competition agreement requiring the defendants to refrain from competing in any market in which plaintiff participated. When the plaintiff sought a preliminary injunction to prevent the defendants from breaching this alleged non-competition covenant, the trial court found that the plaintiff's underlying complaints about the defendants' equipment and services did not rise to the level of a fundamental breach. However, the defendants' argument that the plaintiff had failed to pay the defendants as required by the contract did create such a

---

6. For further discussion of the concept of "fundamental breach" see Chapter 3, *supra*, § C.1.

breach, entitling the defendants to avoid the contract and the consequences of any unfulfilled obligations thereunder.

Notes

4–13. For an exhaustive—if now slightly dated—discussion of fundamental breach, see Robert Koch, *The Concept of Fundamental Breach of Contract Under the United Nations Convention on Contracts for the International Sale of Goods (CISG), in* REVIEW OF THE CONVENTION ON CONTRACTS FOR THE INTERNATIONAL SALE OF GOODS (CISG) 177–354 (1998). For a critical analysis of attempts to harmonize the meaning of fundamental breach in early cases applying the concept under the CISG, see Clemens Pauly, *The Concept of Fundamental Breach as an International Principle to Create Uniformity of Commercial Law*, 19 J.L. & COM. 221 (2000).

4–14. A buyer seeking to avoid a contract due to a nonconformity constituting a fundamental breach must notify the seller within a reasonable time after the buyer discovers or should gave discovered the nonconformity, unless the seller already knew about or "could not have been unaware" of the nonconformity and did not disclose it to the buyer prior to tendering the goods. *See* CISG arts. 26, 39(1) & 40. For an excellent exploration of express and implied notice of avoidance, as well as a party's ability to revoke its notice of avoidance, see Christopher M. Jacobs, Note, *Notice of Avoidance Under the CISG: A Practical Examination of Substance and Form Considerations, the Validity of Implicit Notice, and the Question of Revocability*, 64 U. PITT. L. REV. 407 (2003).

2. Timeliness

Article 47(1) empowers, but does not require, a buyer to extend the time within which its seller must perform. If the buyer grants the seller an extension, Article 47(2) forbids the buyer from pursuing any other remedy for the seller's breach until the seller fails to perform, or notifies the buyer that it will not perform, within the extended time. However, proving an exception to the pessimistic axiom that "no good deed goes unpunished," Article 47(2) does not forbid the buyer whose seller does perform within the extension from recovering damages the buyer suffered due to the seller's delay. Article 63 similarly empowers a seller to grant its buyer extra time within which to perform, restrains a seller who has granted an extension from taking other steps before its buyer fails to perform or repudiates, and allows the patient seller to recover delay damages even when the buyer performs within the extension the seller granted.

The following case addresses both timeliness and fundamental breach under Article 49. Later in this chapter, we will revisit it to illustrate a seller's damages when the buyer improperly refuses to take delivery of contracted-for goods.

VALERO MARKETING & SUPPLY
CO. v. GREENI OY

2006 WL 891196 (D.N.J. Apr. 4, 2006).

DEBEVOISE, SENIOR DISTRICT JUDGE

I. FACTS

This is an action for breach of contract. Plaintiff Valero Marketing & Supply Company ("Valero") is a corporation incorporated in the State of Delaware with its principal place of business in Texas. At all times material to this action it leased shore tanks at the Stolthaven facility located in Perth Amboy, New Jersey, where it blended components purchased from third parties into various grades of reformulated gasoline. Defendant Greeni Trading Oy ("Greeni") is an international petroleum trading company incorporated under the laws of Finland.

In August, 2001, Ilkka Kokko, Managing Director of Greeni and an experienced petroleum products trader, had a stock of naptha [sic] to sell. One of the brokers with whom he communicated was Cees van der Hout of Starsupply Petroleum Feedstocks, Inc. ("Starsupply") in New Jersey. Van der Hout in turn communicated with Valero's trader, Stuart Burt, who was responsible for Valero's blending operations at Stolthaven. Van der Hout informed Burt of the characteristics of the naptha being offered and in due course negotiated a contract between the parties. He dealt with each party, and there were no direct dealings between the parties. Through him on or about August 15, 2001, the parties agreed that between September 10–20, 2001, Greeni would deliver 25,000 metric tons of naptha to Valero's shore tanks at Stolthaven. At that time the naptha was in stock in Hamburg, Germany....

The terms of the agreement are reflected in van der Hout's deal sheet and were confirmed in a faxed communication from van der Hout to Kokko. The confirmation detailed the agreement in terms of, *inter alia,* product, quantity, quality, timing of delivery (September 10 to 20, 2001) and pricing. The vessel on which the naptha would be shipped was subject to acceptance by Valero's Marine Department ("which shall not be unreasonably withheld") and [] title and risk of loss or damage to the naptha would remain with Greeni until the product passed at the flange connection between the vessel's manifold connection and the shore line at the discharge port.

On or about August 17, 2001, Valero sent to Greeni a written confirmation containing similar provisions. Of particular significance in the present case are the provisions for delivery "during the period of 09/10/2001–09/20/2001" and "from a vessel 'TBN' provided by the Seller which is subject to Buyer's approval and terminal acceptance. Such acceptance shall not be unreasonably withheld." Greeni expressed no objections to Valero's confirmation, and Kokko communicated with ship brokers to obtain a vessel to transport the naptha.

Brokers brought to Kokko's attention the Bear G. He was familiar with the Bear G, having chartered it ten or fifteen times previously to transport petroleum products and having had no problems. In early August 2001, prior to entering into the naptha contract, Greeni and Valero entered into negotiations for the sale of vacuum gas oil ("VGO") by Greeni to Valero. The VGO was to be transported from Europe to Valero's facilities in Corpus Christi, Texas. Greeni nominated Bear G to transport the VGO, and Valero accepted the nomination.

.... On August 30, Greeni nominated Bear G to Valero. Starsupply informed Valero. Jason Welch, who was in charge of Valero's operations and plant, asked Valero's Lawrence R. Smith to vet the vessel....

Smith was [] not aware that Valero had recently approved Bear G for a shipment of VGO. He was aware that approximately a year previously Bear G had discharged a cargo at a Valero facility in Corpus Christi. He called the facility to ask about that delivery, but no one called him back, and he pursued the matter no further.

Smith completed his vetting in about an hour, basing his decision to reject Bear G primarily on account of its age and Valero's policy of not approving vessels more than fifteen years old. Smith informed Welsh of his decision, and on the same day as the nomination Welsh notified Aija Antola of Greeni that: "[w]e have received your nomination of the vessel 'Bear G.' Unfortunately, this vessel does not meet Valero's criteria for acceptance at this time. We kindly ask that you renominate another vessel for our review."

This decision caused consternation at Greeni. Kokko sought an explanation from Starsupply and directly from Welch. No explanation was forthcoming other than Bear G did not meet Valero's criteria. What the criteria were was never explained. Valero stated that the decision could not be reversed.

Greeni concluded that it could not at that point find a different vessel. Bear G had a capacity of 56,000 tons. The Valero cargo was 25,000 tons. Greeni had naptha in Tallinn, Estonia, of the same grade and quality as the naptha in Hamburg. On August 28 it entered into a sale of a portion of the Tallinn naptha to Northville for delivery in the New York harbor, and negotiations resulted in a September 7 sale of the balance of the Tallinn naptha to Tosco for delivery in the New York harbor. Bear G was to deliver the entire load.

[The Bear G was delayed four days before it could depart from Hamburg with the combined load. One of the vessels chartered to carry the naptha from Tallinn to Bear G did not have enough of the right kind of hose to transfer the naptha to Bear G, and it lost two days finding the proper hoses. Two more days were lost because the facility at Hamburg where loading was to occur lacked the capability to do so, and loading was transferred to another facility.]

As a result of these delays Bear G did not sail from Hamburg until September 10, the first day of the delivery window, with an estimated time of arrival in New York harbor of September 21—a day after the close of the delivery window. In the event, Bear G encountered a severe storm and was delayed an additional day.

On September 12 Greeni nominated Bear G to Tosco and Northville. Both buyers rejected Bear G, not because of any deficiency in Bear G, but because its size did not permit it to unload at the Tosco and Northville docks. The parties agreed that the naptha would be transferred to barges and delivered to the buyers by the barges. The buyers successfully obtained barges for which Greeni paid.

As between Greeni and Valero, Valero refused to permit Bear G to unload at Stolthaven, and it was apparent that in any event Bear G was not going to arrive within the September 10–20 window. After discussions through van der Hout, Valero's Burt on September 14 authorized van der Hout to present a take-it-or-leave-it proposition. As for the manner of delivery:

> It was stipulated in the contract that the vessel nomination was subject to Valero's Marine Department's approval. Since Greeni elected to charter the vessel "Bear G," which was unacceptable to Valero's Marine department, the only way to deliver the contracted volume was by lightering barge(s). Although there was no contractual obligation to do so Valero's operational department agreed that if this was possible to try to locate barges for this operation. It was, however, made clear that Valero wanted Greeni to ultimately take on the chartering of said barges and didn't want to be held responsible for any operational delays since the barge market has been very tight for quite some time.

As for the time of delivery and price:

> In view of the current e.t.a. of the "Bear G" on September 20, it has become impossible to make delivery of the naptha within the contractual delivery window.

In view of these facts Valero is willing to accept the total volume of product delivered by Greeni to their terminal no later than midnight on September 24. For this accommodation the contract price will be adjusted by a discount of $0.0175 per US gallon. After this time Valero is not obligated to take any more volume under this contract. For all barrels delivered on September 20, Valero will of course pay the full contract price.

Kokko recognized that it would be very difficult to locate and unload Valero's naptha by lightering operations by the September 24 date, but he felt he had no alternative but to accept the offer. The barge market was indeed tight, partly for seasonal reasons and partly because of pressures resulting from the World Trade Center catastrophe [*i.e.*, the terrorist attacks of September 11, 2001, that destroyed the World Trade Center*]. Valero made a few perfunctory efforts to identify barges that Greeni could charter. Greeni made strenuous efforts from its offices in Helsinki to secure barges but was unsuccessful. It had secured none by the time that Bear G arrived in the Port of New York and was ready to unload at 3:30 a.m. on September 22. Had Valero accepted direct delivery Greeni could have commenced delivery to Valero during the afternoon or evening of September 22.

Valero asserts that as a result of Greeni's failure to deliver any naptha to Valero by September 24, Valero was unable to blend naptha with other components and deliver finished gasoline to the market by the end of September. It was thus unable to execute the sales plan based upon Mr. Burt's calculations made in August. It instead purchased quantities of Greeni's naptha in late September and early October and blended this product with the components on hand. Valero then delivered 294,000 barrels (mb) of 87 RFG on various dates in October rather than by the end of September as originally planned. Mr. Burt testified that being required to effect these sales when prices were falling resulted in a loss, computed conservatively, of $246,900.

Greeni effected deliveries to Northville and Tosco in accordance with their agreements. The original contract between Valero and Greeni provided for the sale of 10,642,170 U.S. gallons of naptha (plus or minus 10% at seller's option) priced against October 2001 NYMEX less discount of $0.1515 per gallon. Greeni sold the naptha originally destined for Valero to the following entities for the following prices and with a claimed mitigation loss (in addition to a claim for demurrage and lightering) as follows:

---

* For discussion of the effect of the terrorist attacks on international trade procedures, see Bart S. Fisher, *Commentary on Homeland Defense—Controlling the Border of Trade Revisited*, 17 TRANSNAT'L LAW. 141 (2004).

Sales	Loss
4,090,855 gallons to Glencore at October 2001 NYMEX less discount of $0.1800 per gallon.	$116,560.87
4,933,351 gallons to Valero at October 2001 NYMEX less discount of $0.1775 per gallon.	$128,267.13
1,959,241 gallons to Valero at November 2001 NYMEX less discount of $0.1575 per gallon.	$80,328.88
TOTAL	$325,156.88

Valero, charging that Greeni breached the contract by shipping via the rejected Bear G and failing to meet the delivery schedule, sues for the losses it incurred by reason of the failure of Greeni to deliver the 25,000 metric tons of naptha to it between September 10 and 20, 2001, or at least by September 24, 2001. Greeni, charging that Valero breached the contract by rejecting Bear G unreasonably and refusing to accept the naptha within a reasonable time after the expiration of the window date, sues for the losses it incurred on its sales effected below the contract price. . . .

III. DISCUSSION

A. *Reasonableness of Rejection of Bear G:* The original agreement between Valero and Greeni provided that the vessel selected by Greeni "is subject to Buyer's acceptance. . . . Such acceptance shall not be unreasonably withheld." The reasonableness of Valero's rejection of Bear G is a factual question. Weighing the evidence, the court concludes that Valero's rejection of Bear G was unreasonable. . . .

. . . . Valero undertook not to unreasonably withhold acceptance of the vessel that Greeni nominated. This obligation requires more than applying internal rules, such as age, which are sometimes applied and sometimes not applied. It requires some effort to ascertain the current condition of the nominated vessel, an effort that was not made here. In view of the fact that there has not been established a valid reason to distinguish between the transportation of naptha and VGO, Valero's acceptance of Bear G in early August and its rejection of Bear G on August 30 cannot be found to be reasonable.

The rejection of Bear G was in violation of the contract between the parties.

B. *Late Delivery:* Article 30 of the CISG provides that "[t]he seller must deliver the goods—as required by the contract" and in circumstances where a period of time for delivery is fixed in the contract, Article 33(b) further mandates that "[t]he seller must deliver the goods—at any time during that period." Bear G arrived in New York Harbor at 3:30 a.m. on September 22, 2001, and would have been ready to commence discharging its cargo at 2:00 or 3:00 p.m. the afternoon of the 22nd. Thus even if Valero had accepted Bear G and allowed it to discharge its cargo at the Stolthaven terminal, delivery would have been outside the September 10–20 contractual window.

The naptha to have been delivered during the window period was to have been blended with other components at Stolthaven. Specifically, Valero intended to use this naptha and other components on hand in its leased storage tanks, such as MTBE, to blend approximately 550,000 barrels of 87 octane reformulated gasoline ("A4" or "87 RFG") and sell it on the cash market prior to September 30, 2001.

Valero claims that as a result of Greeni's failure to perform, it was unable to blend the naptha and deliver any 87 RFG to the cash market prior to the end of September as it had planned. Valero asserts that it would have been able to sell the blended 87 RFG into the cash market prior to September 30, 2001, and that, as a result of Greeni's failure to perform within the contractual windows of either the original agreement or the modified agreement, it was deprived of the opportunity to sell 87 RFG into the cash market.

The fact that Valero breached the contract when it rejected Bear G had no effect upon the timing of Bear G's arrival in New York harbor, because Greeni proceeded just as it would have proceeded had Valero accepted Bear G. Bear G arrived outside the window for three reasons: i) it lost two days because it had to transfer loading operations to a different terminal in Hamburg; ii) it lost two days because it had to obtain additional hoses and nozzles in order to load onto Bear G the fuel being sold to Northville and Tosco; and iii) the hurricane encountered in the Atlantic delayed Bear G an additional day.

If Valero had accepted Bear G, the vessel could have proceeded directly to the Stolthaven terminal on September 22 and commenced unloading. The question must be addressed whether under the CISG this delivery outside the window would have constituted a breach of the contract. If the late delivery would not have been a breach of the contract, then Valero would have had no basis to demand new terms from Greeni, and it would have been obligated to receive the naptha and pay Greeni damages for its failure to do so. The damages would be computed on the basis of the price specified in the original agreement.

If the late delivery was a breach of the contract, then it must be determined what remedies were available to Valero under the CISG. . . .

. . . . In general "[t]he seller must deliver the goods, hand over any documents relating to them and transfer the property in the goods, as required by the contract and this convention." As to the time of delivery, Article 33 provides: "The seller must deliver the goods: (a) If a date is fixed by or determinable from the contract on that date." In the present case the delivery date was "fixed by" the contract—September 10–20, 2001. Article 47(1) provides that "[t]he buyer may fix an additional period of time of reasonable length for performance by the seller of his obligation." This is what Valero purported to do by means of the second agreement.

The fact that Greeni did not deliver (and even if Bear G had been accepted, would not have delivered) the naptha by the agreed upon date, does not end the inquiry. Article 49 sets forth the circumstances when a buyer may declare the contract "avoided."[4]
. . .

In the present case Article 49(1)(b) would not have provided grounds for Valero to avoid the contract because, except for Valero's wrongful rejection of Bear G, Greeni could have, and undoubtedly would have, delivered the naptha within the additional period of time (September 24) fixed by Valero. Valero was entitled to avoid the contract for failure to deliver within the September 10–20 window only if the failure to do so amounted "to a fundamental breach of contract." . . .

Valero introduced evidence concerning the volatility of petroleum product prices. Stuart Burt described the complex calculations which he undertakes to establish the price he will pay for the various components of the blend that he proposes to prepare from the various component products. Valero produced evidence supporting its contention that Greeni's failure to deliver naptha either within the original window or by September 24 caused Valero to sell 87 RFG into the cash market. Valero faced a falling price, and the delay pushed its sale of the mix from the September market into the October market resulting in a heavy loss. If that were all that there were to the scenario, that is, that Greeni's non-delivery caused these loses, Greeni's breach would be deemed fundamental. It would have resulted in such detriment to Valero as to deprive it of what it was entitled to expect under the contract, and Greeni and a reasonable person in the petroleum industry would have foreseen such a result.

But the foregoing does not reflect what actually happened in this case. The delay attributable to Greeni . . . is at most a two day delay. It was ready and able to effect delivery of the naptha on

---

4. The term "avoided" is used in CISG as distinguished from "cancelled" or "terminated."

September 22 and would have done so had not Valero prevented delivery by wrongful rejection of Bear G. Had delivery been effected on September 22 the litany of horrors Valero described in its post trial brief would not have taken place. Valero could have commenced mixing and using the supplies of naptha it already had on hand; the naptha on Bear G would have been available almost immediately thereafter; and Valero could have comfortably introduced its 87 RFG into the September market. Confirmation of this conclusion is found in the fact that Valero was willing to take delivery as late as September 24, albeit at a somewhat reduced price. Mr. Burt testified had such a delivery been made, he could have fully met his plan. . . .

Thus Greeni's two-day delay in delivering the naptha was not a fundamental breach and did not give Valero the right to avoid the contract under Article 49(1)(a). Further, under Article 49(1)(b) of the CISG, the buyer may declare the contract avoided "If the seller does not deliver the goods within the additional period of time fixed by the buyer in accordance with paragraph (1) of Article 47 or declares that he will not deliver within the period is fixed." Paragraph (1) of Article 47 permits the buyer to "fix an additional period of time of reasonable length for performance by the seller of his obligations."

However, when granting the extension of time, the buyer "is precluded not only from avoiding the contract but also from resorting to such remedies as demanding a price reduction . . ." John C. Duncan, Jr., *Nachfrist was ist? Thinking Globally and Acting Socially: Considering Time Extension Principles of the U.N. Convention on Contracts for the International Sale of Goods in Revising the Uniform Commercial Code*, 2000 BYU L. REV. 1363, 1384. Further, "[t]he buyer may not claim avoidance or price reduction as long as the additional period of time lasts. . . ." UNCITRAL Digest art. 49, ¶ 8.

In summation, Valero breached the contract by unreasonably rejecting Bear G. As a consequence Greeni is deemed to have been ready, able and willing to deliver the naptha when Bear G arrived in New York Harbor on September 22, 2001. Greeni was in breach of the contract by failing to effect delivery within the September 10–20 window.[5] The breach, however, was not fundamental and did not enable Valero to avoid the contract. Valero did not have the right to demand that Greeni enter into a new contract. The second contract is of no effect and the parties are bound by the original

---

5. The Court rejects Greeni's force majeure defense. With the possible exception of the storm, the circumstances upon which Greeni relies were not impediments beyond Greeni's control and which it could not reasonably have been expected to take into account within the meaning of Article 79(1) of the CISG, and in any event Greeni did not give the notice required by Article 79(4).

contract. Valero is entitled to recover any damages it would have suffered from a two day delivery delay (and none have been shown), and Greeni is entitled to recover damages it incurred as a result of Valero's failure to accept and pay for the naptha in accordance with the contract and any other damages it suffered by reason of Valero's wrongful failure to accept Bear G. . . .

Notes

4–15.   The foregoing excerpt from *Valero Marketing* raises at least three important issues this chapter has not previously addressed.

(a) *Breach and the seller's right to cure.* First, the CISG allows a buyer unilaterally to decrease the price it pays for nonconforming goods (or demand a refund of any price paid in advance) to the extent that the nonconformity decreases the value of the goods. CISG art. 50; *cf. S.V. Braun, Inc. v. Alitalia–Linee Aeree Italiane, S.p.A.*, No. 91 Civ. 8484 (LBS), 1994 WL 121680, at *5 (S.D.N.Y. Apr. 6, 1994) (finding Article 50 inapposite because the buyer reduced price due to receiving fewer goods than the contract required, rather than due to any deficiency in the quality of the goods received). However, as the *Valero Marketing* court pointed out with the help of Professor Duncan's article, a buyer cannot resort to Article 50 if the seller is able to cure the nonconformity in accordance with Article 48 or if the buyer refuses to accept the seller's attempt to cure in accordance with Article 48. *See* CISG art. 50. In *Valero Marketing*, the only nonconformity of which Valero rightfully complained was Greeni's failure to deliver the naphtha (the court's persistent misspelling notwithstanding) during the original delivery window: September 10–20, 2001. However, Valero subsequently extended Greeni's original delivery window until midnight September 24, 2001 (as Article 47(1) empowered Valero to do). *See Valero Marketing*, 2006 WL 891196, at *4. When Greeni attempted to deliver the naphtha on the afternoon of September 22, Valero refused to accept delivery. Under those circumstances, Valero relinquished its right to insist on a lower price-per-gallon. *See id.*; *see also* Harry M. Flechtner, *More U.S. Decisions on the U.N. Sales Convention: Scope, Parol Evidence, "Validity" and Reduction of Price Under Article 50*, 14 J.L. & Com. 153, 170–71 & n.68 (1995) (reading Articles 35 & 37 to support the argument that Article 50 only empowers a buyer to reduce price "where the goods fail to meet the quality obligations of the contract").

(b) *Use of secondary authority.* Second, the relative dearth of reported U.S. decisions applying the CISG often leads U.S. courts to refer to secondary authority to guide or support their reading of the CISG. Notice the different ways the *Valero Marketing* and *Magellan International* courts use the law review articles by Professors Duncan and Walt, respectively. In *Magellan International*, the court cites Professor Walt's policy argument (specific performance should be widely available under the CISG) in a footnote. In *Valero Marketing*, the court cites Professor Duncan's doctrinal analysis—in lieu of its own reading of Section III of the CISG—as the rationale for reaching its decision.

(c) *Use of foreign decisions.* Third, the relative dearth of reported U.S. decisions applying the CISG also leads U.S. courts to seek guidance from foreign courts and arbitral bodies. We see evidence of this in the *Valero Marketing* court's citation to the UNCITRAL Digest. The Digest, which is available at http://www.uncitral.org/uncitral/en/case_ law/digests/cisg.html, publishes discussions of each CISG article, footnoting relevant judicial and arbitral decisions. UNCITRAL's website also includes case abstracts in chronological order at http://www. uncitral.org/uncitral/en/case_law/abstracts.html. Another excellent source for CISG case abstracts and analysis is the CISG Database maintained by Pace Law School's Institute of International Commercial Law at http://www.cisg.law.pace.edu/.

4–16. Article 50 warrants further discussion. Professor Flechtner offers the following analysis from the perspective of one accustomed to common law contract remedies and UCC Article 2:

[T]he price reduction under Article 50 seems to be based on a principle unknown to the common law. To phrase the matter in a fashion that echoes the traditional description of common law remedy principles, one could say that Article 50 puts an aggrieved buyer in the position she would have been in had she purchased the goods actually delivered rather than the ones promised-assuming she would have made the same relative bargain for the delivered goods. For example, if at the time non-conforming goods were delivered the contract price was 80% of the market price of conforming goods, the buyer can buy the non-conforming goods for 80% of their market value. Put another way, expectation damages are designed to preserve for an aggrieved party the benefit of her bargain; reduction in price under Article 50 attempts to preserve the proportion of her bargain.

Alternatively one could view the Article 50 remedy as a modification of the sales contract. From this perspective a seller could be seen as offering such a modification by shipping nonconforming goods. The buyer accepts the offer by keeping the goods at an implied price proportional to the original contract price. The "modification" view, however, should be handled with care. There are important differences between the fictitious modification permitted by Article 50 and an actual modification. For one thing, a buyer who accepts non-conforming goods and reduces the price under Article 50 is entitled to recover damages beyond the amount of the price reduction—although this could be rationalized as part of the implied price term of the modification. Additionally, the seller might be bound to a price reduction under Article 50 even if she made it clear that she did not intend to be so bound. Thus suppose a seller shipped non-conforming goods accompanied by notice that, if the buyer was unwilling to pay full price despite the non-conformity, the goods should be returned to the seller. It is not clear whether this expedient would prevent the buyer from keeping the goods and reducing the price under Article 50.

Flechtner, *supra*, 14 J.L. & Com. at 174–75 (footnotes omitted).

4–17. Recall the essential facts of the problem presented in note 4–5, *supra*. On or about March 1, 2006, Mastiff, a Canadian corporation, contracted to sell two 65,000–pound capacity pulpwood trailers for US$35,000 each to Bunyan, a Minnesota corporation; the contract requires the trailers to be a specific length (based on the standard length to which felled trees are cut before transport); and the contract is silent about what remedy or remedies Bunyan can seek if Mastiff breaches. Suppose that the contract required Mastiff to deliver the trailers to Bunyan no later than July 1, 2006.

(a) If Mastiff notified Bunyan on June 15 that it could not deliver the trailers on or before July 1, would the CISG have required Bunyan to grant Mastiff additional time within which to perform? If the CISG did not require Bunyan to grant Mastiff additional time within which to perform, did the CISG entitle Bunyan to do so without waiving its right to recover any damages it suffered due to Mastiff's delay?

(b) If the CISG did not require Bunyan to grant Mastiff additional time within which to perform, and Bunyan did not elect to do so, could Bunyan avoid the contract solely on the basis of Mastiff's tardiness? If Mastiff informed Bunyan that it could deliver on or before August 1, should Bunyan be able to avoid the contract solely because Mastiff missed the delivery deadline by one month or less?

(c) Suppose, instead, that Mastiff timely delivered the trailers to Bunyan, but that the trailers were ten feet shorter than the contractually-specified length, posing transport safety problems that will either require Bunyan to change the way it cuts felled trees or change the way it transports the cut timber. Should Bunyan be able to avoid its contract with Mastiff because the trailers Mastiff delivered to Bunyan are ten feet shorter than the contractually-specified length?

4–18. Recall the facts of the problem presented in note 4–12, *supra*. Now, suppose that Chanceaux kept her promise to sell and Bonhomme shipped "Snapdragons" to Lüzz as agreed. Promptly after receipt, Lüzz had San Francisco-based art expert Jin Lou, who Bonhomme had recommended, inspect the painting. Jin concluded that Lüzz's painting was not an original Monet; it was most likely a copy of a previously-undiscovered Monet original. Despite being a beautiful painting, Jin estimated it would sell at auction for no more than US$250,000.

(a) Should Lüzz be able to avoid his contract with Chanceaux, return the painting, demand a refund of his US$1.25 million, and refuse to pay the balance of the purchase price? If so, how should he do so?

(b) Suppose that, despite his great disappointment over the painting's apparent provenance, Lüzz wants to purchase it at its "fair market value." Should Lüzz be able to reduce the contract price to US$250,000, keep the painting, and compel Chanceaux to refund the other US$1 million Lüzz already paid (perhaps with some offset for extra shipping costs Chanceaux incurred thinking the painting was worth US$12.5 million)? If so, how should he do so?

E. DAMAGES

As discussed at the outset of this chapter, disappointed buyers and sellers have the right to recover monetary damages from their breaching contract partners.

JOHN Y. GOTANDA, AWARDING DAMAGES UNDER THE UNITED NATIONS CONVENTION ON THE INTERNATIONAL SALE OF GOODS: A MATTER OF INTERPRETATION

37 Geo. J. Int'l L. 95, 99–104 (2005).

The Convention's damages provisions seek to give an aggrieved party its expectation interest.[21] Article 74 provides that a claimant may recover, for breach of contract, "a sum equal to the loss, including loss of profit, suffered ... as a consequence of the breach." The goal of this provision is to place the claimant in the same economic position they would have been in if the breach had not occurred. In other words, it is designed to give the claimant the benefit of the bargain.

Article 74 provides the basic principle for the recovery of damages under the Convention, although it does not provide specific guidelines for the calculation of damages.... Instead, article 74 grants a tribunal the authority to determine the claimant's "loss ... suffered ... as a consequence of the breach" based on the circumstances of the particular case. It also explicitly provides that damages for breach of contract include lost profits....

Articles 75 and 76 set forth guidelines on how damages are to be calculated in instances where the basic measure of damages

---

21. *See* E. Allan Farnsworth, *Damages and Specific Relief*, 27 Am. J. Comp. L. 247, 249 (1979); Jeffrey S. Sutton, Comment, *Measuring Damages Under* the United Nations Convention on the *International Sale of Goods*, 50 Ohio St. L.J. 737, 742 (1989).

under article 74 may not adequately compensate the injured party. Article 75 provides a method for calculating damages when the contract has been avoided and the "buyer has bought goods in replacement or the seller has resold the goods." Here, the claimant "may recover the difference between the contract price and the price in the substitute transaction as well as any further damages recoverable under article 74." However, a claimant may use this method only if the resale or cover purchase was made "in a reasonable manner and within a reasonable time after avoidance[.]" The purpose of these requirements is to prevent the unfairness of having a party pay for loss which the other party caused through hasty or malicious conduct.

Article 76 provides a different method for calculating damages if the contract has been avoided but the claimant has not bought goods in replacement or resold the goods under article 75. It provides that:

> If . . . there is a current price for the goods, the party claiming damages may . . . recover the difference between the price fixed by the contract and the current price at the time of avoidance as well as any further damages recoverable under article 74. If, however, the party claiming damages has avoided the contract after taking over the goods, the current price at the time of such taking over shall be applied instead of the current price at the time of avoidance.

The price to be used in determining damages under this article is "the price prevailing at the place where delivery of the goods should have been made or, if there is no current price at that place, the price at such other place as serves as a reasonable substitute, making due allowance for differences in the cost of transporting the goods." This method of measuring damages . . . allows the claimant to calculate its damages independently from any cover transaction.[35] If the contract does not fix a price and there is no current price within the meaning of article 76, damages may be calculated under article 74.[36]

The Convention . . . limits the recovery of damages through the doctrines of causation, foreseeability, and avoidability.

In order to recover damages, a causal link must exist between the breach and the loss suffered.[39] Article 74 limits damages for

35. *See* PETER SCHLECHTRIEM, UNIFORM SALES LAW: THE UN CONVENTION ON CONTRACTS FOR THE INTERNATIONAL SALE OF GOODS 97 (1986).

36. Victor Knapp, *Damages*, *in* C.M. BIANCA & M.J. BONELL, COMMENTARY ON THE INTERNATIONAL SALES LAW, THE 1980 VIENNA SALES CONVENTION 558 (1987).

39. *See* FRITZ ENDERLEIN & DIETRICH MASKOW, INTERNATIONAL SALES LAW: UNITED NATIONS CONVENTION ON CONTRACTS FOR THE INTERNATIONAL SALE OF GOODS 298 (1992).

breach of contract to those that were "foreseeable." The Convention employs both an objective and subjective test by stating:

> [D]amages may not exceed the loss which the party in breach foresaw or ought to have foreseen at the time of the conclusion of the contract, in light of the facts and matters of which he then knew or ought to have known, as a possible consequence of the breach of contract.

The latter (the objective test) asks whether a reasonable party in the same situation could expect the loss from its non-performance.[42]

The relevant time to determine whether the loss was foreseeable is at the time the contract was concluded. That is, "[t]he facts and matters must have existed at the time of the conclusion of the contract and/or must be foreseeable at the conclusion of the contract, like seasonal market fluctuations, difficulties in transport caused by bad weather...."[43]

It is also important to note that article 74 "gauge[s] foreseeability in terms of *possible consequences*."[44] Thus, a claimant need not show awareness that the loss was a "probable result" or a substantial probability, only that it was a possible result of the breach.

The Convention also embraces the concept of avoidability....

[Article 77] provides that a party must undertake reasonable steps to minimize its loss....

... [T]he failure of a party to mitigate its losses does not preclude any recovery. Rather, the failure to mitigate results in the claimant's damages being reduced by the amount which should have been mitigated.

Notes

4–19. A party can only recover under Article 75 or 76 if it avoided the contract. Article 74 imposes no such eligibility requirement. Any breach may give rise to Article 74 damages.

4–20. In addition to Professor Gotanda's helpful article, another good, quite recent, source of guidance on CISG damages questions is BRUNO ZELLER, DAMAGES UNDER THE CONVENTION ON CONTRACTS FOR THE INTERNATIONAL SALE OF GOODS (2005). To compare and contrast CISG

---

42. Liu Chengwei, *Remedies for Non-performance: Perspectives from CISG, UNIDROIT Principles and PECL* § 14.2.5 (Sept. 2003), *available at* http://www.cisg.law.pace.edu/cisg/biblio/chengwei–74.html.

43. ENDERLEIN & MASKOW, *supra* note 39, at 301 (emphasis omitted).

44. ALBERT H. KRITZER, GUIDE TO PRACTICAL APPLICATIONS OF THE UNITED NATIONS CONVENTION ON CONTRACTS FOR THE INTERNATIONAL SALE OF GOODS 477 (1994) (emphasis added).

damages to those available to disappointed sellers and buyers under UCC Article 2, see, *e.g.*, Harry M. Flechtner, *Remedies Under the New International Sales Convention: The Perspective from Article 2 of the U.C.C.*, 8 J.L. & Com. 53 (1988), and Kathryn S. Cohen, Comment, *Achieving a Uniform Law Governing International Sales: Conforming the Damage Provisions of the United Nations Convention on Contracts for the International Sale of Goods and the Uniform Commercial Code*, 26 U. Pa. J. Int'l Econ. L. 601 (2005).

4–21.　Professor Gotanda's article is a follow-up to one he published a year earlier: John Y. Gotanda, *Recovering Lost Profits in International Disputes*, 36 Geo. J. Int'l L. 61 (2004). While this earlier article offers some helpful insights into recovering lost profits for the breach of international contracts not governed by the CISG, the CISG discussion is restated and augmented in the more recent article excerpted above.

1.　Buyer's Damages

The following case illustrates one court's application of Article 74 in favor of a disappointed buyer whose seller delivered substantially nonconforming goods.

DELCHI CARRIER SPA v. ROTOREX CORP.

71 F.3d 1024 (2d Cir. 1995).

Winter, Circuit Judge:

Rotorex Corporation, a New York corporation, appeals from a judgment of $1,785,772.44 in damages for lost profits and other consequential damages awarded to Delchi Carrier SpA following a bench trial before Judge Munson. The basis for the award was Rotorex's delivery of nonconforming compressors to Delchi, an Italian manufacturer of air conditioners. Delchi cross-appeals from the denial of certain incidental and consequential damages. We affirm the award of damages; we reverse in part on Delchi's cross-appeal and remand for further proceedings.

Background

In January 1988, Rotorex agreed to sell 10,800 compressors to Delchi for use in Delchi's "Ariele" line of portable room air conditioners. The air conditioners were scheduled to go on sale in the spring and summer of 1988. Prior to executing the contract, Rotorex sent Delchi a sample compressor and accompanying written performance specifications. The compressors were scheduled to be delivered in three shipments before May 15, 1988.

Rotorex sent the first shipment by sea on March 26. Delchi paid for this shipment, which arrived at its Italian factory on April 20, by letter of credit. Rotorex sent a second shipment of compressors on or about May 9. Delchi also remitted payment for this shipment by letter of credit. While the second shipment was en route, Delchi discovered that the first lot of compressors did not conform to the sample model and accompanying specifications. On May 13, after a Rotorex representative visited the Delchi factory in Italy, Delchi informed Rotorex that 93 percent of the compressors were rejected in quality control checks because they had lower cooling capacity and consumed more power than the sample model and specifications. After several unsuccessful attempts to cure the defects in the compressors, Delchi asked Rotorex to supply new compressors conforming to the original sample and specifications. Rotorex refused, claiming that the performance specifications were "inadvertently communicated" to Delchi.

In a faxed letter dated May 23, 1988, Delchi cancelled the contract. Although it was able to expedite a previously planned order of suitable compressors from Sanyo, another supplier, Delchi was unable to obtain in a timely fashion substitute compressors from other sources and thus suffered a loss in its sales volume of Arieles during the 1988 selling season. Delchi filed the instant action under the United Nations Convention on Contracts for the International Sale of Goods ("CISG" or "the Convention") for breach of contract and failure to deliver conforming goods. On January 10, 1991, Judge Cholakis granted Delchi's motion for partial summary judgment, holding Rotorex liable for breach of contract.

After three years of discovery and a bench trial on the issue of damages, Judge Munson, to whom the case had been transferred, held Rotorex liable to Delchi for $1,248,331.87. This amount included consequential damages for: (i) lost profits resulting from a diminished sales level of Ariele units, (ii) expenses that Delchi incurred in attempting to remedy the nonconformity of the compressors, (iii) the cost of expediting shipment of previously ordered Sanyo compressors after Delchi rejected the Rotorex compressors, and (iv) costs of handling and storing the rejected compressors. The district court also awarded prejudgment interest under CISG art. 78.

The court denied Delchi's claim for damages based on other expenses, including: (i) shipping, customs, and incidentals relating to the two shipments of Rotorex compressors; (ii) the cost of obsolete insulation and tubing that Delchi purchased only for use with Rotorex compressors; (iii) the cost of obsolete tooling purchased only for production of units with Rotorex compressors; and (iv) labor costs for four days when Delchi's production line was idle because it had no compressors to install in the air conditioning units. The court denied an award for these items on the ground that it would lead to a double recovery because "those costs are accounted for in Delchi's recovery on its lost profits claim." It also denied an award for the cost of modification of electrical panels for use with substitute Sanyo compressors on the ground that the cost was not attributable to the breach. Finally, the court denied recovery on Delchi's claim of 4000 additional lost sales in Italy.

On appeal, Rotorex argues ... that Delchi is not entitled to lost profits because it maintained inventory levels in excess of the maximum number of possible lost sales, that the calculation of the number of lost sales was improper, and that the district court improperly excluded fixed costs and depreciation from the manufacturing cost in calculating lost profits. Delchi cross-appeals, claiming that it is entitled to the additional out-of-pocket expenses and the lost profits on additional sales denied by Judge Munson.

DISCUSSION

The district court held, and the parties agree, that the instant matter is governed by the CISG, a self-executing agreement between the United States and other signatories, including Italy.[1] Because there is virtually no caselaw under the Convention, we look to its language and to "the general principles" upon which it is based. See CISG art. 7(2). The Convention directs that its interpretation be informed by its "international character and ... the need to promote uniformity in its application and the observance of good faith in international trade." See CISG art. 7(1); see generally JOHN HONNOLD, UNIFORM LAW FOR INTERNATIONAL SALES UNDER THE 1980 UNITED NATIONS CONVENTION 60–62 (2d ed. 1991) (addressing principles for interpretation of CISG). Caselaw interpreting analogous provisions of Article 2 of the Uniform Commercial Code ("UCC") may also inform a court where the language of the relevant CISG provisions tracks that of the UCC....

.... The agreement between Delchi and Rotorex was based upon a sample compressor supplied by Rotorex and upon written specifications regarding cooling capacity and power consumption. After the problems were discovered, Rotorex's engineering representative, Ernest Gamache, admitted in a May 13, 1988 letter that the specification sheet was "in error" and that the compressors would actually generate less cooling power and consume more energy than the specifications indicated. Gamache also testified in a deposition that at least some of the compressors were nonconform-

1. Generally, the CISG governs sales contracts between parties from different signatory countries. However, the Convention makes clear that the parties may by contract choose to be bound by a source of law other than the CISG, such as the Uniform Commercial Code. See CISG art. 6 ("The parties may exclude the application of this Convention or ... derogate from or vary the effect of any of its provisions.") If, as here, the agreement is silent as to choice of law, the Convention applies if both parties are located in signatory nations. See CISG art. 1.

ing. The president of Rotorex, John McFee, conceded in a May 17, 1988 letter to Delchi that the compressors supplied were less efficient than the sample and did not meet the specifications provided by Rotorex. Finally, in its answer to Delchi's complaint, Rotorex admitted "that some of the compressors ... did not conform to the nominal performance information." There was thus no genuine issue of material fact regarding liability, and summary judgment was proper.

Under the CISG, if the breach is "fundamental" the buyer may either require delivery of substitute goods, CISG art. 46, or declare the contract void, CISG art. 49, and seek damages.... In granting summary judgment, the district court held that "[t]here appears to be no question that [Delchi] did not substantially receive that which [it] was entitled to expect" and that "any reasonable person could foresee that shipping non-conforming goods to a buyer would result in the buyer not receiving that which he expected and was entitled to receive." Because the cooling power and energy consumption of an air conditioner compressor are important determinants of the product's value, the district court's conclusion that Rotorex was liable for a fundamental breach of contract under the Convention was proper.

We turn now to the district court's award of damages following the bench trial....

The CISG provides:

Damages for breach of contract by one party consist of a sum equal to the loss, including loss of profit, suffered by the other party as a consequence of the breach. Such damages may not exceed the loss which the party in breach foresaw or ought to have foreseen at the time of the conclusion of the contract, in the light of the facts and matters of which he then knew or ought to have known, as a possible consequence of the breach of contract.

CISG art. 74. This provision is "designed to place the aggrieved party in as good a position as if the other party had properly performed the contract." HONNOLD, *supra*, at 503.

Rotorex argues that Delchi is not entitled to lost profits because it was able to maintain inventory levels of Ariele air conditioning units in excess of the maximum number of possible lost sales. In Rotorex's view, therefore, there was no actual shortfall of Ariele units available for sale because of Rotorex's delivery of nonconforming compressors. Rotorex's argument goes as follows. The end of the air conditioner selling season is August 1. If one totals the number of units available to Delchi from March to August 1, the sum is enough to fill all sales. We may assume that the evidence in the record supports the factual premise. Nevertheless, the argument is fallacious. Because of Rotorex's breach, Delchi had to shut down its manufacturing operation for a few days in May, and the date on which particular units were available for sale was substantially delayed. For example, units available in late July could not be used to meet orders in the spring. As a result, Delchi lost sales in the spring and early summer. We therefore conclude that the district court's findings regarding lost sales are not clearly erroneous. . . .

Rotorex contends, in the alternative, that the district court improperly awarded lost profits for unfilled orders from Delchi affiliates in Europe and from sales agents within Italy. We disagree. The CISG requires that damages be limited by the familiar principle of foreseeability established in *Hadley v. Baxendale*, 156 Eng. Rep. 145 (1854). CISG art. 74. However, it was objectively foreseeable that Delchi would take orders for Ariele sales based on the number of compressors it had ordered and expected to have ready for the season. The district court was entitled to rely upon the documents and testimony regarding these lost sales and was well within its authority in deciding which orders were proven with sufficient certainty.

Rotorex also challenges the district court's exclusion of fixed costs and depreciation from the manufacturing cost used to calculate lost profits. The trial judge calculated lost profits by subtracting the 478,783 lire "manufacturing cost"—the total variable cost—of an Ariele unit from the 654,644 lire average sale price. The CISG does not explicitly state whether only variable expenses, or both fixed and variable expenses, should be subtracted from sales revenue in calculating lost profits. However, courts generally do not include fixed costs in the calculation of lost profits. *See Indu Craft, Inc. v. Bank of Baroda*, 47 F.3d 490, 495 (2d Cir. 1995) (only when the breach ends an ongoing business should fixed costs be subtracted along with variable costs); *Adams v. Lindblad Travel, Inc.*, 730 F.2d 89, 92–93 (2d Cir. 1984) (fixed costs should not be included in lost profits equation when the plaintiff is an ongoing business whose fixed costs are not affected by the breach). This is, of course, because the fixed costs would have been encountered whether or not the breach occurred. In the absence of a specific provision in the CISG for calculating lost profits, the district court was correct to use the standard formula employed by most American courts and to deduct only variable costs from sales revenue to arrive at a figure for lost profits.

In its cross-appeal, Delchi challenges the district court's denial of various consequential and incidental damages, including reimbursement for: (i) shipping, customs, and incidentals relating to the first and second shipments—rejected and returned—of Rotorex compressors; (ii) obsolete insulation materials and tubing purchased for use only with Rotorex compressors; (iii) obsolete tooling purchased exclusively for production of units with Rotorex compressors; and (iv) labor costs for the period of May 16–19, 1988, when the Delchi production line was idle due to a lack of compressors to install in Ariele air conditioning units. The district court denied damages for these items on the ground that they "are accounted for in Delchi's recovery on its lost profits claim," and, therefore, an award would constitute a double recovery for Delchi. We disagree.

The Convention provides that a contract plaintiff may collect damages to compensate for the full loss. This includes, but is not limited to, lost profits. . . .

An award for lost profits will not compensate Delchi for the expenses in question. Delchi's lost profits are determined by calculating the hypothetical revenues to be derived from unmade sales less the hypothetical variable costs that would have been, but were not, incurred. This figure, however, does not compensate for costs actually incurred that led to no sales. Thus, to award damages for costs actually incurred in no way creates a double recovery and instead furthers the purpose of giving the injured party damages "equal to the loss." CISG art. 74.

The only remaining inquiries, therefore, are whether the expenses were reasonably foreseeable and legitimate incidental or consequential damages.[2] The expenses incurred by Delchi for shipping, customs, and related matters for the two returned shipments of Rotorex compressors, including storage expenses for the second shipment at Genoa, were clearly foreseeable and recoverable incidental expenses. These are up-front expenses that had to be paid to get the goods to the manufacturing plant for inspection and were thus incurred largely before the nonconformities were detected. To deny reimbursement to Delchi for these incidental damages would effectively cut into the lost profits award. The same is true of unreimbursed tooling expenses and the cost of the useless insulation and tubing materials. These are legitimate consequential damages that in no way duplicate lost profits damages.

The labor expense incurred as a result of the production line shutdown of May 16–19, 1988 is also a reasonably foreseeable result of delivering nonconforming compressors for installation in air

---

2. The UCC defines incidental damages resulting from a seller's breach as "expenses reasonably incurred in inspection, receipt, transportation and care and custody of goods rightfully rejected, any commercially reasonable charges, expenses or commissions in connection with effecting cover and any other reasonable expense incident to the delay or other breach." U.C.C. § 2–715(1) (1990). It defines consequential damages resulting from a seller's breach to include "any loss resulting from general or particular requirements and needs of which the seller at the time of contracting had reason to know and which could not reasonably be prevented by cover or otherwise." U.C.C. § 2–715(2)(a).

conditioners. However, Rotorex argues that the labor costs in question were fixed costs that would have been incurred whether or not there was a breach. The district court labeled the labor costs "fixed costs," but did not explore whether Delchi would have paid these wages regardless of how much it produced. Variable costs are generally those costs that "fluctuate with a firm's output," and typically include labor (but not management) costs. *Northeastern Tel. Co. v. AT & T*, 651 F.2d 76, 86 (2d Cir. 1981). Whether Delchi's labor costs during this four-day period are variable or fixed costs is in large measure a fact question that we cannot answer because we lack factual findings by the district court. We therefore remand to the district court on this issue.

The district court also denied an award for the modification of electrical panels for use with substitute Sanyo compressors. It denied damages on the ground that Delchi failed to show that the modifications were not part of the regular cost of production of units with Sanyo compressors and were therefore attributable to Rotorex's breach. This appears to have been a credibility determination that was within the court's authority to make. We therefore affirm on the ground that this finding is not clearly erroneous.

Finally, Delchi cross-appeals from the denial of its claimed 4000 additional lost sales in Italy. The district court held that Delchi did not prove these orders with sufficient certainty. The trial court was in the best position to evaluate the testimony of the Italian sales agents who stated that they would have ordered more Arieles if they had been available. It found the agents' claims to be too speculative, and this conclusion is not clearly erroneous.

CONCLUSION

We affirm the award of damages. We reverse in part the denial of incidental and consequential damages. We remand for further proceedings in accord with this opinion.

Notes

4–22. Although the Second Circuit's attention was focused on Article 74, the trial court also considered whether Delchi's purchase of the Sanyo compressors constituted cover under Article 75:

> Once Delchi's attempts to remedy the nonconformity failed, it was entitled to expedite shipment of previously ordered Sanyo compressors to mitigate its damages. Indeed, [the CISG] requires such mitigation.... The shipment of previously ordered Sanyo compressors *did not constitute cover* under [CISG] article 75, because the Sanyo units were previously ordered, and hence can not be said to have replaced the nonconforming Rotorex compressors.

Delchi Carrier, SpA v. Rotorex Corp., No. 88–CV–1078, 1994 WL 495787, at *5 (N.D.N.Y. Sept. 9, 1994) (emphasis added), *aff'd in part* and rev'd in part on other grounds, *71 F.3d 1024 (2d Cir. 1995). Cover is a common buyers' remedy under UCC Article 2. Disappointed buyers often purchase replacement goods and sue breaching sellers for the difference between the cover price and the contract price.* See UCC § 2–712; see, e.g., Hessler v. Crystal Lake Chrysler–Plymouth, Inc., *338 Ill.App.3d 1010, 273 Ill.Dec. 96, 788 N.E.2d 405, 417–18 (2003);* Walck Bros. Ag. Serv., Inc. v. Hillock, *5 A.D.3d 1058, 774 N.Y.S.2d 218, 219– 20 (2004).*

4–23. CISG Article 76's contract-market price differential damages also have a counterpart in UCC Article 2. Disappointed buyers who do not cover and whose sellers have repudiated or failed to deliver (neither of which was the case in *Delchi Carriers*) can sue the breaching seller for the difference between the market price at the time the buyer learns of the seller's repudiation or breach and place of tender or delivery and the contract price. *See* UCC § 2–713; *see, e.g., TexPar Energy, Inc. v. Murphy Oil USA, Inc.,* 45 F.3d 1111, 1114 (7th Cir. 1995); *Egerer v. CSR West, LLC,* 116 Wash.App. 645, 67 P.3d 1128, 1131–32 (2003).

4–24. Recall the essential facts of the problem presented in note 4–5, *supra.* On or about March 1, 2006, Mastiff, a Canadian corporation, contracted to sell two 65,000–pound capacity pulpwood trailers for US$35,000 each to Bunyan, a Minnesota corporation; the contract requires the trailers to be a specific length (based on the standard length to which felled trees are cut before transport); and the contract is silent about what remedy or remedies Bunyan can seek if Mastiff breaches. Suppose that Bunyan made a US$7,000 downpayment on each trailer when they executed the contract; the contract required Mastiff to deliver the trailers to Bunyan no later than July 1, 2006; and Mastiff failed to deliver the trailers on or before July 1. Assuming that Mastiff's failure to timely deliver the trailers entitled Bunyan to avoid the contract, what damages should Bunyan be able to recover if:

(a) Bunyan notified Mastiff that it was avoiding their contract and purchased replacement trailers from Mackenzie Trailers for US$40,000 each, which Mackenzie was able to deliver before Bunyan lost any contracts?

(b) Bunyan notified Mastiff that it was avoiding their contract and purchased replacement trailers from Mackenzie for US$40,000 each, but Mackenzie could not deliver until August 1, causing Bunyan to lose two profitable sawmill contracts?

(c) Bunyan did not notify Mastiff that it was avoiding their contract and did not purchase replacement trailers from another seller, despite losing two profitable July sawmill contracts, and Mastiff delivered on August 1?

(d) Bunyan notified Mastiff that it was avoiding their contract but did not purchase replacement trailers within a reasonable time on or after Mastiff's breach or repudiation because the market price for comparable trailers had risen to US$70,000 each.

4–25. Recall the essential facts of the problem presented in note 4–18, *supra*. Chanceaux, who resides in France, agreed to sell an oil painting attributed to Claude Monet to Lüzz, who resides in Nevada, for US$12.5 million, subject to a mutually-acceptable expert confirming that the painting Lüzz received was the one Lüzz contracted to purchase; Lüzz paid Chanceaux US$1.25 million by wire, after which Chanceaux's agent, Bonhomme, shipped the painting to Lüzz; promptly after receipt, the mutually-acceptable expert, Jin, inspected the painting and concluded that it was not an original Monet; Jin estimated it would sell at auction for no more than US$250,000.

(a) If Lüzz notified Chanceaux that he would not accept the painting because it was not, according to Jin, an original Monet, what damages should Lüzz be able to recover from Chanceaux?

(b) Suppose that, having publicly announced the imminent addition of a new masterpiece to his collection, Lüzz arranged to purchase an oil painting by Henri Matisse that reminded Lüzz of his beloved wife, Eleanor. The Matisse, which had previously sold at auction for just over US$12 million appraised at US$14.5 million. Lüzz bought it for US$15 million, including commissions, shipping, insurance, etc. If Lüzz notified Chanceaux that he would not accept "Snapdragons" because it was not an original Monet, what damages should Lüzz be able to recover from Chanceaux in light of Lüzz's purchase of the Matisse to replace "Snapdragons"?

2. Seller's Remedies

Recall from the prior excerpt from *Valero Marketing* that the district court found that Valero had breached its contract to purchase naphtha from Greeni by unreasonably rejecting Greeni's nomination of the "Bear G" as the vessel to transport the naphtha from Hamburg to Stolthaven and by refusing to accept delivery from Greeni once the "Bear G" arrived with its cargo. The excerpt that follows focuses on Greeni's damages.

VALERO MARKETING & SUPPLY CO. v. GREENI OY

2006 WL 891196 (D.N.J. Apr. 4, 2006).

DEBEVOISE, SENIOR DISTRICT JUDGE

.... Greeni is entitled to recover damages it incurred as a result of Valero's failure to accept and pay for the naptha in accordance with the contract and any other damages it suffered by reason of Valero's wrongful failure to accept Bear G.

C. Damages: Greeni computes its damages as follows:

Sales	Loss
4,090,855 gallons to Glencore at October 2001 NYMEX less discount of $0.1800 per gallon.	$116,560.87
4,933,351 gallons to Valero at October 2001 NYMEX less discount of $0.1775 per gallon.	$128,267.13
1,959,241 gallons to Valero at November 2001 NYMEX less discount of $0.1575 per gallon.	$80,328.88
Other Costs	
Lightering charges	$77,867.70
Demurrage charges (settlement plus fees and costs)	$52,787.05
Total Damages (not including interest)	$455,811.63

Valero objects to Greeni's computation of mitigation damages of $325,156.88 and proposes an alternative in the event it were assumed that the prices set forth in the August 15, 2001, agreement were applied. The actual amount that Greeni received as a result of its three mitigation sales was $4,888,331.42. If Greeni had delivered the cargo by September 24, based upon the August 15 agreement, the approximate price would have been 48.12 cpg. Greeni would have delivered 10,642,170 gallons to Valero and the total amount it would have realized would have been $5,121,012.20. The difference of $232,680.78 would be the amount of damages. Valero contends that the standard against which damages should be measured, however, is not the price set forth in the August 15 agreement but, rather, the price set forth in the September 14 agreement. On that basis, the loss would be $46,442.81. As explained above, for at least two reasons Valero did not have the right under the CISG to demand a reduction in price. The delay in delivery was not a fundamental breach, and consequently, Valero was not entitled to avoid the contract under Article 49. When granting the extension of time under Article 47(1) Valero was not entitled to insist upon a price decrease.

Valero's computation of mitigation damages applying the August 15 agreement figures is the more reasonable appraisal, and mitigation damages in the amount of $232,680.78 will be awarded. To this will be added lightering charges in the amount of $77,867.70. They would not have been incurred had Valero not rejected Bear G.

Had Greeni incurred extra demurrage charges because of the rejection of Bear G and the resulting extension of time of retention of the vessel it would be entitled to recover those extra charges. However, the charter party, the demurrage invoices and the London Arbitration Award each demonstrates that Greeni Oy and not Greeni Trading Oy was the charterer of Bear G and entitled to the claim on account of demurrage. It did not pursue the demurrage claim in this action and there is no evidence that it assigned the claim to Greeni. Therefore, that element of the damage claim will be rejected.

The damage award will consist of $232,680.78 for mitigation damages and $77,867.70 for lightering charges for a total of $310,548.48.

IV. CONCLUSION

For the reasons set forth above judgment will be entered in favor of Greeni and against Valero on Valero's complaint and judgment will be entered in favor of Greeni and against Valero on Greeni's counterclaim in the amount of $310,548.48 together with prejudgment interest and costs. The court will file an appropriate order.

Notes

4–26.   In *Chicago Prime Packers, Inc. v. Northam Food Trading Co.*, 320 F. Supp. 2d 702 (N.D. Ill. 2004), *aff'd*, 408 F.3d 894 (7th Cir. 2005), Chicago Prime, a Colorado-based meat wholesaler, contracted to sell about 40,000 pounds of pork product to Northam, another meat wholesaler located in Montreal, Quebec. Northam, in turn, contracted to resell the pork to Beacon. Northam refused to pay Chicago Prime for the pork because much of it was found to be rancid by the time Beacon began to process it. Chicago Prime sued for the unpaid price. The district court found that Northam bore the burden of proving that the pork was nonconforming before the risk of loss shifted from Chicago Prime to Northam and held that, having failed to satisfy that burden, Northam was obliged to pay Chicago Prime for the pork. *See Chicago Prime Packers*, 320 F. Supp. 2d at 710–15. The Seventh Circuit affirmed the district court's allocating the burden of proof to Northam and found no clear error in the district court's holding that Northam failed to prove the pork was nonconforming at a point in time that would excuse Northam from paying Chicago Prime. *See Chicago Prime Packers*, 408 F.3d at 897–900.

4–27.   An issue that arises with some frequency under the CISG is the exchange rate a court should use when calculating a buyer's or seller's damages. In a dispute between, for example, a Maryland seller and a Virginia buyer, the finder of fact will award U.S. dollars and the court will enter judgment requiring the losing party to pay the prevailing party in U.S. dollars, implicitly based on the value of U.S. dollars as of the judgment date. But, what about a dispute between a Maryland seller and a German buyer? While the parties might have agreed that the prevailing party in any dispute arising out of their transaction would recover U.S. dollars, it is as or more likely that they would not have done so. If the German buyer prevails in a U.S. court, what exchange rate should the court use to translate the judgment into German currency? The following excerpt illustrates how one U.S. court grappled with this issue:

> [T]he general rule is that the exchange rate as of the date of the award should be used. *See* RESTATEMENT (SECOND) OF CONFLICT OF LAWS § 144 (1971); *see also Vlachos v. M/V Proso,* 637 F.Supp. 1354, 1376 (D. Md. 1986). Some courts, however, use the exchange rate on the day of breach. *See Middle East Banking Co. v. [State St. Bank Int'l],* 821 F.2d 897, 902 (2d Cir. 1987) (noting that New York courts apply the "breach-day rule"). The CISG is silent on this issue, and it is proper for courts to resort to private international law in such situations. *See* Joanne M. Darkey, *A U.S. Court's Interpretation of Damage Provisions Under the U.N. Convention on Contracts for the International Sale of Goods: A Preliminary Step,* 15 J.L. & COM. 139, 150 (1995). ... [T]he parties agree that private international law would apply the choice of law rules of the forum, Maryland, and that since Maryland's choice of law rules apply the law of the place of contract, Maryland substantive law should apply. We agree that in the absence of controlling language in the CISG, Maryland substantive law applies. But unfortunately there does not appear to be any Maryland law on this topic. . . .
>
> There is no clear resolution of this issue that is dictated by the CISG or by Maryland law. And, we can discern no particular equitable advantage to either of the two rules—it is not clear that either position more fairly compensates an injured party or does so under the discrete facts here. Under these particular circumstances, the district court's decision to use the exchange rate as of the date of breach was not an abuse of discretion and we decline to disturb it.

Schmitz-Werke Gmbh + Co. v. Rockland Indus., Inc., 37 F.App'x 687, 693–94 (4th Cir. 2002). *See generally* Jeffrey R. Hartwig, *Schmitz–Werke Gmbh & Co. v. Rockland Industries, Inc. and the United Nations Convention on Contracts for the International Sale of Goods (CISG): Diffidence and Developing International Legal Norms,* 22 J.L. & COM. 22 (2003) (arguing that the Fourth Circuit ignored its obligation to international uniformity by choosing to uphold the district court's resort to non-CISG law rather than divining a rule that promoted the CISG's remedial principles).

3. Additional Monetary Remedies

Both the *Delchi Carriers* and *Valero Marketing* courts awarded the prevailing party prejudgment interest. CISG Article 78 specifically authorizes such an award. However, the CISG does not provide a prejudgment interest rate, nor does it provide a means for determining the prejudgment interest rate. In the excerpted portion of the following case, the court squarely addresses calculating prejudgment interest.

CHICAGO PRIME PACKERS, INC. v. NORTHAM FOOD TRADING CO.

320 F. Supp. 2d 702 (N.D. Ill. 2004), *aff'd*, 408 F.3d 894 (7th Cir. 2005).

.... Chicago Prime is clearly entitled to prejudgment interest. However, Article 78 does not specify the rate of interest to be applied or how the rate should be determined; and the parties have not addressed the issue. The court's research has revealed that the interest issue under the CISG has been the subject of great controversy. In fact, "[t]he interest issue, while relatively mundane-sounding, has been the subject of up to 30 percent of total CISG cases worldwide." Tom McNamara, *U.N. Sale of Goods Convention: Finally Coming of Age?*, COLO. LAW., Feb. 2003, at 11, 19 (citation omitted); *see also* Louis F. Del Duca & Patrick Del Duca, *Practice Under the Convention on International Sale of Goods (CISG): A Primer for Attorneys and International Traders (Part II)*, 29 U.C.C.L.J. 99, 157 (1996) (stating that "[42] of the 142 cases reported thus far involve issues as to what interest rate should be applicable to overdue payments or refunds"). One author outlined nine different approaches that courts have used (or authors have suggested) in determining the rate of interest under the CISG, including using the law applicable to the contract in the absence of the CISG, the law of the creditor's place of business, the law of payment currency, trade usages observed in international sale, general principles of full compensation and the law of the forum. *See* Christian Thiele, *Interest on Damages and Rate of Interest Under Article 78 of the U.N. Convention on Contracts for the International Sale of Goods*, *available at* http://www.cisg.law.pace. edu/cisg/biblio/thiele.html (updated July 5, 2001). Another author, finding that the current approaches do not fully satisfy the objectives of a default rule (such as international uniformity), suggests that adjudicators should "customize" the rate by awarding the actual borrowing or savings rate or the lending rate in the absence of evidence of borrowing costs. Karin L. Kizer, *Minding the Gap: Determining Interest Rates Under the U.N. Convention for the International Sale of Goods*, 65 U. CHI. L. REV. 1279, 1302–05 (1998).

However, because there is no single approach used by all courts and the parties have failed to address the interest issue or provide information necessary to "customize" a rate, this court will award interest according to the principles used by federal courts in determining choice of law issues. It is well-settled that "[a] federal court sitting in diversity jurisdiction must apply the substantive law of the state in which it sits," including its choice of law. *Land v. Yamaha Motor Corp., U.S.A.*, 272 F.3d 514, 516 (7th Cir. 2001) (citing *Erie R.R. v. Tompkins*, 304 U.S. 64 (1938)); *see also Allen & O'Hara, Inc. v. Barrett Wrecking, Inc.*, 964 F.2d 694, 695 n.3 (7th Cir. 1992) ("In diversity cases, federal courts look to state law to determine the availability of and rules for computing prejudgment interest.").

In contract disputes, Illinois follows the *Restatement (Second) of Conflict of Laws*, which refers courts either to a choice of law provision in the contract at issue, or to the place of performance. *Midwest Grain Prods. of Ill., Inc. v. Productization, Inc.*, 228 F.3d 784, 787 (7th Cir. 2000) (citing *Esser v. McIntyre*, 169 Ill. 2d 292, 661 N.E.2d 1138, 1141 (1996)). In this case, there is no choice of law provision found in the contract but performance undoubtedly took place in Illinois. The contract was one for the purchase of ribs and the ribs were delivered to Northam's agent in Illinois. "In Illinois, prejudgment interest, whether grounded in a statute or equity, is based on the concept of fairness and is awarded to make the plaintiff whole for the loss of use of money wrongfully withheld." *Platinum Tech., Inc. v. Fed. Ins. Co.*, 282 F.3d 927, 933 (7th Cir. 2002) (citing *In re Estate of Wernick*, 127 Ill. 2d 61, 535 N.E.2d 876, 888 (1989)). The Illinois Interest Act, 815 ILCS § 205, provides a statutory rate of 5% per annum, calculated from the time the money was due under the contract:

> Creditors shall be allowed to receive at the rate of a five (5) per centum per annum for all moneys after they become due on any bond, bill, promissory note, or other instrument of writing; on money lent or advanced for the use of another; on money due on the settlement of account from the day of liquidating accounts between the parties and ascertaining the balance. . . .

Id. § 205/2.

Coincidently, the result of applying Illinois choice of law rules in this case is to apply the law of Illinois, the forum state. Using the forum's interest rate is a common choice in CISG cases, notwithstanding its tension with the CISG's goal of promoting international uniformity. *See* McNamara, *supra*, at 19 ("In the absence of direction, courts have often awarded interest according to the applicable law of the forum jurisdiction.").

The undisputed contract price for the ribs was $178,200.00, which is evidenced in the Confirmation and the Invoice. Based on the statutory rate of 5% and the finding that $178,200.00 was due under the contract on May 1, 2001, simple prejudgment interest is $27,242.63. Therefore, Chicago Prime is entitled to damages in the amount of $178,200.00 plus prejudgment interest in the amount of $27,242.63.

Notes

4–28. In addition to prejudgment interest, the plaintiff-seller in *Chicago Prime Packers* also sought to recover attorneys' fees from the defendant-buyer. *See Chicago Prime Packers*, 320 F. Supp. 2d at 715. While CISG Article 78 explicitly authorizes a court to award prejudgment interest, the Convention is silent about attorneys' fees. Following an earlier Seventh Circuit decision, the *Chicago Prime Packers* court refused to award Chicago Prime its attorneys' fees. *See id.* at 717. In the case on which the *Chicago Prime Packers* court relied, Judge Richard Posner explained the unavailability of attorneys' fees (at least, unless the parties expressly provided to the contrary in their contract) as follows:

> Article 74 of the Convention provides that "damages for breach of contract by one party consist of a sum equal to the loss, including loss of profit, suffered by the other party as a consequence of the breach," provided the consequence was foreseeable at the time the contract was made.... There is no suggestion in the background of the Convention or the cases under it that "loss" was intended to include attorneys' fees, but no suggestion to the contrary either. Nevertheless it seems apparent that "loss" does not include attorneys' fees incurred in the litigation of a suit for breach of contract, though certain prelitigation legal expenditures, for example expenditures designed to mitigate the plaintiff's damages, would probably be covered as "incidental" damages. *Sorenson v. Fio Rito*, 90 Ill.App.3d 368, 413 N.E.2d 47, 50–52 (1980); *cf. Tull v. Gundersons, Inc.*, 709 P.2d 940, 946 (Colo. 1985); RESTATEMENT (SECOND) OF CONTRACTS § 347 cmt. c (1981).

> The Convention is about contracts, not about procedure. The principles for determining when a losing party must reimburse the winner for the latter's expense of litigation are usually not a part of a substantive body of law, such as contract law, but a part of procedural law.... [N]ot only is the question of attorneys' fees not "expressly settled" in the Convention, it is not even mentioned. And there are no "principles" that can be drawn out of the provisions of the Convention for determining whether "loss" includes attorneys' fees; so by the terms of the Convention itself the matter must be left to domestic law (i.e., the law picked out by "the rules of private international law," which means the rules governing choice of law in international legal disputes).

> U.S. contract law is different from, say, French contract law, and the general U.S. rule on attorneys' fee shifting (the "American rule") is different from the French rule (loser pays). But no one would say that French contract law differs from U.S. *because* the

winner of a contract suit in France is entitled to be reimbursed by the loser, and in the U.S. not. That's an important difference but not a contract-law difference. It is a difference resulting from differing procedural rules of general applicability.

The interpretation of "loss" for which Zapata contends would produce anomalies; this is another reason to reject the interpretation. On Zapata's view the prevailing plaintiff in a suit under the Convention would (though presumably subject to the general contract duty to mitigate damages, to which we referred earlier) get his attorneys' fees reimbursed more or less automatically (the reason for the "more or less" qualification will become evident in a moment). But what if the defendant won? Could he invoke the domestic law, if as is likely other than in the United States that law entitled either side that wins to reimbursement of his fees by the loser? Well, if so, could a winning plaintiff waive his right to attorneys' fees under the Convention in favor of domestic law, which might be more or less generous than Article 74, since Article 74 requires that any loss must, to be recoverable, be foreseeable, which beyond some level attorneys' fees, though reasonable ex post, might not be? And how likely is it that the United States would have signed the Convention had it thought that in doing so it was abandoning the hallowed American rule? To the vast majority of the signatories of the Convention, being nations in which loser pays is the rule anyway, the question whether "loss" includes attorneys' fees would have held little interest; there is no reason to suppose they thought about the question at all.

For these reasons, we conclude that "loss" in Article 74 does not include attorneys' fees. . . .

Zapata Hermanos Sucesores, S.A. v. Hearthside Baking Co., 313 F.3d 385, 388–89 (7th Cir. 2002); *see also* Harry M. Flechtner, *Recovering Attorneys' Fees as Damages Under the U.S. Sales Convention: The Role of Case Law in the New International Commercial Practice, with Comments on* Zapata Hermanos v. Hearthside Baking, 22 Nw. J. Int'l L. & Bus. 121, 156–59 (2002) (arguing that U.S. courts should not award attorneys' fees to prevailing parties under Article 74 and opining that the district court in *Zapata Hermanos* erred by awarded Zapata its attorneys' fees).

Foreign courts and arbitral tribunals, as well as distinguished commentators, are divided on the recoverability of attorneys' fees under the CISG. *See* John Y. Gotanda, *Awarding Damages Under the United Nations Convention on the International Sale of Goods: A Matter of Interpretation*, 37 Geo. J. Int'l L. 95, 112–16 (2005) (collecting cases and commentary). That said,

> Most courts and tribunals that have resolved contract disputes governed by the Convention have allowed the successful claimant to recover litigation expenses. . . . [I]n many of these decisions the court or tribunal did not explain whether the source of authority

for awarding fees and costs to the prevailing party was based on article 74 or applicable procedural law. One decision where the court did make such a distinction was the decision of the Amtsgericht Viechtach of April 11, 2002. In that case, the court held the seller was entitled to attorneys' fees because the word "loss" in article 74 encompasses the cost of pursuing one's rights.... [T]he Amtsgericht Viechtach decision and a subsequent decision from a District Court in Berlin stand for the notion that article 74 allows for the recovery of attorneys' fees.

Id. at 115–16 (footnotes omitted).

4–29. Recall the essential facts of the problem presented in note 4–18, *supra.* Chanceaux, who resides in France, agreed to sell an oil painting attributed to Claude Monet to Lüzz, who resides in Nevada, for US$12.5 million, subject to a mutually-acceptable expert confirming that the painting Lüzz received was the one Lüzz contracted to purchase. Lüzz paid Chanceaux US$1.25 million by wire, after which Chanceaux's agent, Bonhomme, shipped the painting to Lüzz. Promptly after receipt, the mutually-acceptable expert, Jin, inspected the painting and concluded that it was not an original Monet; Jin estimated it would sell at auction for no more than US$250,000. Suppose that Lüzz notified Chanceaux that he would not accept the painting because it was not, according to Jin, an original Monet, and that Lüzz would make appropriate arrangements to return the painting to Chanceaux, at Lüzz's expense, upon Chanceaux's refund of Lüzz's US$1.25 million. Suppose further that Chanceaux refused to refund Lüzz's US$1.25 million and demanded that he remit the balance due because, by the terms of their contract, Lüzz agreed to pay the full purchase price provided that a mutually-acceptable expert confirmed that the painting Lüzz received was the original "Snapdragons" attributed to Claude Monet, not that the painting Lüzz received was by Claude Monet.

(a) If Lüzz refused to pay the US$11.25 million balance due, and Chanceaux successfully sued Lüzz for breach of contract, what monetary damages should Chanceaux be able to recover from Lüzz?

(b) Assuming that their contract was silent about the remedies to which an injured party would be entitled, should Chanceaux be able to recover prejudgment interest from Lüzz? What about her attorneys' fees and other litigation expenses?

F. MITIGATION OF DAMAGES— A COMPARATIVE VIEW

There are parallels between common law and European approaches to mitigation of damages, in so far as neither legal tradition would permit the nonbreaching party to recover damages that he or she has already voluntarily mitigated. The nonbreaching party should be compensated commensurate with the loss suffered, but not beyond that measure—*tout le préjudice mais rien que le préjudice*.[45] However, the French Civil Code contains no provision generally *requiring* a claimant to mitigate his or her loss.[46] Indeed, mitigation as a duty has only been raised in such specialized areas of French law as leasing,[47] insurance,[48] and, of course, international sale of goods.[49] In contrast, Germany,[50] Italy,[51] and Belgium[52] have more recently accepted a duty to mitigate. Mitigation of damages is also included in the PRINCIPLES OF EUROPEAN CONTRACT LAW[53] prepared by the Commission on European Contract Law. The UNIDROIT PRINCIPLES contains the following provisions:

Article 7.4.5

Where the aggrieved party has terminated the contract and has made a replacement transaction within a reasonable time and in a reasonable manner it may recover the difference between the contract price and the price of the replacement transaction as well as damages for any further harm.

Article 7.4.8

(1) The non-performing party is not liable for harm suffered by the aggrieved party to the extent that the harm could have been reduced by the latter party's take reasonable steps.

(2) The aggrieved party is entitled to recover any expenses reasonably incurred in attempting to reduce the harm.

Notes

4–30. Assume that on 1 May *Herr A*, a German national traveling on business, requests *B GmbH*, a German company, to reserve a hotel room in Frankfurt for 1 June, at a cost of € 200. On 14 May, *A*

---

45. *See* Solène Le Pautremat, *Mitigation of Damage: A French Perspective*, 55 Int'l & Comp. L.Q. 205, 206 (2006) (citing Cass civ (20 Dec 1966) D 1967, 169; Cass 2ème civ (23 Jan 2003) Bull Civ II, No 20; Cass 1ère civ (25 Mar 2003) Bull inf).

46. Hanotiau, *Régime Juridique et Portée de l'Obligation de Modérer le Dommage dans les Ordres Juridiques Nationaux et le Droit du Commerce International*, REVUE DE DROIT DES AFFAIRES INTERNATIONALES 393, 398 (1987). The civil law concept of good faith has sometimes been invoked in lieu of a principle of mitigation. *See* Le Pautremat, *Mitigation of Damage*, 55 Int'l & Comp. L.Q. at 207 (citing Court of Appeal of Paris (22 June 2001) D 2002, 843, in which claimant, declining to exercise contractual option that would have terminated contract with debtor, was held to be acting in bad faith).

47. Code Civ., art. 1760.

48. Insurance Code, art. L172–23.

49. CISG, arts. 75, 77 (in force in France since 1988).

50. BGB 254(2).

51. Italian Civ. Code, art. 1227(2).

52. *See* Le Pautremat, *Mitigation of Damage*, 55 Int'l & Comp. L.Q. at 212 (suggesting that Belgian mitigation principle is "subspecies of contributory negligence," or is enforced "on the ground of 'abuse of right' ").

53. Principles of European Contract Law, art. 9:505(1), (2).

discovers that *B* has failed to make the reservation. *A* makes his own reservation on 25 May, but can only find a comparable room at € 300. If *A* had made his own reservation on 15 May, a comparable room would have been available at € 250. Under German law, what damages could *A* recover against *B*? What result under the UNIDROIT Principles? Under the European Principles?

4–31. The facts are the same as in 4–30, except that *A* makes his own reservation on 15 May at the Intercontinental Hotel, a luxury hotel, for € 500. Under German law, what damages could *A* recover? What result under the UNIDROIT Principles? Under the European Principles?

4–32. Assume that on 1 May *Herr A* had contracted with American Express Travel Services (AMEX) to reserve a hotel room in New York for 1 June, at a cost of US$400. On 14 May, *A* discovers that AMEX has failed to make the reservation. *A* makes his own reservation on 25 May, but can only find a comparable room at US$500. Assume that, if *A* had made his own reservation on 15 May, a comparable room would have been available at US$450. Under U.S. law, what damages could *A* recover against *B*? What result under the UNIDROIT Principles? Under the CISG?

4–33. The facts are the same as in 4–32, except that *A* makes his own reservation on 15 May at a boutique hotel on the East Side of Manhattan, for US$600. Under U.S. law, what damages could *A* recover? What result under the UNIDROIT Principles? Under the CISG?

SELECTED BIBLIOGRAPHY

1. INTRODUCTION

C. AUBRY & C. RAU, IV COURS DE DROIT CIVIL FRANÇAIS: OBLIGATIONS (Louisiana State Law Institute, trans. 6th ed. 1965).

KLAUS PETER BERGER, THE CREEPING CODIFICATION OF THE LEX MERCATORIA (1999).

C.M. BIANCA & M.J. BONELL, COMMENTARY ON THE INTERNATIONAL SALES LAW: THE 1980 VIENNA SALES CONVENTION (1987).

MICHAEL JOACHIM BONELL, AN INTERNATIONAL RESTATEMENT OF CONTRACT LAW: THE UNIDROIT PRINCIPLES OF INTERNATIONAL COMMERCIAL CONTRACTS (3d ed. 2005).

MICHAEL JOACHIM BONNELL (ed.), THE UNIDROIT PRINCIPLES IN PRACTICE: CASELAW AND BIBLIOGRAPHY ON THE UNIDROIT PRINCIPLES OF COMMERCIAL CONTRACTS (2d ed. 2005).

LARRY A. DIMATTEO ET AL., INTERNATIONAL SALES LAW: AN ANALYSIS OF CISG JURISPRUDENCE (2005).

FRITZ ENDERLEIN & DIETRICH MASKOW, INTERNATIONAL SALES LAW (1992).

FRANCO FERRARI, THE SPHERE OF APPLICATION OF THE VIENNA SALES CONVENTION (1995).

RALPH H. FOLSOM, MICHAEL WALLACE GORDON & JOHN A. SPANOGLE, JR., INTERNATIONAL BUSINESS TRANSACTIONS (2d ed. 2001).

HENRY GABRIEL, CONTRACTS FOR THE SALE OF GOODS: A COMPARISON OF THE DOMESTIC AND INTERNATIONAL LAW (2004).

VIVIAN GROSSWALD CURRAN, COMPARATIVE LAW: AN INTRODUCTION (2002).

ARTHUR HARTKAMP ET AL. (eds.), TOWARDS A EUROPEAN CIVIL CODE (2d ed. 1998).

JOHN O. HONNOLD, UNIFORM LAW FOR INTERNATIONAL SALES UNDER THE 1980 UNITED NATIONS CONVENTION (3d ed. 1999).

NORBERT HORN, HEIN KÖTZ & HANS G. LESER (eds.), GERMAN PRIVATE AND COMMERCIAL LAW: AN INTRODUCTION (1982) (trans. Tony Weir).

INTERNATIONAL INSTITUTE FOR THE UNIFICATION OF PRIVATE LAW, UNIDROIT PRINCIPLES OF INTERNATIONAL COMMERCIAL CONTRACTS (2004).

ALBERT H. KRITZER, GUIDE TO PRACTICAL APPLICATIONS OF THE UNITED NATIONS CONVENTION ON CONTRACTS FOR THE INTERNATIONAL SALE OF GOODS (1989).

G. GREGORY LETTERMAN, UNIDROIT's RULES IN PRACTICE: STANDARD INTERNATIONAL CONTRACTS AND APPLICABLE RULES (2001).

JOSEPH LOOKOFSKY, UNDERSTANDING THE CISG IN THE USA (2d ed. 2004).

DANIEL BARSTOW MAGRAW & REED R. KATHREIN, THE CONVENTION FOR THE INTERNATIONAL SALE OF GOODS: A HANDBOOK OF BASIC MATERIALS (2d ed. 1990).

BARRY NICHOLAS, THE FRENCH LAW OF CONTRACT (2d ed. 1992).

JAN RAMBERG, INTERNATIONAL COMMERCIAL TRANSACTIONS (2000).

PETAR SARCEVIC & PAUL VOLKEN (eds.), THE INTERNATIONAL SALE OF GOODS REVISITED (2001).

PETER SCHLECHTRIEM, UNIFORM SALES LAW: THE UN CONVENTION ON CONTRACTS FOR THE INTERNATIONAL SALE OF GOODS (1986).

PETER SCHLECHTRIEM & INGEBORG SCHWENZER (eds.), COMMENTARY ON THE UN CONVENTION ON THE INTERNATIONAL SALE OF GOODS (CISG) (2d (English) ed. 2005).

Fatima Akaddaf, *Application of the United Nations Convention on Contracts for the International Sale of Goods (CISG) to Arab Islamic Countries: Is the CISG Compatible With Islamic Law Principles?*, 13 PACE INT'L L. REV. 1 (2001).

Camilla Baasch Andersen, *Furthering the Uniform Application of the CISG: Sources of Law on the Internet*, 10 PACE INT'L L. REV. 403 (1998).

James E. Bailey, *Facing the Truth: Seeing the CISG as an Obstacle to a Uniform Law of International Sales*, 32 CORNELL INT'L L.J. 273 (1999).

Michael Joachim Bonell, *Soft Law and Party Autonomy: The Case of the UNIDROIT Principles*, 51 LOY. L. REV. 229 (2005).

————, *From UNIDROIT Principles 1994 to UNIDROIT Principles 2004: A Further Step Towards a Global Contract Law*, 37 U.C.C.L.J. 1 (2004).

_____, *The UNIDROIT Principles of International Commercial Contracts: Why? What? How?*, 69 Tul. L. Rev. 1121 (1995).

_____ & Fabio Liguori, *The U.N. Convention on the International Sale of Goods: A Critical Analysis of Current International Case Law (Part I)*, 1 Unif. L. Rev. 147 (1996).

_____, *The U.N. Convention on the International Sale of Goods: a Critical Analysis of Current International Case Law (Part II)*, 1 Unif. L. Rev. 359 (1996).

_____, *The U.N. Convention on the International Sale of Goods: A Critical Analysis of Current International Case Law*, 2 Unif. L. Rev. 385 (1997).

Ronald A. Brand, *CISG Article 31: When Substantive Law Rules Affect Jurisdictional Results*, 25 J.L. & Com. 181 (2005).

_____, *Professional Responsibility in a Transnational Transactions Practice*, 17 J.L. & Com. 301 (1998).

_____ & Harry M. Flechtner, *Arbitration and Contract Formation in International Trade: First Interpretations of the U.N. Sales Convention*, 12 J.L. & Com. 239 (1993).

Michael G. Bridge, *Uniformity and Diversity in the Law of International Sale*, 15 Pace Int'l L. Rev. 55 (2003).

_____, *The Bifocal World of International Sales: Vienna and Non-Vienna*, *in* Making Commercial Law: Essays in Honor of Roy Goode 277 (Ross Cranston ed. 1997).

Gabrielle S. Brussel, *The 1980 United Nations Convention on Contracts for the International Sale of Goods: A Legislative Study of the North–South Debates*, 6 N.Y. Int'l L. Rev. 53 (1993).

James J. Callaghan, *U.N. Convention on Contracts for the International Sale of Goods: Examining the Gap–Filling Role of CISG in Two French Decisions*, 14 J.L. & Com. 183 (1995).

CISG Advisory Council, *CISG Advisory Council Opinion No. 4: Contracts for the Sale of Goods to be Manufactured or Produced and Mixed Contracts (Article 3 CISG)*, 17 Pace Int'l L. Rev. 79 (2005).

_____, *CISG Advisory Council Opinion No. 1: Electronic Communications Under CISG*, 15 Pace Int'l L. Rev. 453 (2003).

S.K. Date–Bah, *Vienna Sales Convention 1980–Developing Countries' Perspectives*, *in* Current Developments in International Transfers of Goods & Services 87 (L. Rao Penna et al. eds. 1994).

Louis F. Del Duca, *Globalization, Regionalization and Transplants in Commercial and Consumer Law*, 23 Penn St. Int'l L. Rev. 491 (2005).

Larry A. DiMatteo, *An International Contract Law Formula: The Informality of International Business Transactions Plus the*

Internationalization of Contract Law Equals Unexpected Contractual Liability, 23 SYRACUSE J. INT'L L. & COM. 67 (1997).

Larry A. DiMatteo et al., *The Interpretive Turn in International Sales Law: An Analysis of Fifteen Years of CISG Jurisprudence*, 24 NW. J. INT'L L. & BUS. 299 (2004).

E. Allan Farnsworth, *The American Provenance of the UNIDROIT Principles*, 72 TUL. L. REV. 1985 (1998).

Franco Ferrari, *Remarks on the UNCITRAL Digest's Comments on Article 6 CISG*, 25 J.L. & COM. 13 (2005).

_____, *What Sources of Law for Contracts for the International Sale of Goods? Why One Has to Look Beyond the CISG*, 25 INT'L REV. L. & ECON. 314 (2005).

_____, *The Relationship Between International Uniform Contract Law Conventions*, 22 J.L. & COM. 57 (2003).

_____, *"Forum Shopping" Despite International Uniform Contract Law Conventions*, 51 INT'L & COMP. L.Q. 689 (2002).

_____, *The Relationship Between the UCC and the CISG and the Construction of Uniform Law*, 29 LOY. L.A. L. REV. 1021 (1996).

_____, *Specific Topics of the CISG in the Light of Judicial Application and Scholarly Writing*, 15 J.L. & COM. 1 (1995).

_____, *Uniform Interpretation of the 1980 Uniform Sales Law*, 24 GA. J. INT'L & COMP. L. 183 (1994).

Harry M. Flechtner et al., *Transcript of a Workshop on the Sales Convention: Leading CISG Scholars Discuss Contract Formation, Validity, Excuse for Hardship, Avoidance, Nachfrist, Contract Interpretation, Parol Evidence, Analogical Application, and Much More*, 18 J.L. & COM. 191 (1999).

Harry M. Flechtner & Joseph Lookofsky, *Viva* Zapata*! American Procedure and CISG Substance in a U.S. Circuit Court of Appeal*, 7 VINDOBONA J. INT'L COM. L. & ARB. 93 (2003).

Angelo Forte, *The United Nations Convention on Contracts for the International Sale of Goods: Reason and Unreason in the United Kingdom*, 26 U. BALT. L. REV. 51 (1997).

David Frisch, *Commercial Common Law, the United Nations Convention on Contracts for the International Sale of Goods, and the Inertia of Habit*, 74 TUL. L. REV. 495 (1999).

Henry D. Gabriel, *A Primer on the United Nations Convention on the International Sale of Goods: From the Perspective of the Uniform Commercial Code*, 7 IND. INT'L & COMP. L. REV. 2 (1997).

Karen B. Gianuzzi, *The Convention on Contracts for the International Sale of Goods: Temporarily Out of "Service"?*, 28 L. & POL'Y INT'L BUS. 991 (1997).

Clayton P. Gillette & Robert E. Scott, *The Political Economy of International Sales Law*, 25 INT'L REV. L. & ECON. 446 (2005).

Roy Goode, *Rule, Practice, and Pragmatism in Transnational Commercial Law*, 54 INT'L & COMP. L.Q. 539 (2005).

Eduardo Grebler, *The Convention on International Sale of Goods and Brazilian Law: Are Differences Irreconcilable?*, 25 J.L. & COM. 467 (2005).

John Gregory, Note, *Uniform Contract Law of the People's Republic of China: First Comparative Look*, 12 FLA. J. INT'L L. 467 (1998–2000).

Annemarie Großhans, *Reflections on the Scope of the Applicability of the 1980 U.N. Convention on Contracts for the International Sale of Goods*, 9 VINDOBONA J. INT'L COM. L. & ARB. 223 (2005).

Philip Hackney, Note, *Is the CISG Achieving Uniformity?*, 61 LA. L. REV. 473 (2001).

Sunil R. Harjani, *The Convention on Contracts for the International Sale of Goods in United States Courts*, 23 HOUS. J. INT'L L. 49 (2000).

Helen Elizabeth Hartnell, *Rousing the Sleeping Dog: The Validity Exception to the Convention on Contracts for the International Sale of Goods*, 18 YALE J. INT'L L. 1 (1993).

Jeffrey R. Hartwig, Note, Schmitz–Werke GmbH & Co. v. Rockland Industries, Inc. *and the United Nations Convention on Contracts for the International Sale of Goods (CISG): Diffidence and Developing International Legal Norms*, 22 J.L. & COM. 22 (2003).

Andreas Heldrich & Beghard M. Rehm, *Modernisation of the German Law of Obligations: Harmonisation of Civil Law and Common Law in the Recent Reform of the German Civil Code*, in COMPARATIVE REMEDIES FOR BREACH OF CONTRACT 123 (Nili Cohen & Ewan McKendrick eds. 2005).

Robert A. Hillman, *Applying the United Nations Convention on Contracts for the International Sales of Goods: The Elusive Goal of Uniformity*, in REVIEW OF THE John Honnold, *The Draft Convention on Contracts for the International Sales of Goods: An Overview*, 27 AM. J. COMP. L. 223 (1979).

John Honnold, *The Sales Convention: Background, Status, and Application*, 8 J.L. & COM. 1 (1988).

————, *The New Uniform Law for International Sales and the U.C.C.: A Comparison*, 18 INT'L LAW. 21 (1984).

————, *The United Nations Commission on International Trade Law: Mission and Methods*, 27 AM. J. COMP. L. 201 (1979).

Martin Karollus, *Judicial Interpretation and Application of the CISG in Germany 1988–1994*, 1 Rev. CISG 51 (1995).

Troy Keily, *Harmonisation and the United Nations Convention on Contracts for the International Sale of Goods*, Nordic J. Com. L. (2003), *available at* http://www.njcl.fi/1_2003/article3.pdf.

Monica Kilian, *CISG and the Problem with Common Law Jurisdictions*, 10 J. Transnat'l L. & Pol'y 217 (2001).

Rolf Knieper, *Celebrating Success by Accession to CISG*, 25 J.L. & Com. 477 (2005).

Stefan Kröll, *Selected Problems Concerning the CISG's Scope of Application*, 25 J.L. & Com. 39 (2005).

Herbert Kronke, *The UN Sales Convention, The UNIDROIT Contract Principles and the Way Beyond*, 25 J.L. & Com. 451 (2005).

Henry Landau, *Background to the U.S. Participation in United Nations Convention on Contracts for the International Sale of Goods*, 18 Int'l Law. 29 (1984).

Ole Lando, *CISG and its Followers: A Proposal to Adopt Some International Principles of Contract Law*, 53 Am. J. Comp. L. 379 (2005).

————, *A Vision of a Future World Contract Law: Impact of European and UNIDROIT Contract Principles*, 37 U.C.C.L.J. 2 (2004).

Roland Loewe, *The Sphere of Application of the United Nations Sales Convention*, 10 Pace Int'l L. Rev. 79 (1998).

Joseph Lookofsky, *In Dubio Conventione? Some Thoughts About Opt–Outs, Computer Programs and Preemption Under The 1980 Vienna Sales Convention (CISG)*, 13 Duke J. Comp. & Int'l L. 258 (2003).

————, *The Limits of Commercial Contract Freedom: Under the UNIDROIT "Restatement" and Danish Law*, 46 Am. J. Comp. L. 485 (1998).

Henning Lutz, *The CISG and Common Law Courts: Is There Really a Problem?* 35 Victoria U. Wellington L. Rev. 711 (2004).

Henry Mather, *Choice of Law for International Sales Issues Not Resolved by the CISG*, 20 J.L. & Com. 155 (2001).

Peter J. Mazzacano, *Canadian Jurisprudence and the Uniform Application of the U. N. Convention on Contracts for the International Sale of Goods*, 18 Pace Int'l L. Rev. (forthcoming 2006), *available at* http://cisgw3.law.pace.edu/cisg/biblio/mazzacano1.html.

Francesco G. Mazzotta, *Why Do Some American Courts Fail to Get It Right?*, 3 Loy. U. Chi. Int'l L. Rev. 85 (2005).

————, *The International Character of the UN Convention on Contracts for the International Sale of Goods: An Italian Case Example*, 15 PACE INT'L L. REV. 437 (2003).

Lars Meyer, *Soft Law for Solid Contracts? A Comparative Analysis of the Value of the UNIDROIT Principles of International Commercial Contracts and the Principles of European Contract Law to the Process of Contract Law Harmonization*, 34 DENV. J. INT'L L. & POL'Y 119 (2006).

Catherine Mitchell, *Leading a Life of its Own? The Roles of Reasonable Expectation in Contract Law*, 23 OXFORD J. LEGAL STUD. 639 (2003).

John S. Mo, *The Code of Contract Law of the People's Republic of China and the Vienna Sales Convention*, 15 AM. U. INT'L L. REV. 209 (1999).

Sally Moss, *Why the United Kingdom Has Not Ratified the CISG*, 25 J.L. & COM. 483 (2005).

Note, *Unification and Certainty: The United Nations Convention on Contracts for the International Sale of Goods*, 97 HARV. L. REV. 1984 (1984).

Luke Nottage, *Who's Afraid of the Vienna Sales Convention (CISG)? A New Zealander's View from Australia and Japan*, 36 VICT. U. WELLINGTON L. REV. 815 (2005).

Rodrigo Novoa, Culpa in Contrahendo: *A Comparative Law Study: Chilean Law and the United Nations Convention on Contracts for the International Sale of Goods (CISG)*, 22 ARIZ. J. INT'L & COMP. L. 3 (2005).

L. Scott Primak, *Computer Software: Should the U. N. Convention on Contracts for the International Sale of Goods Apply? A Contextual Approach to the Question*, 11 COMPUTER/L.J. 197 (1991).

Willibald Posch, *Uniform Law of International Sales of Goods*, *in* 1 REMEDIES FOR INTERNATIONAL SELLERS OF GOODS (Dennis Campbell & Susan Meek eds. 1998 & Supp. 2001).

Bradley L. Richards, Note, *Contract for the International Sale of Goods: Applicability of the United Nations Convention*, 69 IOWA L. REV. 209 (1983).

Arthur Rossett, *Critical Reflections on the United Nations Convention on Contracts for the International Sale of Goods*, 45 OHIO STATE L.J. 265 (1984).

Peter Schlechtriem, *Requirements of Application and Sphere of Applicability of the CISG*, 36 VICTORIA U. WELLINGTON L. REV. 781 (2005).

_____, *Vienna Sales Convention 1980—Developed Countries' Perspectives*, in CURRENT DEVELOPMENTS IN INTERNATIONAL TRANSFERS OF GOODS & SERVICES 103 (L. Rao Penna et al. eds. 1994).

Ingeborg Schwenzer, *The Danger of Domestic Pre–Conceived Views with Respect to the Uniform Interpretation of the CISG: The Question of Avoidance in the Case of Non–Conforming Goods and Documents*, 36 VICTORIA U. WELLINGTON L. REV. 795 (2005).

Rajeev Sharma, *The United Nations Convention on Contracts for the International Sale of Goods: The Canadian Experience*, 36 VICTORIA U. WELLINGTON L. REV. 847 (2005).

Lucia Carvahal Sica, *Gap-Filling in the CISG: May the UNIDROIT Principles Supplement the Gaps in the Convention?*, NORDIC J. COM. L. (2006), *available at* http://www.njcl.fi/1_2006/article2.pdf.

Michael P. Van Alstine, *Consensus, Dissensus, and Contractual Obligation Through the Prism of Uniform International Sales Law*, 37 VA. J. INT'L L. 1 (1996).

Steven Walt, *Implementing CISG's Scope Provisions: Validity and Three–Party Cases*, 35 U.C.C.L.J. 43 (2002).

Bruno Zeller, *The UN Convention on Contracts for the International Sale of Goods (CISG)–A Leap Forward Toward Unified International Sales Laws*, 12 PACE INT'L L. REV. 79 (2000).

Jacob Ziegel, *The Scope of the Convention: Reaching Out to Article One and Beyond*, 25 J.L. & COM. 59 (2005).

Sara G. Zwart, *The New International Law of Sales: A Marriage Between Socialist, Third World, Common, and Civil Law Principles*, 13 N.C. J. INT'L L. & COM. REG. 109 (1988).

2. CONTRACT FORMATION

Paul Amato, *U.N. Convention on Contracts for the International Sale of Goods—The Open Price Term and Uniform Application: An Early Interpretation by the Hungarian Courts*, 13 J.L. & COM. 1 (1993).

Rod N. Andreason, Note, MCC–Marble Ceramic Center: *The Parol Evidence Rule and Other Domestic Law Under the Convention on Contracts for the International Sale of Goods*, 1999 BYU L. REV. 351 (1999).

Omri Ben–Shahar, *An Ex–Ante View of the Battle of the Forms: Inducing Parties to Draft Reasonable Terms*, 25 INT'L REV. L. & ECON. 350 (2005).

Peter J. Calleo, Note, *The Inapplicability of the Parol Evidence Rule to the United Nations Convention on Contracts for the International Sale of Goods*, 28 HOFSTRA L. REV. 799 (2000).

CISG Advisory Council, *CISG Advisory Council Opinion No. 3: Parol Evidence Rule, Plain Meaning Rule, Contractual Merger Clause and the CISG*, 17 PACE INT'L L. REV. 61 (2005).

Vivian Grosswald Curran, *The Interpretive Challenge to Uniformity*, 15 J.L. & COM. 175 (1995) (reviewing CLAUDE WITZ, LES PREMIÈRES APPLICATIONS JURISPUDENTIELLES DU DROIT UNIFORME DE LA VENTE INTERNATIONALE (1995)).

Pedrag Cvetkovic, *The Characteristics of an Offer in CISG and PECL*, 14 PACE INT'L L. REV. 121 (2002).

Louis F. Del Duca, *Implementation of Contract Formation Statute of Frauds, Parol Evidence, and Battle of Forms CISG Provisions in Civil and Common Law Countries*, 38 U.C.C.L.J. 55 (2006).

———, *Implementation of Contract Formation Statute of Frauds, Parol Evidence, and Battle of Forms CISG Provisions in Civil and Common Law Countries*, 25 J.L. & COM. 133 (2005).

——— & Patrick Del Duca, *Internationalization of Sales Law—Practice Under the Convention on International Sale of Goods—A Primer for Attorneys and International Traders, in* NEW DEVELOPMENTS IN INTERNATIONAL COMMERCIAL AND CONSUMER LAW: PROCEEDINGS OF THE 8TH BIENNIAL CONFERENCE OF THE INTERNATIONAL ACADEMY OF COMMERCIAL AND CONSUMER LAW 37 (Jacob S. Ziegel ed. 1998).

Frank Diedrich, *Maintaining Uniformity in International Law Via Autonomous Interpretation: Software Contract and the CISG*, 8 PACE INT'L L. REV. 303 (1996).

Franco Ferrari, *Gap-Filling and Interpretation of the CISG: Overview of International Case Law*, 7 VINDOBONA J. INT'L COM. L. & ARB. 63 (2003).

Harry M. Flechtner, *The U.N. Sales Convention (CISG) and MCC–Marble Ceramic Center, Inc. v. Ceramica Nuova D'Agostino, S.P.A.: The Eleventh Circuit Weighs in on Interpretation, Subjective Intent, Procedural Limits to the Convention's Scope, and the Parol Evidence Rule*, 18 J.L. & COM. 259 (1999).

———, *More U.S. Decisions on the U.N. Sales Convention: Scope, Parol Evidence, "Validity" and Reduction of Price Under Article 50*, 14 J.L. & COM. 153 (1995).

Henry Gabriel, *The Battle of the Forms: A Comparison of the United Nations Convention for the International Sale of Goods and the Uniform Commercial Code: The Common Law and the Uniform Commercial Code*, 49 BUS. LAW. 1053 (1994).

Wolfgang Hahnkamper, *Acceptance of an Offer in Light of Electronic Communications*, 25 J.L. & COM. 147 (2005).

Matt Jamison, *The On–Sale Bar and the New UCC Article 2: Arguments for Defining a Commercial Offer for Sale Pursuant to the United Nations Convention on Contracts for the International Sale of Goods*, 5 N.C. J.L. & TECH. 351 (2004).

Burt A. Leete, *Contract Formation Under The United Nations Convention on Contracts for the International Sale of Goods and the Uniform Commercial Code: Pitfalls for the Unwary*, 6 TEMP. INT'L & COMP. L.J. 193 (1992).

Joseph Lookofsky, *Walking the Article 7(2) Tightrope Between CISG and Domestic Law*, 25 J.L. & COM. 87 (2005).

Henry Mather, *Firm Offers Under the UCC and CISG*, 105 DICK. L. REV. 31 (2000).

Alberto Monti, *A Comment on "An Ex–Ante View of the Battle of the Forms: Inducing Parties to Draft Reasonable Terms,"* 25 INT'L REV. L. & ECON. 371 (2005).

David H. Moore, Note, *The Parol Evidence Rule and the United Nations Convention on Contracts for the International Sale of Goods: Justifying* Beijing Metals & Minerals Import/Export Corp. v. American Business Center, Inc., 1995 BYU L. REV. 1347 (1995).

John E. Murray, Jr., *Essay on the Formation of Contracts and Related Matters under the United Nations Convention on Contracts for the International Sale of Goods*, 8 J.L. & COM. 11 (1988).

Ch. Pamboukis, *The Concept and Function of Usages in the United Nations Convention on the International Sale of Goods*, 25 J.L. & COM. 107 (2005).

Vivica Pierre & John Pierre, *A Comparison of the Rules on Formation of Sales Contract Under the Louisiana Civil Code and the United Nations Convention on Contracts for the International Sale of Goods: What Buyers and Sellers Should Know*, 20 S.U. L. REV. 189 (1993).

Giesela Rühl, *The Battle of the Forms: Comparative and Economic Observations*, 24 U. PA. J. INT'L ECON. L. 189 (2003).

Rob Schultz, *Rolling Contract Formation Under the UN Convention on Contracts for the International Sale of Goods*, 35 CORNELL INT'L L.J. 263 (2001–02).

Kevin C. Stemp, *A Comparative Analysis of the "Battle of Forms,"* 15 TRANSNAT'L L. & CONTEMP. PROBS. 243 (2005).

Charles Sukurs, Note, *Harmonizing the Battle of the Forms: A Comparison of the United States, Canada, and the CISG*, 34 VAND. J. TRANSNAT'L L. 1481 (2001).

Maria del Pilar Perales Viscasillas, *"Battle of the Forms" Under the 1980 United Nations Convention on Contracts for the International Sale of Goods: A Comparison with Section 2-207 and the UNIDROIT Principles*, 10 PACE INT'L L. REV. 97 (1998).

Gregory C. Walker, Note, *Trade Usages and the CISG: Defending the Appropriateness of Incorporating Custom Into International Commercial Contracts*, 24 J.L. & Com. 263 (2005).

Janet Walker, *Agreeing to Disagree: Can We Just Have Words? CISG Article 11 and the Model Law Writing Requirement*, 25 J.L. & Com. 153 (2005).

3. PERFORMANCE AND BREACH

COMMISSION ON EUROPEAN CONTRACT LAW, THE PRINCIPLES OF EUROPEAN CONTRACT LAW (2003).

UGO DRAETTA, RALPH B. LAKE & VED P. NANDA, BREACH AND ADAPTATION OF INTERNATIONAL CONTRACTS: AN INTRODUCTION TO LEX MERCATORIA (1992).

ROY GOODE ET AL., TRANSNATIONAL COMMERCIAL LAW: INTERNATIONAL INSTRUMENTS AND COMMENTARY (2004).

JAMES GORDLEY (ed.), THE ENFORCEABILITY OF PROMISES IN EUROPEAN CONTRACT LAW (2001).

RENÉ FRANZ HENSCHEL, THE CONFORMITY OF GOODS IN INTERNATIONAL SALES (2005).

SONJA A. KRUISINGA, (NON-)CONFORMITY IN THE 1980 UN CONVENTION ON CONTRACTS FOR THE INTERNATIONAL SALE OF GOODS: A UNIFORM CONCEPT? (2004).

HENRY MATHER, CONTRACT LAW AND MORALITY (1999).

RICHARD A. POSNER, ECONOMIC ANALYSIS AND THE LAW (6th ed. 2003).

Andrew Babiak, Note, *Defining "Fundamental Breach" Under the United Nations Convention on Contracts for the International Sale of Goods*, 6 TEMP. INT'L & COMP. L.J. 113 (1992).

Jürgen Basedow, *Towards a Universal Doctrine of Breach of Contract: The Impact of the CISG*, 25 INT'L REV. L. & ECON. 487 (2005).

Michael Bridge, *A Comment on "Towards a Universal Doctrine of Breach: The Impact of CISG,"* 25 INT'L REV. L. & ECON. 501 (2005).

————, *Issues Arising Under Articles 64, 72 and 73 of the United Nations Convention on Contracts for the International Sale of Goods*, 25 J.L. & Com. 405 (2005).

David W. Barnes, *The Anatomy of Contract Damages and Efficient Breach Theory*, 6 S. CAL. INTERDISCIPLINARY L.J. 397 (1998).

Wayne R. Barnes, *Contemplating a Civil Law Paradigm for a Future International Commercial Code*, 65 LA. L. REV. 677 (2005).

Robert Bejesky, *The Evolution in and International Convergence of the Doctrine of Specific Performance in Three Types of States*, 13 IND. INT'L & COMP. L. REV. 353 (2003).

Robert L. Birmingham, *Breach of Contract, Damage Measures, and Economic Efficiency*, 24 RUTGERS L. REV. 273 (1970).

Nayiri Boghossian, *A Comparative Study of Specific Performance Provisions in the United Nations Convention on Contracts for the International Sale of Goods, in* PACE REVIEW OF THE CONVENTION ON CONTRACTS FOR THE INTERNATIONAL SALE OF GOODS 3 (1999–2000).

John M. Catalano, Comment, *More Fiction Than Fact: The Perceived Differences in the Application of Specific Performance Under the United Nations Convention on Contracts for the International Sale of Goods*, 71 TUL. L. REV. 1807 (1997).

CISG Advisory Council, *CISG Advisory Council Opinion No. 2: Examination of the Goods and Notice of Non–Conformity Articles 38 and 39*, 16 PACE INT'L L. REV. 377 (2004).

Dagmar Coester–Waltjen, *The New Approach to Breach of Contract in German Law, in* COMPARATIVE REMEDIES FOR BREACH OF CONTRACT 135 (Nili Cohen & Ewan McKendrick eds. 2005).

Franco Ferrari, *Fundamental Breach of Contract under the UN Sales Convention—25 Years of Article 25 CISG*, 25 J.L. & COM. 489 (2006).

Silvia Ferreri, *Remarks Concerning the Implementation of the CISG by the Courts (The Seller's Performance and Article 35)*, 25 J.L. & COM. 223 (2005).

Henry Deeb Gabriel, *The Buyer's Performance under the CISG: Articles 53–60 Trends in the Decisions*, 25 J.L. & COM. 273 (2005).

Daniel Girsberger, *The Time Limits of Article 39 CISG*, 25 J.L. & COM. 241 (2005).

Donald L. Grace, Force Majeure, *China & the CISG: Is China's New Contract Law a Step in the Right Direction?*, 2 SAN DIEGO INT'L L.J. 173 (2001).

Oliver Wendell Holmes, Jr., *The Path of the Law*, 10 HARV. L. REV. 457 (1897).

Richard Hyland, *Pacta Sunt Servanda: A Meditation*, 34 VA J. INT'L L. 405 (1994).

Sarah Howard Jenkins, *Discharge of Contract—Performance and Tender: What are the Operative Principles for a Global Community?*, 54 FLA. L. REV. 451 (2002).

Amy H. Kastely, *The Right to Require Performance in International Sales: Towards an International Interpretation of the Vienna Convention*, 63 WASH. L. REV. 607 (1988).

Catherine Kessedjian, *Competing Approaches to Force Majeure and Hardship*, 25 Int'l Rev. L. & Econ. 415 (2005).

Robert Koch, *The Concept of Fundamental Breach of Contract Under the United Nations Convention on Contracts for the International Sale of Goods (CISG)*, in Review of the Convention on Contracts for the International Sale of Goods (CISG) 177 (1998).

Henrik Lando & Caspar Rose, *On the Enforcement of Specific Performance in Civil Law Countries*, 24 Int'l Rev. L. & Econ. 473 (2004).

Ole Lando, *Comparative Law and Lawmaking*, 75 Tul. L. Rev. 1015 (2001).

————, *Salient Features of The Principles of European Contract Law: A Comparison with the UCC*, 13 Pace Int'l L. Rev. 339 (2001).

Niklas Lindström, *Changed Circumstances and Hardship in the International Sale of Goods*, Nordic J. Com. L. (2006), *available at* http://www.njcl.fi/1_2006/commentary1.pdf.

Laura E. Longobardi, Note, *Disclaimer of Implied Warranties: The 1980 United Nations Convention on Contracts for the International Sale of Goods*, 53 Fordham L. Rev. 863 (1985).

Joseph Lookofsky, *Impediments and Hardship in International Sales: A Commentary on Catherine Kessedjian's "Competing Approaches to Force Majeure and Hardship,"* 25 Int'l Rev. L. & Econ. 434 (2005).

Ian R. Macneil, *Efficient Breach of Contract: Circles in the Sky*, 68 Va. L. Rev. 947 (1982).

Edmond Meynial, *De la Sanction Civile Des Obligations de Faire Ou de Ne Pas Faire*, 56 Revue Pratique de Droit Français 385 (1884).

Fabio Morosini, *Globalization & Law: Beyond Traditional Methodology of Comparative Legal Studies and an Example from Private International Law*, 13 Cardozo J. Int'l & Comp. L. 541 (2005).

Clemens Pauly, *The Concept of Fundamental Breach as an International Principle to Create Uniformity of Commercial Law*, 19 J.L. & Com. 221 (2000).

Joseph M. Perillo, *Force Majeure and Hardship Under the UNIDROIT Principles of International Commercial Contracts*, 5 Tul. J. Int'l & Comp. L. 5 (1997).

————, *UNIDROIT Principles of International Commercial Contracts: The Black Letter Text and a Review*, 63 Fordham L. Rev. 281 (1994).

Teija Poikela, *Conformity of Goods in the United Nations Convention on Contracts for the International Sale of Goods*, NORDIC J. COM. L. (2003), *available at* http://www.njcl.fi/1_2003/article5.pdf.

Paul J. Powers, *Defining the Undefinable: Good Faith and the United Nations Convention on Contracts for the International Sale of Goods*, 18 J.L. & COM. 333 (1999).

Keith A. Rowley, *A Brief History of Anticipatory Repudiation in American Contract Law*, 69 U. CIN. L. REV. 565 (2001).

Mathias Reimann, *The Progress and Failure of Comparative Law in the Second Half of The Twentieth Century*, 50 AM. J. COMP. L. 671 (2002).

————, *Beyond National Systems: A Comparative Law for the International Age*, 75 TUL. L. REV. 1103 (2001).

Bernard Rudden & Philippe Juilhard, *La Théorie de la violation efficace*, 8 REVUE INTERNATIONALE DE DROIT COMPARÉ 1016 (1986).

Peter Schlechtriem, *Subsequent Performance and Delivery Deadlines—Avoidance of CISG Sales Contracts Due to Non–Conformity of the Goods*, 18 PACE INT'L L. REV. 83 (2006).

Tatsiana Seliazniova, Translation, *Prospective Non–Performance or Anticipatory Breach of Contract (Comparison of the Belarusian Approach to CISG Application and Foreign Legal Experience)*, 24 J.L. & COM. 111 (2004).

Mercédeh Azeredo da Silveira, *Anticipatory Breach Under the United Nations Convention on Contracts for the International Sale of Goods*, NORDIC J. COM. L. (2005), available at http://www.njcl.fi/2_2005/article1.pdf.

Scott D. Slater, *Overcome by Hardship: The Inapplicability of the UNIDROIT Principles' Hardship Provision to CISG*, 12 FLA. J. INT'L L. 231 (1998).

Zoi Valioti, *Passing of Risk in International Sales Contracts: A Comparative Examination of the Rules on Risk Under the United Nations Convention on Contracts for the International Sale of Goods (Vienna 1980) and INCOTERMS 2000*, NORDIC J. COM. L. (2004), *available at* http://www.njcl.fi/2_2004/article3.pdf.

Steven Walt, *For Specific Performance Under the United Nations Sales Convention*, 26 TEX. INT'L L.J. 211 (1991).

Jonathan Yovel, *The Seller's Right to Cure a Failure to Perform: An Analytical Comparison of the Respective Provisions of the CISG and the PECL*, NORDIC J. COM. L. (2005), *available at* http://www.njcl.fi/1_2005/commentary1.pdf.

Reinhard Zimmermann, *Remedies for Non–Performance: The Revised German Law of Obligations, Viewed Against the Background of the Principles of European Contract Law,* 6 EDINBURGH L. REV. 271 (2002).

4. CONTRACT REMEDIES

SIR GUENTER H. TREITEL, REMEDIES FOR BREACH OF CONTRACT 51 (1988).

BRUNO ZELLER, DAMAGES UNDER THE CONVENTION ON CONTRACTS FOR THE INTERNATIONAL SALE OF GOODS (2005).

Fabio Bortolotti, *Remedies Available to the Seller and Seller's Right to Require Specific Performance (Articles 61, 62 and 28),* 25 J.L. & COM. 335 (2005).

Michael Bridge, *A Comment on "Towards a Universal Doctrine of Breach: The Impact of CISG,"* 25 INT'L REV. L. & ECON. 501 (2005).

————, *Issues Arising Under Articles 64, 72 and 73 of the United Nations Convention on Contracts for the International Sale of Goods,* 25 J.L. & COM. 405 (2005).

John M. Catalano, Comment, *More Fiction Than Fact: The Perceived Differences in the Application of Specific Performance Under the United Nations Convention on Contracts for the International Sale of Goods,* 71 TUL. L. REV. 1807 (1997).

Lui Chengwei, *Recovery of Interest,* NORDIC J. COM. L. (2003), *available at* http://www.njcl.fi/1_2003/article1.pdf.

CISG Advisory Council, *CISG Advisory Council Opinion No. 5: The Buyer's Right to Avoid the Contract in Cases of Non–Conforming Goods or Documents,* NORDIC J. COM. L. (2005), *available at* http://www.njcl.fi/2_2005/commentary2.pdf.

Kathryn S. Cohen, Comment, *Achieving a Uniform Law Governing International Sales: Conforming the Damage Provisions of the United Nations Convention on Contracts for the International Sale of Goods and the Uniform Commercial Code,* 26 U. PA. J. INT'L ECON. L. 601 (2005).

John Dawson, *Specific Performance in France and Germany,* 57 MICH. L. REV. 495 (1959).

Larry A. DiMatteo, *The CISG and the Presumption of Enforceability: Unintended Contractual Liability in International Business Dealings,* 22 YALE J. INT'L L. 111 (1997).

John C. Duncan, Jr., Nachfrist Was Ist?: *Thinking Globally and Acting Socially; Considering Time Extension Principles of the U.N. Convention on Contracts for the International Sale of Goods in Revising the Uniform Commercial Code,* 2000 BYU L. REV. 1363.

Sieg Eiselen, *Proving the Quantum of Damages*, 25 J.L. & COM. 375 (2005).

Johan Erauw, *CISG Articles 66–70: The Risk of Loss and Passing It*, 25 J.L. & COM. 203 (2005).

David C. Fagan, *The Remedial Provisions of the Vienna Convention of the International Sale of Goods 1980: A Small Business Perspective*, 2 J. SMALL & EMERGING BUS. L. 317 (1998).

E. Allan Farnsworth, *A Common Lawyer's View of His Civilian Colleagues*, 57 LA. L. REV. 227 (1996).

————, *Damages and Specific Relief*, 27 AM. J. COMP. L. 247 (1979).

————, *Legal Remedies for Breach of Contract*, 70 COLUM. L. REV. 1145 (1970).

John Felemegas, *An Interpretation of Article 74 CISG By the U.S. Circuit Court of Appeals*, 15 PACE INT'L L. REV. 91 (2003).

Harry M. Flechtner, *Buyers' Remedies in General and Buyers' Performance–Oriented Remedies*, 25 J.L. & COM. 339 (2005).

————, *Recovering Attorneys' Fees as Damages Under the U.S. Sales Convention: The Role of Case Law in the New International Commercial Practice, with Comments on* Zapata Hermanos v. Hearthside Baking, 22 NW. J. INT'L L. & BUS. 121 (2002).

————, *Remedies Under the New International Sales Convention: The Perspective from Article 2 of the U.C.C.*, 8 J.L. & COM. 53 (1988).

Alejandro M. Garro, *The Buyers "Safety Valve" under the CISG: Article 40: What is the Seller Supposed to Know and When?* 25 J.L. & COM. 253 (2005).

John Y. Gotanda, *Awarding Damages Under the United Nations Convention on the International Sale of Goods: A Matter of Interpretation*, 37 GEO. J. INT'L L. 95 (2005).

————, *Recovering Lost Profits in International Disputes*, 36 GEO. J. INT'L L. 61 (2004).

Bernhard Grossfeld, *Money Sanctions for Breach of Contract in a Communist Economy*, 72 YALE L.J. 1326 (1963).

Shael Herman, *Specific Performance: A Comparative Analysis (1)*, 7 EDINBURGH L. REV. 1 (2003).

————, *Specific Performance: A Comparative Analysis (2)*, 7 EDINBURGH L. REV. 194 (2003).

Robert A. Hillman, *Remedies and the CISG: Another Perspective*, 25 INT'L REV. L. & ECON. 411 (2005).

Christopher M. Jacobs, Note, *Notice of Avoidance Under the CISG: A Practical Examination of Substance and Form Considerations, the Validity of Implicit Notice, and the Question of Revocability*, 64 U. PITT. L. REV. 407 (2003).

Avery Katz, *Remedies for Breach of Contract under the CISG*, 25 INT'L REV. L. & ECON. 378 (2005).

Troy Keily, *How Does the Cookie Crumble?: Legal Costs Under a Uniform Interpretation of the United Nations Convention on Contracts for the International Sale of Goods*, NORDIC J. COM. L. (2003), *available at* http://www.njcl.fi/1_2003/commentary2.pdf.

Andrew J. Kennedy, *Recent Developments: Nonconforming Goods Under the CISG—What's a Buyer to Do?*, 16 DICK. J. INT'L L. 319 (1998).

Ericson P. Kimbel, Nachfrist *Notice and Avoidance Under the CISG*, 18 J.L. & COM. 301 (1999).

Karin L. Kizer, *Minding the Gap: Determining Interest Rates Under the U.N. Convention for the International Sale of Goods*, 65 U. CHI. L. REV. 1279 (1998).

Robert Koch, *The Concept of Fundamental Breach of Contract Under the United Nations Convention on Contracts for the International Sale of Goods (CISG)*, *in* REVIEW OF THE CONVENTION ON CONTRACTS FOR THE INTERNATIONAL SALE OF GOODS (CISG) 177 (1998).

Ari Korpinen, *On Legal Uncertainty Regarding Timely Notification of Avoidance of the Sales Contract*, NORDIC J. COM. L. (2005), *available at* http://www.njcl.fi/1_2005/article1.pdf.

Helmut Koziol, *Reduction in Damages According to Article 77 CISG*, 25 J.L. & COM. 385 (2005).

Anthony T. Kronman, *Specific Performance*, 45 U. CHI. L. REV. 351 (1978).

Henrik Lando & Caspar Rose, *On the Enforcement of Specific Performance in Civil Law Countries*, 24 INT'L REV. L. & ECON. 473 (2004).

Solène Le Pautremat, *Mitigation of Damage: A French Perspective*, 55 INT'L & COMP. L.Q. 205 (2006).

Chengwei Liu, *Effects of Avoidance: Perspectives from the CISG, UNIDROIT Principles and PECL and Case Law*, NORDIC J. COM. L. (2005), *available at* http://www.njcl.fi/1_2005/article2.pdf.

Ulrich Magnus, *The Remedy of Avoidance of Contract Under CISG: General Remarks and Special Cases*, 25 J.L. & COM. 423 (2005).

_____, *Remarks on Good Faith: The United Nations Convention on Contracts for the International Sale of Goods and the International Institute for the Unification of Private Law, Principles of International Commercial Contracts*, 10 PACE INT'L L. REV. 89 (1998).

Lucinda Miller, *Penalty Clauses in England and France: A Comparative Study*, 53 INT'L & COMP. L.Q. 79 (2004).

Arthur G. Murphey, Jr., *Consequential Damages in Contracts for the International Sale of Goods and the Legacy of* Hadley, 23 GEO. WASH. J. INT'L L. & ECON. 415 (1989).

Damien Nyer, *Withholding Performance for Breach in International Transactions: An Exercise in Equations, Proportions or Coercion?*, 18 PACE INT'L L. REV. 29 (2006).

Alejandro Osuna–Gonzàlez, *Buyer's Enabling Steps to Pay the Price: Article 54 of the United Nation's Convention on Contracts for the International Sale of Goods*, 25 J.L. & COM. 299 (2005).

Clemens Pauly, *The Concept of Fundamental Breach as an International Principle to Create Uniformity of Commercial Law*, 19 J.L. & COM. 221 (2000).

Julie M. Philippe, *French and American Approaches to Contract Formation and Enforceability: A Comparative Perspective*, 12 TULSA J. COMP. & INT'L L. 357 (2005).

Catherine Piche, *The Convention on Contracts for the International Sale of Goods and the Uniform Commercial Code Remedies in Light of Remedial Principles Recognized Under U.S. Law: Are the Remedies of Granting Additional Time to the Defaulting Parties and of Reduction of Price Fair and Efficient Ones?*, 28 N.C. J. INT'L L. & COM. REG. 519 (2003).

Peter A. Piliounis, *The Remedies of Specific Performance, Price Reduction and Additional Time (*Nachfrist*) Under the CISG: Are These Worthwhile Changes or Additions to English Sales Law?*, 12 PACE INT'L L. REV. 1 (2000).

Jan Ramberg, *To What Extent Do INCOTERMS 2000 Vary Articles 67(2), 68 and 69?* 25 J.L. & COM. 219 (2005).

————, *Breach of Contract and Recoverable Losses, in* MAKING COMMERCIAL LAW: ESSAYS IN HONOR OF ROY GOODE 191 (Ross Cranston ed. 1997).

Annemieke Romein, *The Passing of Risk: A Comparison Between the Passing of Risk Under the CISG and German Law* (1999), available at http://www.cisg.law.pace.edu/cisg/biblio/romein.html.

Djakhongir Saidov, *Damages: The Need for Uniformity*, 25 J.L. & COM. 393 (2005).

————, *Methods of Limiting Damages Under The Vienna Convention on Contracts for the International Sale of Goods*, 14 PACE INT'L L. REV. 307 (2002).

Sandra Saiegh, *Avoidance Under the CISG and Its Challenges Under International Organizations Commercial Transactions*, 25 J.L. & COM. 443 (2005).

Eric C. Schneider, *Measuring Damages Under the CISG*, 9 PACE INT'L L. REV. 223 (1997).

Alan Schwartz, *The Case for Specific Performance*, 89 YALE L.J. 271 (1979).

Damon Schwartz, *The Recovery of Lost Profits Under Article 74 of the U. N. Convention on the International Sale of Goods*, NORDIC J. COM. L. (2006), *available at* http://www.njcl.fi/1_2006/article1.pdf.

Ingeborg Schwenzer, *Avoidance of the Contract in Case of Non-Conforming Goods (Article 49(1)(a) CISG)*, 25 J.L. & COM. 437 (2005).

———, *The Danger of Domestic Pre-Conceived Views with Respect to Uniform Interpretation of the CISG: The Question of Avoidance in the Case of Non-Conforming Goods and Documents*, 36 VICTORIA U. WELLINGTON L. REV. 795 (2005).

Jianming Shen, *Declaring the Contract Avoided: The U.N. Sales Convention in the Chinese Context*, 10 N.Y. INT'L L. REV. 7 (1997).

———, *The Remedy of Requiring Performance Under the CISG and the Relevance of Domestic Rules*, 13 ARIZ. J. INT'L & COMP. L. 253 (1996).

Chang-Sop Shin, *Declaration of Price Reduction Under the CISG Article 50 Price Reduction Remedy*, 25 J.L. & COM. 349 (2005).

Jeffery S. Sutton, Comment, *Measuring Damages Under the United Nations Convention on the International Sale of Goods*, 50 OHIO ST. L.J. 737 (1989).

Christian Thiele, *Interest on Damages and Rate of Interest Under Article 78 of the U.N. Convention on Contracts for the International Sale of Goods*, 2 VINDOBONA J. INT'L COM. L. & ARB. 3 (1998).

Marco Torsello, *Substantive and Jurisdictional Aspects of International Contract Remedies: A Comment on Avery Katz's "Remedies for Breach of Contract Under the CISG,"* 25 INT'L REV. L. & ECON. 397 (2005).

Thomas S. Ulen, *The Efficiency of Specific Performance: Toward a Unified Theory of Contract Remedies*, 83 MICH. L. REV. 341 (1984).

Elbi Janse van Vuuren, *Termination of International Commercial Contracts for Breach of Contract: The Provisions of the UNI-*

DROIT Principles of International Commercial Contracts, 15 ARIZ. J. INT'L & COMP. L. 583 (1998).

S.M. Waddams, *The Choice of Remedy for Breach of Contract, in* GOOD FAITH AND FAULT IN CONTRACT LAW 470 (Jack Beatson and Daniel Friedmann eds. 1995).

Evelien Visser, *Favor Emptoris: Does the CISG Favor the Buyer?*, 67 UMKC L. REV. 77 (1998).

Bruno Zeller, *Remarks on the Manner in Which the UNIDROIT Principles May be Used to Interpret or Supplement Article 76 of the CISG*, NORDIC J. COM. L. (2003), *available at* http://www. njcl.fi/1_2003/commentary1.pdf.

Jacob S. Ziegel, *Remedial Provisions in the Vienna Sales Convention: Some Common Law Perspectives, in* INTERNATIONAL SALES: THE UNITED NATIONS CONVENTION ON CONTRACTS FOR THE INTERNATIONAL SALE OF GOODS (Nina M. Galston & Hans Smit eds. 1984).

*

Index

References are to Pages

---

†